NINETY YEARS AND GROWING

The Story of Lincoln National

Michael C. Hawfield

GUILD PRESS OF INDIANA
6000 Sunset Lane
Indianapolis, IN 46208

Library of Congress
Catalog Card Number
95-79933

ISBN 1-878208-68-3

Manufactured in the United States of America.

PREFACE

The idea of producing a new history of Lincoln National belongs to Ladonna Huntley James, second vice president and director of the company's Corporate Communications Department. Although a fine history of Lincoln National had been written by Mark E. Neely Jr. in 1980, a new history seemed appropriate in view of the dynamic changes that had occurred in the company since that time. The occasion of the opening of a new Lincoln Museum and the ninetieth anniversary of the company's founding appeared to offer an ideal opportunity to bring the Lincoln National story up to date and to examine the company's traditions in different ways.

It has been the goal of this project not only to relate the principal events in the evolution of the company through the mid-1990s and the extraordinary success that it has attained, but also to emphasize the qualities of leadership that Lincoln National has evinced since its beginnings. This success is best seen in the careers of those who led the company as well as in the many experiences of those who served the company in scores of different roles, representing advancements in the insurance industry, technology, science, business, education, the arts and human services. It has also been an objective of this project to express as much of the personal or "human" quality of the company's history as possible. Thus, throughout the history are "sidebars" of stories about Lincoln National's experiences that do not easily fit in the narrative of the company's growth, but which are as revealing about the character of the company as its business record.

Lincoln National's is an extraordinary story of a very successful business, rich in traditions and character. It is a story that serves as a model for appreciating the principal developments in the insurance industry in this country for nearly a century.

Relating the history of Lincoln National would not be possible without the generous help of dozens of individuals who have revealed the great complexities and many nuances of the company's evolution. Foremost among those who have guided me was Scott Bushnell, assistant vice president for Corporate Communications. Without dominating the historian's work or attempting to make the story fit a predetermined mold, his insights into the many facets of the company's life, from technical issues to corporate culture, his probing questions and his natural sense of historical process have constantly kept me from straying toward easy answers to complex questions and facile explanations of highly complicated events. It is not too much to say that without his assistance this history could not have been completed.

Central to the research for this book have been the numerous interviews conducted in the course of a year and a half. To these former and present employees, agents and others who know Lincoln National I am especially indebted for the valuable time given so freely and, above all, the absolute candor with which they responded to questions and told the stories of their time with the company. It was a special pleasure to meet at length with former CEOs Walter O. Menge, Henry F. Rood and Thomas A. Watson, as well as the current CEO, Ian M. Rolland. Their forthright comments on the people and events that shaped the company under their leadership have been invaluable. But their view is only from the top. Other views — from the trenches, as it were — are equally valuable. For these I am deeply grateful to the nearly eighty individuals who also gave freely of their time and insights to illuminate the rich history of Lincoln National from many different perspectives. Among the first were the members of a special committee of volunteers whose task was to give me guidance in identifying critical issues and open the doors to important research contacts. Chaired by Ladonna Huntley James, the committee included Scott Bushnell, John Steinkamp, Barbara Taylor, John Cantrell, Barbara Wachtman, Dr. Donald Chambers, John Behrendt, Michael Snyder, Larry Edris, Marcia DuMond and Joan Marquardt.

I am grateful for the interviews given in the corporate center by Kenneth Dunsire, Robert Anker, Richard Robertson, Ladonna Huntley James, Mary Johnson, Suzanne Womack, Jack Hunter, Judy Davis, Michael Keefer, Barbara Kowalczyk, Leonard Helfrich, George Davis, Wilburn Smith, Barbara Taylor, Marcia DuMond, Don Van Wyngarden, Karen Bohnstedt and Linda Zimmer-Smith. At Lincoln Life, interviews and technical discussions included Art Page, Kathy Kolb, Jon Boscia, Marilyn Scherer, Kelly Clevenger, Robert Nikels, Neil Clay, Carl Baker, Carolyn Nightingale, Steve Lewis, Gary McPhail, Reed Miller, Mary McDonald, George Dunn, Larry Edris, Roy Chang, Lew Dotterer, Luann Boyer, Marti Philips, Barbara Kowalczyk, Ed Martin, Michael McMath, Phil Hartman, Ruth Cook and Debbie Carter. At Lincoln National (UK), Managing Director Jeff Nick gave important insight to global issues and at Lincoln National Reinsurance those who gave valuable time in interviews were Joni Wood-Lehman, Gabriel Shaheen, Jess Mast, Thomas West, James Schibley, Dinah Wright, Joanne Collins, Dr. Donald Chambers, John Cantrell, Barbara Wachtman and Jane Kite. In Lincoln National Investment Management I was helped especially by Thomas McMeekin, Dennis Blume and Marybeth Montgomery. At American States Insurance interviews given by former CEOs John Phelan and Edwin Goss, current CEO Cedric McCurley and Robert Coffin were particularly helpful. I was also privileged to meet with numerous leading Lincoln National agents, such as Robert Penland, Robert Loeb, Von Burba, Robert Wyman, Richard Vicars, Terri Magli and Sam Dichter. Former officers such as Gathings Stewart, Dave Silletto, Michael Marchese, Marilyn Vachon, Cliff Gamble, William Bogardus and Dave Martin were most generous with their time, and I am especially thankful to Allen Steere who gave many hours not only for interviews, but also in reading and commenting on the manuscript. Important insight was also given by several individuals who have been associated with Lincoln National, such as Chip Chandler of McKinsey & Company, Judy Norrell of Julia J. Norrell and Associates, and William B. Harmon Jr., of Davis & Harmon. I am especially grateful to Doug Rood and his mother, Ruth, for making available many of the personal effects of Henry Rood pertaining to his career with Lincoln National.

For assistance throughout the project I am deeply grateful to Joan Marquardt who has been an invaluable guide to the archival resources of Lincoln National and an enthusiastic researcher of photographs and documents. Thanks to her familiarity with the company's collections and her keen interest in the history of Lincoln National, many useful items that would have gone unnoticed were uncovered.

I am also greatly indebted to Ann Baker of the Corporate Communications Department for her efficient and pleasant help in resolving a host of administrative matters, and to Marlene Condron for her careful reading of the manuscript. For their many kind services helping me to solve a host of problems, I am thankful to Joyce Byrer, Cindy O'Brien, Bob Jones, Gene Monteith, Mark Bontrager, Amy Haycox, Susie Weisheit, Pam Paschal, Susan Bishop and Diane Mierau.

I am grateful also to the staff of the Lincoln Museum — Joan Flinspach, Gerald Prokopowicz, Carolyn Texley, Jim Eber and YvonneWhite, who accepted me as one of their own during the project.

TABLE OF CONTENTS

LEADERSHIP

In 1905 a group of Fort Wayne business leaders came together in a meeting room of the Commercial Club on Calhoun Street to create a life insurance company — something about which none of them knew very much. They included bankers, attorneys, wholesalers, hoteliers, manufacturers, physicians and brokers. Few had ever purchased life insurance and some had even lost their investments in earlier insurance schemes that had gone astray. Indeed, it was an age when the life insurance business was highly suspect, under investigation and scorned in the popular press. What these business leaders shared in common, however, was the ability to envision an insurance enterprise based on dependability and honesty. One later recalled, "We set our hearts on building in Fort Wayne a life insurance company at which no one could ever point the finger of scorn." Real success, it was noted, "would be due to real service, and that unusual success would be due to unusual service." They named the company after the nation's greatest leader, Abraham Lincoln, and soon adopted the motto, "Its name indicates its character." On this foundation of trust, integrity and service, the company pinned its fortune. The vision of these leaders was fully realized.

Lincoln National Corporation today is Indiana's largest publicly traded business and the state's oldest insurance company. In the industry and in the marketplace, Lincoln National is also one of the most highly respected insurance companies in the nation. Nationally, it is a major financial services company with assets in excess of $55 billion and revenues of $6 billion. Income from operations in 1994 was $389.8 million. Through its businesses Lincoln National is the world's largest life-health reinsurer and the nation's leading writer of individual annuities. In early 1995 the company purchased Delaware Management Holdings, Inc., of Philadelphia, which significantly expanded the company's foundation in the arena of investment management.

The company's strong record of growth is deeply rooted in its earliest experiences, from its willingness to explore non-traditional and innovative concepts to its drive to exert leadership in the industry. In its earliest decades, the Lincoln National's growth rate outstripped those of competitors, including the oldest firms in the country. This growth was due largely to the dynamic role Lincoln National Life played in the field of reinsurance, one of the first complementary lines of business it developed. In later years growth was centered on expansion of the distribution systems, development of new lines of business and the creation of the holding company that allowed for greater flexibility in business activity. In the past two decades the dramatic changes that have transformed Lincoln National into a financial services corporation have been in response to rapid and profound changes in the national and global economy. What sets the company apart has been its ability not only to survive in difficult, rapidly changing economic and social conditions, but also to adapt, turning challenges into new opportunites for growth.

Although the company could not have grown and prospered without the efforts of thousands of individuals who daily solved myriad problems, settled innumerable conflicts and disputes, tackled the critical clerical foundations of the business, created the new products and lines of business, envisioned and energized novel sales efforts, served on countless committees and participated in endless studies, it has been the half-dozen men who gave direction and became the embodiment of all that Lincoln National represented. A survey of the careers of the six individuals who shaped and molded the firm since 1905 provides a useful chronological framework for understanding the principal events in the life of Lincoln National during the past nine decades.

THE FRATERNAL

The beginnings of Lincoln National, however, were not very auspicious. The roots of Lincoln National lie in an insurance enterprise known as the Fraternal Assurance Society of America. In April 1902 an energetic promoter named Wilbur Wynant came to Fort Wayne and organized the Fraternal Assurance Society of America. Wynant was a slightly shady turn-of-the- century financial entrepreneur. A native of Jay County, Indiana, he had been a teacher and a railroad brakeman, but somewhere along the line he learned a little about life insurance. He also knew the great attraction fraternal organizations held for people in late Victorian America, especially middle-class working people with strong ethnic ties. To these people fraternal organizations of all kinds made sense as a hedge against what they perceived to be corrupt big businesses. This was especially true for insurance plans, which were particularly popular: By 1905 there were nearly six hundred fraternals in the United States with a membership of more than four million representing in excess of $6 billion in life insurance. In these first years of the twentieth century fraternal insurance totalled three-fourths of the amount held in force by legal reserve insurance companies. Some of the fraternals were

Wilbur Wynant, who also invested in natural gas and oil schemes. Caricature from *Some Fort Wayne Phizes.*

well managed and survive to the present as respected mutual protection organizations. Others, however, were less successful. Wynant, for example, founded at least nine fraternal companies, among which were the Protected Home Circle fraternal insurance society in Pennsylvania and the Supreme Tribe of Ben Hur in Indiana, before coming to Fort Wayne.

Although the fraternal was supposed to be a not-for-profit, mutual benefit organization, in reality many early fraternals were profit-making schemes for the organizers. The Wilbur Wynant fraternal in Fort Wayne was this type of organization. Wynant attracted to his scheme several well known but middling businessmen of Fort Wayne at the turn-of-the-century. Leading the group was Perry Randall, an attorney and hotelier who had been engaged in numerous local ventures. He was joined by several notable professional men, including Dr. Calvin H. English, the Rev. J. Webster Bailey of Plymouth Congregational Church, and attorney Daniel B. Ninde, the Allen County prosecutor and son of prominent

judge, Lindley M. Ninde. In keeping with the popularity of fraternal trappings, the officers of the Fraternal Assurance Society sported grand titles meant to convey the splendor of the group: there was the "Supreme Sergeant At Arms," the "Supreme President," and even in its first year a "Supreme Past President", Wynant, of course, was the "Supreme Manager." All this was perfectly appreciated in an age in which fraternal ritual and bonding were readily accepted.

The concept of the early fraternal was simple but if poorly managed, like a pyramid scheme, was destined to fail for a majority of participants. Initial capital came from the sale of policies and loans. Expenses were supposed to be minimal because everything was undertaken "for mutual benefit" in a fraternal spirit and thus premiums were necessary only to cover "reasonable charges." This was all very attractive to those who already mistrusted big business and who appreciated the notion of paying premiums only to cover what was they assumed necessary to cover policies, the so-called "natural premium." This was fine

until someone died. Because no reserve was required to be held by the company, the death of a policyholder brought an assessment for higher premiums from the surviving members. As assessments for higher premiums grew, sometimes just to cover operating expenses, it became increasingly difficult to attract new policyholders — especially younger, healthier ones. At first, sales were strong, but by 1904 business plummeted in the wake of rapidly rising assessments for higher premiums. Wynant left town in 1905 having taken all that he could from this venture and went on to the Indiana oil boom, which went bust in a few years. Left behind were the directors, a bankrupt company and thousands of worthless policies.

Determined to salvage the enterprise, the directors still judged it a good idea to be in the life insurance business in Fort Wayne in 1905. First, there was little competition from either locally owned or larger companies. There were several good general agents in town, like Max Blitz, Charles Orr and William Paul, but most life insurance business was in the hands

The First President of the Lincoln: Samuel Foster and the Beginnings of the Blouse

Besides serving as a founder and first president of the Lincoln National Life Insurance Company, Samuel Foster made an indelible mark on his adopted city of Fort Wayne and the fashion industry. A native of New York and an 1879 graduate of Yale University, Foster joined his older brother, David, in his Fort Wayne dry goods business. As the sole owner of the Foster Dry Goods Company in 1885, Samuel was struggling. That winter was terrible, too, and business had come to a standstill. Seeking to put idle workers to work, Foster had the men in the store create a pattern for a boy's shirt. With this pattern the men would then cut out the parts of the shirts from the store's stock of fabric and the wives of the store clerks would be employed to assemble the shirts. Business did indeed pick up that year, but Foster found that they could not keep in stock one size in particular: a size 14. A little research revealed that young women were buying and wearing these shirts to play tennis, ride bikes, play croquet or go on picnics.

Foster began to produce the shirtwaist especially for the female market, with new collars, longer sleeves and smaller necks. The home of the American shirtwaist, or blouse, became Fort Wayne, and it spread throughout the United States, reaching a world-famous peak in the highly fashionable styles of the Gibson Girl. By the time of the founding of Lincoln National in 1905, the Foster Shirtwaist Company was one of the leading factories of its kind in the Midwest.

In 1905 Foster also was one of the founders and first president of the German-American Bank, which during World War I changed its name to the more patriotic Lincoln National Bank. Not surprisingly, because of Foster's connections it was in this institution that Lincoln National Life Insurance Company carried out its primary banking needs. An active civic leader, he and his brother David donated the land for the present-day Foster Park in Fort Wayne. When he died, on April 4, 1935, he had served Lincoln National Life as president for its first seventeen years and was chairman of the board for another twelve years. While Foster was always a good counsellor to the company and a highly respected figurehead, his greatest contribution to Lincoln National was to let Arthur Hall develop the company as he saw best.

of other small fraternal and mutual benefit organizations such as the German Beneficial Union and the Bowser Employees' Relief Union. Second, Fort Wayne was far removed from the negative reputation suffered by Eastern companies soon to be caught up in the great insurance reform effort known as the Armstrong Committee. Indeed, in 1904, the Northern Indiana Life Underwriters' Association was organized in Fort Wayne with the aim of upgrading the professional quality of the life insurance business. The formation of Lincoln National was, in fact, a part of what has come to be known as the "new company movement," which witnessed in 1905 an explosion of new insurance companies. In 1905 alone, fifty-five new companies, all in the Midwest and West, were established. Thirteen of these were in Indiana.

The directors of the collapsed

Fraternal Assurance Society thus decided to reorganize as a legal reserve company to assure policyholders of the company's long-term obligation to provide service. Recent Indiana legislation had made it easier for new companies to be established in the state by allowing the reserve to be formed on a full preliminary term valuation basis rather than on a full net premium basis. This enabled the company to use more of its income for ordinary expenses at a time when it most needed operating cash. On May 15, 1905, a preliminary agreement was drawn up by the assessment society's attorney, Daniel Ninde, providing that the new company would be established once $200,000 in capital stock was raised, although it could begin business once $100,000 had been subscribed. Thirty-nine men signed the preliminary agreement to buy stock. These affairs were formalized May 29 when thirty-three of the original group signed the

articles of incorporation for the Lincoln National Life Insurance Company. Samuel Foster, a prominent local manufacturer of women's clothing, was elected president.

The name of the company was suggested by Perry Randall, who insisted that the integrity of a life insurance company was its greatest asset. In 1905 the concepts of integrity and honesty in the insurance industry seemed lost because of the actions of some large eastern companies. Stories of the recently convened Armstrong Committee in New York investigating charges of abuse and mismanagement among life insurance companies filled the pages of the nation's newspapers and magazines with accounts of corruption and scandal, confirming the public's worst apprehension about the industry. This was the "golden age of muckraking," the name given by Theodore Roosevelt to popular writings that thrived on exposing wrong-

Perry A. Randall, the Man who Named Lincoln National

The man who suggested that the new company be named Lincoln National Life Insurance Company was Perry A. Randall, Fort Wayne attorney, businessman and entrepreneur. Born in Avilla, in Noble County, Indiana, in 1847, he came to Fort Wayne at the end of the Civil War to attend the high school, and in 1873 he graduated from the University of Michigan.

Randall was intensely interested in his community and in public works. He was attracted to a scheme to revitalize the canal era by constructing a canal from Fort Wayne to Chicago. Through this plan, especially in Randall's eyes, New York (by way of the Erie Canal and Lake Erie) could thus be directly connected by water to Chicago, and Fort Wayne would be at the center of the commercial waterway. As president of the national Canal Association and a director of the Indiana Rivers and Harbors Congress, Randall lobbied for the project until the day he died. He even took his case to the presidential offices of Teddy Roosevelt, but it all failed.

As a businessman, Randall was best known for the hotel named for him, the Randall Hotel, located on Harrison Street. Known popularly as "the best $2 hotel in Indiana," it was a favorite with travelling salesmen, theater troupes, Buffalo Bill's "Wild West Show" and a variety of fraternal organizations. It was even the site of the first annual meeting of the National Cribbage Association in 1892.

Through it all, Randall remained immersed in civic activities. His greatest project was the Fort Wayne Centennial, which was celebrated one year late. Although civic figures had planned to hold the 100th birthday of the city in the proper year of 1894, the city council failed to come up with the money for the celebration and all the volunteers quit. Randall, however, was not to be undone. He proceeded on his own to make plans and raise the funds for what he called a "monster celebration" in October 1895. Finally, on the morning of October 16, 101 years after the first Fort Wayne had been constructed, the week-long celebration opened with a salute of one hundred cannon shots from the Charles Zollinger Battery of the local militia. Along Calhoun Street, at the intersections of Wayne, Berry and Main streets, triumphal arches were erected and dedicated to "Mad" Anthony Wayne and his adversary, Chief Little Turtle. The Cincinnati Reds played an exhibition game against the Chicago Colts in League Park, and military drills were held in the public parks, sham battles against sham Indians were held and ended with a high-wheeled bicycle parade. The week was punctuated with a grand fireworks display with "theme pieces" spelling out the names of such luminaries as George Washington, Anthony Wayne and, of course, Perry A. Randall.

Randall had made an indelible mark on his contemporaries, but his most lasting contribution was in suggesting the name of the little life insurance company in which he had a hand in organizing. Perry Randall died on February 1, 1916 and his colleagues at Lincoln Life were among those who erected in Swinney Park a statue in his memory as one of the city's great citizens.

doings and abuse especially in giant monopolies like Standard Oil or in large city administrations. Many famous books revealing the ills of America at the turn-of-the-century in the stock market, the political world, the meat-packing industry and the insurance business began as articles in widely read magazines like *McClure's* and the *Arena*. In this atmosphere Randall believed only the name of Abraham Lincoln would so powerfully convey the spirit of integrity in the American tradition to offset such strong negative feelings about insurance. The board agreed and the name was adopted. Although Randall suggested the name, it was another key man who made the noble concept into a reality that remains today. He was Arthur F. Hall, one of the first subscribers and the only person not from Fort Wayne to support the enterprise.

The Lincoln National field force, ca. 1910.

Lincoln National employees take a break in front of the Berry Street office, ca. 1920.

Arthur F. Hall

ARTHUR F. HALL
(1872 - 1942)

The beginnings of Lincoln National cannot be separated from the life of Arthur Hall. Although he did not conceive the company, he was there at its birth and he nurtured it through its first years. Hall was in every way the patriarch of the company. Because he so carefully molded its character in its earliest years, he above all others thoroughly understood the soul and spirit of the company, sensing, as a parent might, how this child of his could wither and die, bloom and blossom, or be injured and renewed like a living thing. It deserved the most personal attention. Just as he became the most noticeable promoter and enthusiastic advocate of Lincoln National in the first two decades when it struggled to establish itself, he became the very personification of the company in the last years of his life, as the middle of the century neared.

Hall was a classic entrepreneur of the turn-of-the-century. He possessed great personal drive, enjoyed business ventures immensely and knew an opportunity when he saw it. Born in Baxter Springs, Kansas, on May 11, 1872, Hall was a year old when his father died the next year and the family returned to his mother's home in Indianapolis. At age fourteen he started as a newsboy for *The Indianapolis Star* and soon had not only two routes, but also hired a boy to help him carry a third. Evidently determined to become a newspaperman, he quit high school in 1889, a year before graduation, to work at the Indianapolis *Journal* as a printer's devil, the lowest job in the company. After eleven years he was promoted to advertising manager and by 1902 had become the assistant business manager. But the paper was sold in 1904 and Hall took a job as a circulation promoter for the *Chicago Tribune*. He also worked for a time with Bobbs-Merrill Publishing Company promoting magazines. These were the difficult times of the Depression of 1903, however, and Hall needed to supplement his income. He decided to try selling life insurance.

Hall joined the Equitable Life Assurance Society of the United States in 1904 as an agent for Marion County, Indiana, but he had difficulty selling, though not for want of effort. In the first months of 1905 the Equitable was experiencing significant troubles at its home office in New York and negative news items which appeared regularly in Indiana newspapers frightened off major policy applicants. Hall, in fact, lost three very large prospects, two for $100,000 and one for $50,000 — very large amounts in 1905 — as a result of the home office problems. So serious was the problem in Indiana that Hall's acquaintance at the Equitable, an experienced insurance man named William B. Paul, lost his agency in Fort Wayne. Both men, unemployed William Paul of Fort Wayne and frustrated Arthur Hall of Indianapolis, were thus very interested when the directors of the Fraternal Assurance Society in Fort Wayne invited them to consider positions to help them reorganize as a legal reserve company. Each man invested $5,000 in the new company — a significant amount and equalling the largest investment by any of the original stockholders. Paul accepted the position of vice president, assuming agency organization duties, and Hall was named secretary and placed in charge of overall office management. It was also part of Hall's contract to have exclusive control for raising the capital for the company as well as selling the necessary number of policies to meet the Insurance Commissioner's requirements for a new company. In addition to his annual salary of $2,600, the board tied Hall's additional compensation to the performance of the company by allowing him to receive a commission on all renewal premiums if scheduled amounts of insurance in force were reached each January 1. The schedule called for $1 million to be in force by 1907 and $53 million by January 1, 1921. If these goals were not met, Hall would not get his commissions. Paying the company secretary in this way was illegal in some states, but not in Indiana, and although Best's *Insurance Reports* criticized the arrangement, the program's success over the years ended any concerns.

Hall was a natural salesman. He arrived in Fort Wayne in March 1905 and at once began raising the required $100,000 in capital. The original subscribers had pledged only $87,000 and some of these tried to get out of their promises in the wake of the demise of the Fort Wayne's White National Bank and the near collapse of the city's First National Bank caused by the depression that began in 1903. But Hall was persistent and as a newcomer to town, successfully relied upon the extensive city contacts of Daniel Ninde and Samuel Foster for access to the new funding sources. The $100,000 required by law was soon raised and on June 12 a charter to do business was granted by the state.

From the moment of incorporation, Hall turned all his energies to the affairs and future of Lincoln National. His first reward was to be named general manager of the company, replacing Paul as vice president less than a month after arriving on the job. Hall later recalled that the directors had, in fact, offered the job "of managing the company to every experienced life insurance man in town, but each in turn wisely shook his head and said, 'It can't be done!' In desperation these gentlemen offered the job to me. With

William B. Paul was well known in the Fort Wayne community as an insurance salesman before the founding of Lincoln National. Caricature from *Some Fort Wayne Phizes*.

fifteen years' business training on a newspaper and a few months' experience selling life insurance, and consequently no insurance knowledge to speak of, I 'rushed in where angels feared to tread,' and accepted the job."

He then demonstrated his zeal for the business and his own infatuation with Abraham Lincoln when he wrote to President Lincoln's son, Robert Todd Lincoln, asking for a photograph of the sixteenth president to be used on the company's letterhead. Mr. Lincoln answered on August 3, 1905:

Replying to your note of July 28th, I find no objection whatever to the use of a portrait of my father upon the letterhead of such a life insurance company named after him as you describe; and I take pleasure in enclosing you, for that purpose, what I regard as a very good photograph of him.

This photograph was none other than the well-known "five-dollar-bill" image of Abraham Lincoln taken by Anthony Berger on Feb. 9, 1864, at the Mathew Brady studio in Washington, D. C..

Hall moved his family to Fort Wayne in September and began to organize and sell Lincoln National in earnest. The first home of Lincoln National was one room in the White National Bank building on Calhoun Street furnished with two straight-back chairs and a cherry table. The staff consisted of Hall and his secretary. Two men who were familiar with the insurance business, Max Blitz and former Fraternal salesman William Bishop, assisted Hall as agents in securing the necessary 250 applications to qualify the company for its license.

Hall's leadership and tireless energy in these difficult days were critical to the survival of the company. For the first six years of its life, between 1905 and 1911, Lincoln National struggled to stay alive. First-year sales were encouraging with $532,000 of life insurance in force and paid premiums of $20,859. The level of business required an increase of clerical staff to eight and a new, larger office was leased on the second floor of the Odd Fellows building on Wayne and Calhoun streets.

One notable reason for its early success was that the company had been spared any claims since its beginning. In 1907, however, the first claim finally was submitted. At the same time, sales expenses were increasing rapidly. Agency expenses, in particular, had pushed the cost of new business to 130 percent. By the end of the year Lincoln National would have been insolvent had it not been for a con-

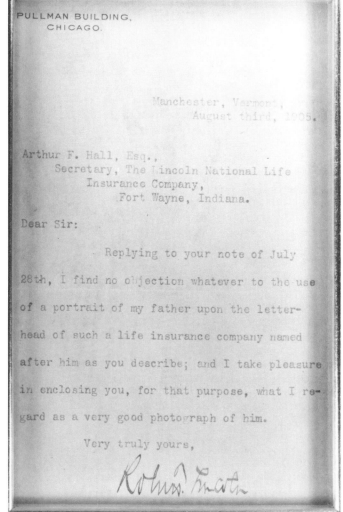

sulting actuary reporting to the insurance commissioner that the value of the office furniture should be included in the balance sheet.

To add to the infant company's woes an Indiana version of the Armstrong Committee began investigating the insurance industry in 1907. Under the leadership of reform-minded Gov. James F. Hanley, measures were put before the Indiana General Asssembly that would severely curtail the amount of first-year premium that could be used to meet acquisition expenses, such as sales commissions, medical examinations and premium taxes. Hall and Foster together lobbied vigorously to ensure defeat of proposed measures, marking the beginning of Lincoln National's strong tradition of working within the regulatory system to balance business and policyholder needs. Sales remained fairly strong after 1907, but overhead expenses continued to plague the company. Hall's immediate answer was to curtail the growth of the field force and focus on office development. But he soon saw the need to reverse himself and this required, for the first time, bringing in new professionals to help him.

This decision was the first evidence of what was one of Hall's greatest attributes. Although he personally worked very hard and put in long hours at his office, Hall was above all else a leader who could attract leaders and then allow them to lead. He had a knack for comprehending the strengths and weaknesses of others while also understanding his own limitations as an insurance professional. Simply stated, he knew when to get help.

Hall firmly believed that Lincoln National ought not to be a one-man company. As he said in an interview given to the *Forbes* reporter in 1935, "I'd rather guide a team of fast-step-pers than try to speed up a team of plugs. I am not managing a life insurance company. What I am managing is a group of men, each of whom thoroughly understands his particular part of a highly technical business, and keeping them in accord and all pepped up to go." Development of an executive organization on which he could rely was one of his "four planks on which The Lincoln was built."

Hall made two critical decisions in 1910: Extend the field force into large cities and hire an actuary. To accomplish the first goal, Hall used all his powers of persuasion to recruit Walter T. Shepard, the superintendent of the Midwestern field force for Security Mutual Life of Binghamton, N.Y. Shepard was a young man already highly regarded in the insurance industry as "a live wire, a man of delightful personality and successful." During the next 23 years "Shep" would create a well organized, aggressive and effective field force centered in the large cities, a field force that played a significant role in the early success of the company.

Hall's greatest coup, however, was convincing the actuary Franklin B. Mead to come to Lincoln National. Mead was the actuary of Michigan State Life Insurance Company in Detroit when Hall met him at an industry meeting. Before this, Mead had worked in Philadelphia at the Security Trust and Life Insurance Company, a firm that specialized in substandard insurance, and his insightful understanding of underwriting issues had become evident in the several formal papers he delivered to the profession. One outstanding presentation given at the 1909 annual meeting of the American Life Convention (a predecessor to the present-day trade association, the American Council of Life Insurance, or ACLI) on measuring risk and liability under disability benefits in life insurance policies was especially well received as Mead addressed this relatively new topic in the innovative manner which would become his hallmark. Opportunities for putting his notions into operation were limited, however, at Michigan State Life. Hall and Lincoln National offered the opportunities he sought.

The impact of the arrival of Shepard and Mead was quickly felt at Lincoln National. Hall became first vice president, Mead was made secretary, and Shepard was superintendent of agents. Thanks to the new men in management and Hall's earlier success in building the surplus, Lincoln National experienced a burst of growth that set the tone for future aggressive expansion and creative ventures. Mead, with his earlier experience with substandard cases, supported medical director Dr. Calvin English, who had already issued Lincoln National's first substandard policy on June 15, 1909. Mead's newly developed statistics allowed the company to rate many "impaired" risks with precision. Sales improved dramatically as the rejection rate fell from the industry norm of 11% to less than 4%. Shepard's agency development efforts were bolstered because agents could place much more business with Lincoln National. In addition, Mead also had developed a strong interest in the potential of reinsurance — that is, accepting part of another company's risk on a policy in exchange for part of the policy's premium. Leaning heavily on his personal connections with other insurance companies, Mead obtained the reinsurance business from forty companies in 1913, and in 1914 he doubled the figure. Lincoln National was not ten years old, and it had already begun to assume a place of special

The Classic Salesman

In later years Arthur Hall like to recall how he had received a note from William Noble, one of the original subscribers, saying that he would not after all be able to fulfill his pledged subscription of $5,000. Hall went immediately to see Noble who asked "What are you doing here?" when Hall entered his office. He replied, "I've come for your check." "But didn't you get my note?" Noble responded. Hall then answered, "Yes, that is why I'm here." Although the discussion then became animated and argumentative, Hall remembered that Noble never actually said "No" to his demands for the check. Finally, Noble said, "Well, Hall, if you go after business the way you've gone after me, I don't see what can keep that company from being a success." So saying, he gave Hall the check for $5,000; Hall took no chances but went immediately by streetcar to Noble's bank and had his check certified.

expertise in the industry that it enjoys to this day.

Lincoln National took another major leap forward in 1913 when it dramatically expanded its business through the acquisition of the Michigan State Life Insurance Company. This company was strong when Hall purchased the controlling interest in the stock and then reinsured the business through a technique known as assumption reinsurance. In addition to expanding the business dramatically by adding $8 million of business in force to the portfolio, the agency force was increased and a new region opened for sales. In the wake of this successful venture, Hall turned his attention to other possible acquisitions. The Pioneer Life Insurance Company of Fargo, North Dakota, founded in 1907, had also been a strong company, but agricultural difficulties in the West left the owners ready to sell. Hall organized a consortium to borrow the money and, as with the Michigan State Life, purchased a controlling interest and reinsured the business. When this deal was completed early in 1917 Lincoln National's insurance in force was $50 million. By the end of the year it had climbed to $63 million, more than double that of the previous year. Talent also came with these early acquisitions, most notably Alfred Dern, an outstanding young executive at the Pioneer who eventually became Lincoln National's director of agencies.

As America entered World War I in

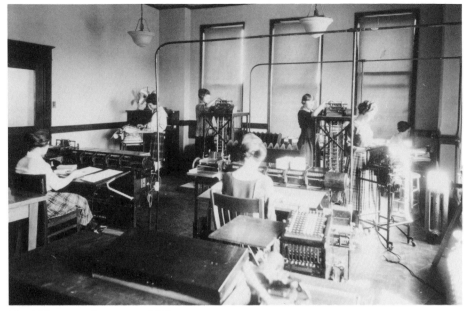

The Addressograph room, ca. 1920.

1917, the Lincoln National Life Insurance Company was healthy and growing quickly. It was well positioned, also, for the aftermath of the war. Despite the obvious consequences of the war for mortality rates, the insurance industry in general benefitted from World War I because Americans came to understand better the value of life insurance, which had been provided by the government to servicemen. The perceived value of life insurance was reinforced in 1918 when the great influenza epidemic killed more Americans than from all causes in the war. Sales of the Lincoln Life product soared after 1918. Insurance in force in 1920 was over

$159 million, an increase of $130 million from 1915.

More importantly, the reinsurance business begun by Lincoln National in 1912 gained a major boost in 1917. First, the Pittsburgh Life and Trust, then the principal life reinsurer in America collapsed. Second, the largest reinsurers in the world were German companies barred from doing business in the United States by the latter's entry into the war. At the spring 1917 meeting of the Medical Section of the American Life Convention, Mead astounded the industry when he rose to announce dramatically that Lincoln National intended to take the place in the reinsurance market of Pittsburgh

---

"Where there's a will, there's a way" — Arthur Hall Jumps from a Train

Tales of travel have been a staple of conversation among the generations of Lincoln National people who have driven the roads, ridden the rails or flown the skies in behalf of the company. Arthur Hall began the tradition. Once, on a snowy winter night in 1907, Hall was returning to Fort Wayne on the Pennsylvania Flyer en route from Pittsburgh to Chicago. He had wearily climbed aboard at 1 a.m. in Upper Sandusky, Ohio, and asked the porter to be sure to wake him five minutes before arriving in Fort Wayne at the scheduled time of 4 a.m.. Hall figured the five minutes would be plenty of time to get up and dressed and make it to his office for an early morning meeting. So exhausted was Hall, however, that the porter could not rouse him. When Hall at last awoke, he saw the familiar walls of Fort Wayne's Pennsylvania station out his window, thinking they had just arrived. He said to the porter, "You sure didn't give me much time to get dressed; we're already in Fort Wayne!" The porter answered, "I've been trying to wake you for twenty minutes. We're not pullin' in, we're pullin' out of Fort Wayne."

The next stop was Plymouth, Indiana, seventy miles west of Fort Wayne, but Hall had to be at his morning meeting. "Open that door," he yelled at the porter, as he grabbed his hat, coat and clothes. Barefooted, he dashed through the train door and threw himself from the steps of the moving train and landed in a snowdrift along the tracks. Clad only in his underwear, he managed to get himself out of the snowdrift, pull on his overcoat, put on his shoes and make his way back to the station. "For the Lord's sake, Mr. Hall, what's happened to you?" the station agent exclaimed when Hall entered the station. As he dressed in front of the pot-bellied stove in the agent's office, Hall told his story, adding the moral tag, "It just goes to show, that where there's a will, there's a way."

Hall's love of roses was turned into a symbol for sales contests.

the rapidly increasing volume of business. Under Mead's guidance the concept of granting lay people the authority to approve clearly acceptable applications was instituted on Feb. 20, 1919. By unburdening the medical director and his professional staff, this pioneering effort in application management allowed the company to serve its agents and customers more efficiently. Similarly, the process of general office management, and especially the training of new personnel, was greatly enhanced when Hall endorsed in 1925 Mead's concept of the training program known today as LOMA (Life Office Management Association). For the benefit of the field force, Shepard began publication of *The Emancipator*, which was designed to offer advice and information to the sales force. Today it is the oldest continuous publication of the company.

Riding a wave of prosperity, Hall was elected president of the company in January 1923 and he enthusiastically set $1 billion of insurance in force as the goal for 1930. He had good reason to believe this could be done. During the first five years of the decade the company had already increased its business to nearly $350 million in force and the annual sales figures, particularly for reinsurance, were increasing more rapidly. The physical manifestation of this growing prosperity was the construction of LNL's own home office building on Harrison Street. Since the beginning in 1905 the company had leased space as needed in several buildings around Fort Wayne. The grand project of erecting its own building began in 1921 and was completed in 1923 with a gala celebration led by Hall and Postmaster General Harry S. New who

Life and Trust and the German reinsurers. The years of peril for Lincoln National were over as it poised for the boom decade of the "Roaring Twenties."

For Hall personally, the decade opened on a somber note. Una Fletcher, his wife and a gifted muscian, died in February 1920, and later that year his mother, Elizabeth, also died. Hall was left with his three small children, William, Arthur and Aileen, but in October of the following year he married Ann O'Rourke, a woman who had worked for Lincoln National since 1907.

Hall continued to attract to the company top professionals, especially people who understood reinsurance.

In 1919 he hired Alva J. McAndless who one day would take Hall's place as the head of Lincoln National. McAndless' first job was to promote reinsurance sales, which he did aggressively throughout the early 1920s. Hall then recruited the bright young actuary Leland J. "Pete" Kalmbach in 1924 who served as Lincoln National's chief reinsurance officer until he left the company in 1947. Kalmbach later became the president of the Massachusetts Mutual Life Insurance Company.

Rapid growth required Hall to focus on the internal development of the company. An urgent difficulty lay in the inability of Dr. English and his Medical Department to keep up with

Arthur Hall and Fort Wayne Aviation

Arthur Hall was a leader in the effort to bring air mail and commercial aviation to Fort Wayne. He was one of the key figures in the creation of Fort Wayne's first airport, called Baer Field (today, Smith Field) in honor of the World War I ace, Paul Max Baer of Fort Wayne. He succeeded in bringing aviation into the local limelight when he was able to get the Ford Trophy Contestants to come to Fort Wayne in 1925 and 1926. Indiana's representative on the National Aeronautic Association, Hall served several years as the president of the Fort Wayne branch. His enthusiasm for local aviation was visible to many early aviators. When the new Harrison Street home office building was erected in 1923, he had special roof-top markers installed to point the way to the airport on the north side of town. In its day, these markers were highly prized by pilots and in recognition of the service Hall was awarded a special certificate of commendation by Charles Lindbergh and Harry Guggenheim of the prestigious Daniel Guggenheim Fund for the Promotion of Aeronautics in 1929. The next year Hall was one of the Fort Wayne leaders instrumental in inaugurating the first air mail service for the city, an important development for the growing insurance company that was anxious to serve its policyholders as quickly as possible.

Lincoln National women celebrating the wedding engagement of one of their colleagues, ca. 1920.

came from New York to dedicate the new home office. Hall was named "one of the twelve greatest living men in life insurance" by the *National Underwriter.*

With the new home office in operation and with expanded staff and professional training programs in place, Hall again turned to acquisition to build the business. Thanks to the reinsurance contacts of McAndless, whose extensive travelling had often taken him to Des Moines, Iowa, Hall learned of the possibility of acquiring the Merchants Life Insurance Company there. He moved quickly and closed the deal in 1928, adding a hefty $80 million of insurance in force.

Hall's efforts to expand the company did not interfere with his desires to develop "The Lincoln family." Like business leaders of his day, Hall had strong patriarchal feelings about the employee force, believing that he had an obligation to see to their overall welfare. Consequently, he instituted publication of *Life With The Lincoln,* a popular company magazine that not only gave information about the business, but also devoted many columns to personal news about employees, the progress of company athletic teams, vacation stories and even lessons on such topics as the virtues of savings and home-owning or the evils of communism. Not infrequently, the president encouraged voter registration and employee turn-out in national elections, and he did not hesitate to do so in the context of his own strongly stated opinions about particular candidates.

In 1923 the employees' Social and Athletic Association was organized, which provided for regular exercise as a part of the daily office routine, supported teams and oversaw the in-house golf practice areas and bowling alleys. The company sponsored a competitive baseball team and a bowling team that in 1922 won the national amateur title. Hall, an excellent bowler himself, was the manager of the bowling team. This was the era of company banquets, picnics, and an occasional minstrel show. In 1931, once the Volsted Act which prohibited the sale and consumption of alcohol was repealed, the president started his popular "Mr. Hall's Party," a biennial event for the executives at his vaca-

tion home in Leland, Michigan. The place was called "The Duck." Very much a man of the 1920s, one of his favorite activities at the "Party" with "the gang," as he liked to call the men who were invited (and they called him "Chief"), was to lead them in a rousing rendition of "Little Liza Jane."

Perhaps the greatest luxury of all in these boom days was the establishment in 1928 of the Lincoln Foundation, marking the beginnings of the company's famous Lincoln Library, today's Lincoln Museum. Inheriting his mother's reverence for the sixteenth president, Hall saw the foundation as a "repayment of the company's debt to Abraham Lincoln." The foundation gave body to the self-image of the insurance company that increasingly turned to the words and spirit of the great president to sell its products and develop its internal strengths. The company's first advertising slogan, "Its Name Indicates Its Character," summed it up perfectly.

Hall also became a prominent community leader in the 1920s. In the previous decade he had served as chair of a variety of boards, but he firmly established himself as one of the top figures in the community in 1920 when he led the effort to attract International Harvester to Fort Wayne over the competitive bids of twenty-six other cities. International Harvester was one of the nation's

largest heavy truck manufacturers, and Hall's success as chairman of the effort gave his adopted community its largest industry for half a century. Henceforth, the president of Lincoln National would be on call for every major fund drive or community development effort.

On Jan. 11, 1929, during the first agents' meeting at the new home office, Hall made an important announcement that illustrated how firmly established the company had become. He explained to the field force that as president he no longer needed personally to supervise the company, now that it was in the capable hands of those he had recruited. Now he "could think and plan about the future." This became a critical issue for the company as it entered the decade of the most serious economic trial the nation had yet faced, the Great Depression. New applications and renewals fell sharply as unemployment lines lengthened, and the many long-term investments in farm mortgages, seemingly so secure a few years earlier, became a serious liability threatening the stability of the company.

The Depression denied Hall the opportunity to "think about and plan the future." His beloved goal of $1 billion of insurance in force by 1930 was shattered. He now had to save the company and all that he and his col-

"The Duck," Hall's home in Leland, Michigan, site of the annual gathering of the executives in the 1930s.

Lincoln National executives enjoying themselves at "The Duck," 1935.

leagues had worked so hard to create. In addition to fending off the first modest attempts by an outsider to acquire a controlling interest in the company, the first issue to face — as it was for the entire industry — was the deteriorating condition of the investment portfolio. Although the company had not invested heavily in the volatile equities market, its traditionally strong place in real estate, and particularly Midwestern agricultural mortgages, caused serious problems as farmers failed to make their mortgage payments and foreclosures increased. Hall, with the considerable help of McAndless, spent a great deal of time restructuring Lincoln National's investment position, which became an issue that would outlive both men. Among Hall's proudest achievements in these years was his successful lobbying in the Indiana General Assembly for more flexible investment regulations for the insurance industry in the state. These greatly helped Lincoln National's ability to remain competitive.

The Depression also had an adverse effect on direct sales. Hall sought to offset this by giving more attention to the development of reinsurance, so much so that some have reflected that by the end of the decade Lincoln National was, in fact, primarily a reinsurance company. In order to expand direct business, however, Hall again turned to his old technique of acquiring other insurance companies and adding their business to the Lincoln National books. The Depression offered the opportunity as several ailing small companies were acquired in 1932 and 1933, including Northern States Life of Hammond, Indiana, Old Line Life Insurance Company of Lincoln, Nebraska, and the Royal Union Life Insurance Company of Des Moines, Iowa, one of the oldest insurance companies in the West. These three acquisitions alone boosted the company's business in force by nearly $200 million at very little initial cost.

The greatest blow of the Depression years, however, was the death of Mead in 1933. Mead clearly was destined to succeed Hall. He and Hall were very much of the same mind about the future direction of the company and the accession of Mead would have placed Lincoln National in the hands of a first rate professional with keen managerial abilities. After 1933, Hall turned increasingly to McAndless and Kalmbach, who also were both top rate professionals and tough businessmen, though of very different character. It was McAndless, in fact, who during the decade recruited Walter Menge and Henry Rood, each of whom would one day run the company. Others who came to Lincoln National in the 1930s and who in later years would be formative figures were Allen Steere, Edward Auer, Gathings Stewart, M. C. "Bud" Ledden, Carl Ashmann, Cecil Cross, Thagrus Burns, Samuel Adams and Gordon Reeves. This was the generation that would help take Lincoln National to its next stage of significant change.

By 1935 the worst effects of the Depression were over for the insurance industry and Lincoln National emerged as one of the strong survivors of the experience. Hall and McAndless had saved most jobs in the company by simply seeking other means than layoffs to achieve necessary austerity, and in 1939 the company achieved

ITS NAME INDICATES ITS CHARACTER

The LINCOLN NATIONAL
LIFE INSURANCE COMPANY
FORT WAYNE, INDIANA

Early Lincoln National advertising focused on values represented by the powerful image of Abraham Lincoln.

Hall and agency head Al Dern celebrate the occasion of Lincoln National Life reaching $ 1 billion insurance in force.

Participants in the Lincoln National Golf Tournament, 1928. Left to right are Joseph Frank (Lincoln National general counsel), Paul Baer (America's first "ace" in World War I), Arthur Hall Jr., Arthur Hall and Leland "Pete" Kalmbach (head of Lincoln National's Reinsurance Department).

the much vaunted goal of $1 billion of life insurance in force. This was the first time a company in the United States had achieved this level of business entirely under the guidance of one man. But Hall also learned in 1938 that he had a serious heart problem. He was warned that if he did not ease his hectic business and community schedule and stop his almost constant smoking, he would not last for very many years. Unwilling, or unable, to change his lifestyle, Hall continued to represent the company publicly, participate in Community Chest drives, lead in the Taxpayers' Research Association, serve the congregation at the Trinity Episcopal Church, and participate in numerous industry committees of the American Life Convention. And he continued to smoke heavily. Understanding the gravity of the situation, however, he saw to the election of McAndless as the president of the company in 1939, thereby designating a successor.

Hall worked at his office until only weeks before his death. When he finally had to stay home, the company remained his passion. In an extraordinarily touching demonstration of his paternal instinct for the welfare of the company he had created and developed into one of the nation's finest life insurers, he called to his home by twos each of the leading men in Lincoln National. He started with those who had been with the company the most years and worked his way down to those who had been with Lincoln National at least ten years. To each couple he gave fatherly advice about the way to give their best to Lincoln National, the way he had done. For each man who experienced this, it was a moment deeply cherished and never to be forgotten. In this way, Hall's unique spirit was continued through decades long after his death and this cannot be underestimated in considering the success of the company in the second half of the twenteth century. Hall died on November 9, 1942.

Hall at the peak of his career, ca. 1935.

"Dame Fortune's Surrender to Arthur F. Hall"

Arthur Hall at the peak of his early career building Lincoln National deeply impressed those with whom he came in contact, especially for his personal qualities as a leader. In the September 1921 issue of the *American Insurance Digest*, in an article entitled "Dame's Fortune's Surrender to Arthur F. Hall," the reporter wrote two passages that tell a great deal about Hall's commanding presence:

Thinking of Mr. Hall personally, one thinks of a trim Vandyke beard, hair that is streaked prematurely with silver, and cigarettes that have about them the aroma of Cairo. Roses are no more becoming to a June bride than that Vandyke to Mr. Hall. As to the gray hair, he wears that with dignity, and the cigarettes, he smokes with frequency.

Physically, Mr. Hall is as slender as he is broad intellectually. His suave and gracious manner alone is enough to woo the heart out of an arctic iceberg, and with it, he combines a rare understanding of the human heart and mind. His ability along this line, flavored with the diplomacy that marks his every move, makes him an extraordinary salesman.

Aerial view of Lincoln National's home office in 1935 displaying on the roof the directions for pilots to the new Fort Wayne airport.

Alva J. McAndless

ALVA J. McANDLESS
(1890 - 1954)

Alva McAndless was well prepared for taking command of Lincoln National when Arthur Hall died in 1942. He had been in charge of the day-to-day operations of the company since Franklin Mead's death nine years earlier. Those closest to Hall knew he had selected McAndless to be his successor by 1935 and this became an open certainty when McAndless was elected president of the company in 1939. Like Hall, McAndless viewed the company in very personal terms. To McAndless, however, it was more than a family; it was his alter ego. It was, indeed, one of his notable habits to speak of company matters in the first person. He, like Hall, was a patriarch who was intimately familiar with every part of the company's operation and knew most of the 1,700 employees of the Home Office and all of the more than 1,200 field agents by name. He was not, like Hall, a gentle patriarch, however. Rather, he was a stern father who did not hesitate to chastise, instruct or discipline the members of the Lincoln National family. There were no parties in Leland for the senior men. Profoundly honest and humble, "Mac" — as he liked to be called, for he hated to be called Alva — was intensely competitive, bluntly straightforward and exceptionally bright. Yet, McAndless was strangely uncomfortable with personnel issues. Later CEOs, Walter Menge and Thomas Watson, recall how McAndless would wait until the day he was scheduled to go on his annual vacation before he would announce the senior staff raises so he would not have to deal with unhappy executives. Sometimes, according to Menge, one might not find out about a raise until the paychecks came out. McAndless was a poor delegator of responsibility, frequently succumbing to the urge to insert himself in every detail of the company, sometimes in upsetting ways. Hall, during his last interviews with the leading executives, had recognized this as his greatest fault and cautioned several of the leading men to work with, or at least be understanding of, McAndless' habits.

McAndless was the guiding force that pulled Lincoln National through the Great Depression, the uncertainties of World War II and the post-war economic slump. His fiscal policies for the company were austere, reflecting the era of economic uncertainty, but he knew how to pursue opportunities for growth and crowned his career with what was then the largest transaction in American life insurance history. His reputation in the industry was superlative and, according to the trade journals, Lincoln National under his guidance was known as one of the best managed insurance companies of any size in the nation. It was one of the most prosperous, too: Just before Hall died, the company reached its long dreamed-of mark of $1 billion of insurance in force, yet by the time McAndless died a little more than a decade later, the Lincoln National was writing that much business each year.

McAndless was the son of prosperous Scotch-Irish immigrants who had settled in the little central Michigan town of Capac, not far from Port Huron. Born on Oct. 23, 1890, McAndless attended the local schools and worked summers on the lake steamers that called at Port Huron. After high school he attended the Ypsilanti Normal School for two years and took a position as a teacher. Although he seems to have enjoyed teaching and talking about history, philosophy and literature, he was unhappy and struggled to raise enough money to attend law school. Having scrimped enough to enjoy a savings balance well over the substantial sum of $1,000, he explored the limits of his rage and frustration when the bank failed and he lost everything. Doggedly reaccumulating the necessary funds, he entered the University of Michigan to become a lawyer at the advanced age of twenty-four. But mathematics sidetracked him. He had the good fortune to study under a professor of applied mathematics who eventually placed him in the class of James W. Glover, destined to be one of the chief luminaries in the field of actuarial science. McAndless did well in this arena. He was elected Phi Beta Kappa and was graduated with honors in 1917, on the eve of America's entry into World War I.

McAndless turned down an offer for a faculty position at the University of Michigan to do actuarial work for the Grange Life Insurance Company of Lansing, Michigan. After about a year, he became the actuary for the Detroit Life Insurance Company. These were important experiences, because he learned a great deal about the reinsurance needs of small insurance companies. While in Detroit he met Mead, who was there to discuss a reinsurance contract. McAndless let him know in no uncertain terms how disappointed he was in the service Lincoln National had been giving Detroit Life. Lincoln National had recently lost its fine medical director, Dr. Bryan Barlow, in an automobile accident and had replaced him with three young physicians just out of the Army and inexperienced in insurance work. As McAndless recalled, he told Mead "the service was pretty awful; it wasn't like the old days when Dr. Barlow was in charge of affairs. I told him that I could send six cases down to The Lincoln and instead of getting a decision on any of them, I would get six letters back. In fact, these M.D.s were the world's marathon letter writers. This disturbed him considerably, and he assured me the condition would be cured." Mead's "cure" was to hire McAndless in December 1919 and put him in charge as assistant secretary for underwriting.

McAndless was an insatiable student of the Lincoln National operation and he fell in love with the rapidly growing company. Two years before McAndless joined Lincoln National, the company had acquired Pioneer Life whose agencies increased Lincoln National's field operation by 50%. To this was added growth as a result of war risks and the influenza epidemic of 1918. Mead urgently needed the additional actuarial expertise of a man like McAndless who became Mead's chief assistant and "reinsurance ambassador." McAndless quickly built upon Mead's great reputation in the field and soon created his own during the 1920s as the head of reinsurance sales. By the end of the decade McAndless had become a powerful figure not only in the company but

McAndless as head of reinsurance operations, ca. 1920.

also in the industry as Lincoln National carefully fostered its image as a "mother hen" offering service especially to smaller companies.

Setting a pattern for later leaders of the company to follow, McAndless worked energetically in all areas of the company, culminating with his involvement in the agency and investment departments in 1929. Clearly favored by Mead, who was his mentor, McAndless advanced rapidly. In 1924 he was elected to the Board of Directors and two years later McAndless assumed Mead's role as secretary of the company, a post which Mead had held since 1912.

It is important to note also that between 1928 and 1933, when Lincoln National embarked on a round of acquisitions, McAndless was either at the beginning or at the center of the deals. It was through his reinsurance connections that he learned of the Merchants Life opportunity in 1928 and he was one of the key senior officers in the 1933 acquisitions of both Northern States Life and Royal Union Life. These were also very tough years for Lincoln National, as they were for many insurance compa-

nies. McAndless played a key role in reducing home office overhead, becoming well known for his many austerity measures. One plague of the Great Depression was incessant rumor-mongering, and Lincoln National was not spared. Stories flew

about in the early 1930s that the company was becoming insolvent and would fold. Walter Menge, who was teaching actuarial sciences at the University of Michigan at the time, recalled frequently running into Lincoln National agents at various meetings who raised questions about the company's possible fate. These difficulties had a marked impact on McAndless, who later vowed that he would run the company in such a way that would never again cause anyone to question its solvency.

In 1933 the double tragedy of Mead's death and the pressures of the Great Depression thrust McAndless into the limelight. He became Hall's right-hand man. McAndless took over day-to-day operations while Hall retained the overall reins of authority and continued his role as persona of the company. McAndless was elected first vice president in 1934 and, although the worst of the Depression was over for the insurance industry by mid-decade, he kept the company in an austerity mode that was difficult for some to manage. His programs of cost control and conservative investments gradually paid off. He was made executive vice president in 1936 and three years later, when Hall knew his health was beginning to fail, McAndless was elected president and designated successor. As Hall explained to the company in *The*

A Lincoln National agent of the 1920s.

A Forceful Presence — The Personality of "Mac"

Perhaps no other chief executive of Lincoln National has caused so much comment about his personality and style of management as has A.J. McAndless. Seldom do those who knew him use terms of subtlety or shadings to describe him. He is clearly remembered as strong and forceful, single-minded and intrusive, brilliant and incisive, and sober and brusque. He was cautious and conservative, but he gave himself unstintingly to community causes. An avid reader of magazines (he was especially fond of *The London Economist,* but enjoyed many others too, from the *New Yorker* and *Atlantic Monthly* to *The Journal of the History of Ideas,* the *Saturday Review of Literature* and the *Atomic Energy Report,* in addition to a host of industry publications), McAndless greatly enjoyed conversations in history, philosophy, economics and current affairs.

"Mac" was an imposing man physically — tall, muscular and large framed, with striking red hair when he was young. When he walked the halls of Lincoln National his distinctive step announced his coming; likewise his somewhat high-pitched voice could be recognized easily. One person recalled that "he had a quick sense of humor, a democratic manner, and when thinking, his tongue was in his cheek. No photograph ever successfully recorded the twinkle in his eye when he was amused."

His style of management, however, is what most consistently is remembered. It was indicative of the deep attachment of the patriarch who had a difficult time allowing too much independence for fear of harm coming to the thing he loved so much. Reaching back to his high school course in Port Huron on "Business and Common Sense Mathematics" he was a tight-fisted governor of the company: "He demanded full value for every dollar spent." His door was always open, though visitors would be cut short if the conversation turned to trivialities. He constantly attended to every detail of the company's operation, making it a point to make rounds every day to see for himself what employees, high and low, were doing. He became renowned for popping in on staff at every level with the question, "What are you doing?" or "How is it coming?" or "What does it show?" Then he might as easily suggest another way of doing the task or interpreting the data. Sometimes he would simply give new direction to the employee without ever informing his or her supervisor, for protocol had no meaning for him. Some employees came to dread hearing that distinctive walk coming down the hall toward their office for fear that "Mac" might appear and hold them accountable for whatever at that moment they were doing. Yet, many noted how he also enjoyed having a late evening meal with the janitorial staff, and he was intensely loyal to employees, seeking every effort to save jobs; on several occasions employees who had fallen ill and were no longer productive were kept on the payroll.

Allen Steere, an attorney who came to Lincoln National during Arthur Hall's last years, remembered one incident when he told McAndless about the complaints made by some stockholders about the company's dividend policy. "Mac demanded to know who had complained, but I told him I couldn't tell him or it would ruin my credibility with the stockholders I had to work with. He was furious that I would not tell, but I knew that the effectiveness of my job prevented me doing what Mac wanted. He came to my office later that day — I still can hear those footsteps coming — he came to my desk and standing tall over me pointed his finger at me, demanding I tell him who had complained. I would not and he walked out. I thought for sure I was in big trouble and I spent some very uncomfortable days. Later, he came back again, still angry and still wagging his finger at me, demanding I reveal who complained. Still, I protested that I could not. Again, he stalked out of the office without a word. But that was the last I ever heard of the issue. It wasn't in him to admit defeat or enjoy being thwarted, but he was wise enough to listen to well meaning counsel. One thing's sure, he never would have respected me or my opinions if I had backed down, for he was an immensely honest and fair man."

McAndless was deeply respected, particularly in the field and in the industry at large, but in the Home Office he was also feared and seldom loved. He understood and accepted that.

Cecil Cross, head of the agency department and Mac's frequent, often bitter opponent, illustrated the depth of feeling McAndless stirred in his top executives when McAndless suddenly died in New Orleans; Cross wept the entire trip as he accompanied the body back to Fort Wayne.

Emancipator, "In bringing about this change in titles, I am substituting a younger man as the 'quarterback' and I shall be the 'coach.' I know that he heartily favors conducting the business in the future with such a relationship existing. I commend our new president to you. He is forty-seven years old and has been with the Company for nineteen years. He is thoroughly seasoned for the task and knows the business of life insurance as well as anyone I know in the business."

When McAndless became CEO of Lincoln National in 1942, the nation was in the dark hours of World War II. The company thrived, however, in

Hall and McAndless toward the end of Hall's career.

McAndless at the Augusta National with golfing legend Bobby Jones (left) and Pete Kalmbach, March 1940.

part because life insurance had become a well established vehicle for financial stability in the previous two decades and the uncertainties of global war caused sales to soar. Within ten years of the war's end, Lincoln National's life insurance in force exceeded $5 billion.

McAndless' reputation was such that he was one of five industry representatives named to the War Committee for Life Insurance, which guided government policy touching on the nation's insurance companies during the war. He achieved professional recognition when he was elected president of the American Life Convention in 1942. His most important contribution to the industry was his leadership in the development of the Revenue Act of 1942 and what came to be known as "The McAndless Plan" for determining taxation of life insurance companies. The original Treasury plan would have put an unfair burden particularly on the investment income of small insurance companies; but McAndless, with assistance from Walter Menge, his top aide, presented a proposal that provided for the least amount of discrimination. Even larger companies which would pay a somewhat higher tax applauded the McAndless concept and its overall benefit to the industry and the federal government. In the words of the American Life Convention directors in 1943, McAndless' "distinct contribution, which more than anything else aided in unifying the business in troublesome times such as now confront the country, constituted a most invaluable service to both the American Life Convention and all other segments of the industry, and is but further tangible evidence of his profound wisdom and judgment."

McAndless even had a widespread reputation for making solid predictions about the state of the economy. In his presidential address of 1942,

Cookie and McAndless' "Football Contest"

Just before he died, McAndless addressed the field force in a way that well expresses his enthusiasm for the tough business of sales, which when well organized and aggressively pursued lay at the heart of the excitement of working in the insurance industry.

"This Cross Month Contest (named in honor of Agency Department Manager Cecil Cross), with its football trappings, makes me think with longing of wonderful times in the past. It takes me back to college days, with all their display of colorful bands and trooping students. It brings before one's eyes a bright pattern of youth and energy and courage. But it arouses also memories and thoughts of people who are near you now and things that happen now.

So I think of Cookie (H.T. Cook) and his football days as I think about you and this particular contest. Not all of you men and women in the field know Cookie, but he is a little guy — and I mean physically — who is in the Home Office agency here in Fort Wayne. Cookie played football in Nebraska a long, long time ago when the rules and penalties were not quite so strict as they are today. Sometimes I have had Cookie talk to a group of agents, and it is his habit always on such occasions to drag in some football ghost out of the glorious past.

One of the best stories was used last year before a group of new agents who were in here for training. I think he told it in somewhat this fashion: 'The coach between halves of a clean, hard-fought contest told the boys to remember that the fellow in front of them was just as dog tired as they were and had been knocked down just as often, and perhaps if they just had the courage and spirit to put one more try into the contest they would start a scoring play.'

McAndless' predictions for the post-war future were notably accurate, at least for the state of the nation's economy in the first decade after the war:

"There will be no more luxurious and extravagant living by the wealthy for there will be fewer wealthy people. Skilled workers will be the chief bene-factors of the war through an advance in their wages, which will be permanent. Taxes will be heavy and interest rates low. In this country federal and state development of poorer areas and renewed flow of capital into backward countries abroad will be featured, and there will be more planning in our econ-omy. There will also be a considerable 'levelling off' of individual incomes."

Throughout his career at Lincoln National, McAndless was seriously involved in community affairs. He took a special interest in health and human services organizations such as the Fort Wayne chapter of the American Red Cross, of which he was president; the Allen County Cancer Society; and several organizations for disadvantaged youths in Chicago and New York. He also was a leader in the Fort Wayne Chamber of Commerce.

After the war, McAndless continued as a leader in the industry and espe-cially the American Life Convention. By 1950 McAndless realized three important tasks confronted the insur-ance industry: "Improving service offered to the public, reducing insur-ance costs, and using financial resources for the greatest economic benefit for the American people." For Lincoln National, a critical task also

McAndless and colleagues at their favoite pastime on the train.

lay in the need to expand its sales force and its market arena dramatical-ly. This McAndless set out to do.

McAndless, whose earlier career was founded in the company's 1930s' acquisitions, sought to expand Lincoln National again in the early 1950s. He learned in 1951 that the Reliance Life Insurance Company of Pittsburgh was available for purchase. The Reliance, controlled by the Mellon National Bank, was a solid, well managed concern with more than $1 billion of insurance in force. Most importantly for McAndless, however, the Reliance had an extensive and effective sales force, particularly in the

East and South where Lincoln National was weak. Negotiations led to an October 1951, agreement for Lincoln National to acquire Reliance for $27.5 million. McAndless and two of his key men, Walter Menge and Cecil Cross, led teams that spent an intensive two weeks travelling to all the Reliance agencies, convincing the field force to remain in place. Once all elements of the deal were completed, Lincoln National had achieved what was then the largest transaction of its kind in the history of life insurance in America. More importantly, McAndless had dramatically reposi-tioned the company in the life insur-

Lincoln National's check to the Mellon National Bank for the acquisition of the Reliance Life Insurance Company, October 12, 1951.

ance marketplace. Lincoln National was now poised for its next major spurt of growth that laid the foundations for the creation of the holding company in 1968.

McAndless did not have long to enjoy his triumphs, though. While playing golf with the agents in New Orleans, he was stricken with a heart attack and died on January 25, 1954. His last speech, given to the agents in New Orleans earlier that same day, sums up his vision of the company in which he so thoroughly enmeshed his own life: "So our management objectives are first, to build for you a great company — a company great in every way; second, to build a company which, even though it is large, has not lost its human touch; and third, to build a company that is a good citizen in the community — community being used in a very broad sense." In many important ways, this vision, which was inherited from Hall, has remained that of the CEOs who succeeded McAndless.

For the Love of Bridge

McAndless was a different man away from the office. He would never, for instance, play bridge at the lunch hour in the office as many of the executives did — bridge being one of the highly popular card games of the 1930s. He thought that would set a bad example in that age of austerity and Spartan habits, since those who did play were apt to take lunch a little early and stay a little late in order to get in a number of hands. But "Mac" loved to play. It came to be known that on those times he was scheduled to go on the road on behalf of reinsurance, he would eat his lunch early so that when he got to the train he could begin playing right away rather than waste time eating lunch on the train. Henry Rood recalled often seeing McAndless happily board the special train headed for an agency convention and begin playing bridge by 8 o'clock in the morning, refusing to stop for lunch, and playing right through to 9 o'clock at night.

The clerical staff at work in the bare office spaces of the Group Department in the Wayne Building, 1954.

Walter O. Menge

WALTER O. MENGE
(1904 -)

With the sudden death of Alva McAndless, the Lincoln National Board of Directors had to move quickly and decisively because there was no clearly designated successor. Several senior officers were likely candidates. Lewis Reitz, the head of reinsurance, believed he was the strongest candidate and well before McAndless died had campaigned for the designation of successor. Vice President Ed Auer was a forceful personality in a very powerful position, and Henry Rood, company actuary who had been with Lincoln National since 1931, was a top flight executive who had done outstanding service in a variety of difficult jobs throughout the company. In the minds of the board members, however, there was only one choice — Walter O.

Menge, whom McAndless had hired in 1937.

As Menge well knew, the company he now guided was the product of half a century of extraordinary growth carried out under the leadership of three men. Hall, Mead and McAndless had led the company in intensely personal ways to a place of national significance. Lincoln National's reputation was one of the highest integrity, coupled with recognition as a creative, innovative force in the industry. To achieve this reputation, Hall, Mead and McAndless had attracted the best young minds in the business, encouraged them to grow and had instilled in them a profound sense of loyalty and dedication to the company and its ideals. Menge understood this because

he had been one of those young men attracted to the vitality of Lincoln National.

Menge brought a new level of dignity, poise and sophistication to Lincoln National Life. Where Hall had been the enthusiastic parent of the company, undaunted in his enthusiasm for the future of Lincoln National and McAndless had been a tough disciplinarian who fostered the company up to the eve of its golden anniversary, Menge was the reserved professional adept at the highest levels of insurance expertise. Understated and reserved, Menge was an intellectual, not unlike Mead in the earlier generation. Menge recognized the vastly increased size of Lincoln National in the mid-1950s precluded him from

An Extraordinary Week in January, 1954

Alva McAndless worked hard when he was with the field force. It was enough of a strain on his normally reticent personality to be glad-handing with the agents. As in everything he did, he threw himself into agency conventions. He would get up in the mornings and have four or five breakfasts with the agents before the day started. These occasions were often stressful because of all the urgent questions the field force had for the company president who was known for his straight answers, no matter how difficult.

The acquisition of the Reliance had been especially fatiguing. For more than a year McAndless and his key men had spared no effort to work with the Reliance agents across the country. Early in 1954, with the merger finally complete, four conventions were held within two weeks in the deep South. It was a gruelling pace. Two meetings were held in Hollywood Beach, Florida, and then the Home Office team wearily boarded the train for New Orleans where two more meetings were to be held.

The first sign of trouble came when First Vice President Walter Menge and McAndless were playing golf with executives from a small company which had reinsurance business with the Lincoln National. At the sixteenth hole, McAndless had to rest, complaining of being "awfully tired," but he insisted on finishing the round. After his usual series of agents' breakfasts early the next morning, January 25, he had the melancholy duty of announcing to the convention that his long-time friend Jerry Klingenberger had died early that morning. Klingenberger was Agency Secretary and had been with Lincoln National for forty-two years. Late that afternoon, McAndless was again on the golf course, this time with Sam Dichter, a top agent from the Los Angeles office, and two agents from Houston, Manny Blum and Al Enderle. At the fourteenth tee McAndless collapsed. Dichter ran to the clubhouse to get help and the golfing partners got the stricken CEO back to the clubhouse, but McAndless refused a doctor's suggestion to go to the hospital. When asked by worried subordinates what to do, Menge ordered that McAndless be taken to the hospital anyway.

At the hospital, Mrs. McAndless was told her husband had had a massive coronary and had been admitted. An offer was made to contact McAndless' physician, an old friend from Michigan, and attempts were made to locate Dr. George Graham, of Lincoln National's medical department, who was attending the convention. Menge recalled, "Then one of the nurses who was helping the doctors at the hospital began protesting that she didn't have any account to charge McAndless' bills to, so I said I would go down to the treasurer's office and make arrangements." In the midst of this hubbub, McAndless died.

The convention was called off and arrangements were made to fly back to Fort Wayne. Menge in the meantime saw that Mrs. McAndless was contacted and telephoned Ed Auer to ask him to send a message to all the directors of Lincoln. This was on Monday; the funeral was scheduled for Thursday. There would be an emergency meeting of the board on Friday. "I did all this," Menge remembered, "because I was first vice president — this I thought was my job and in any case somebody had to take charge."

The board meeting on Friday began somewhat awkwardly for there was no presiding officer. It was agreed, however, that the oldest director, Fort Wayne attorney Fred Shoaff, should preside. He quickly asked for nominations for president of the company and Menge was named. Menge announced, "Now that my name has been put in nomination, I'll leave the room so you can discuss this frankly." Before he got out the door, Shoaff said, "Well, you do not have to leave. We have discussed this among ourselves already, and we've made our decision. You are the president of The Lincoln."

knowing everyone in the various departments. This sometimes led to occasional criticism by those who longed for the old days when Hall and McAndless could greet everyone by name, or sit at his or her desk and do his or her job. The acquisition of the Reliance was a watershed from the past, though. The Lincoln National which Menge inherited was one of the nation's largest life insurance companies and there was no possibility for him to be as intimate with employees as his predecessors had been. He was a strategist, not a warrior in the trenches. And, where Hall and McAndless had envisioned a great life insurance company, Menge foresaw a great financial corporation.

Born in 1904 in Buffalo, New York, to German Lutheran parents, Menge was raised in Detroit and worked from a very young age. Among his fond memories of growing up was the paper route he shared with his brother while in elementary school. He learned some important lessons then. The boys purchased the route from a neighborhood lad for ten cents a customer, or $6 for the sixty houses on the route. The brothers then split the route and increased the customer base to one hundred. After a year, the Menge brothers sold it back to the same boy for fifteen cents a customer, or $15 for the new, enlarged route, realizing a capital gain of $9. During World War I, while still in his early teens, Menge worked in a local grocery and for a company that manufactured Maxwell automobile parts.

After performing well in high school he took his first two years of higher education at the Detroit Junior College (Wayne State University today) as an engineering student. He proved to be a top student and in his sophomore year, at age seventeen, he taught a course in descriptive geometry when the regular instructor became ill. Recognizing in Menge a different ability than engineering, a math teacher encouraged him to think about pursuing actuarial sciences. With his college friend, Alex Wellman, Menge entered the University of Michigan in 1923 as a junior and was able to gain a place in the class of Dr. James W. Glover, a leading authority in the field and McAndless' teacher in the previous decade. Initially, Menge paid his way through school by collecting fraternity

The information booth at the Lincoln National home office, ca. 1930.

The home office as seen from the main rail line into Fort Wayne, ca. 1930.

house laundry to deliver to the cleaners, but after a semester he won a position as an assistant in the Statistical Laboratory at the university. He continued to perform well, and in his senior year he taught a course in statistics and was graduated in 1925. That summer he worked for a fraternal insurance company, the Macaabees, and there met Elsie Cramer, the woman who became his wife. He continued his work at Michigan and completed his M.S. in the next year.

Menge left the university in 1926 to become the actuary for the Grange Life Insurance Company of Lansing, just as McAndless had done in 1919. There, again as had McAndless before

him, Menge came under the tutelage of company President Nathan P. Hall, a central Michigan farmer-businessman whose homespun philosophies of frugality, prudence and common sense made a lasting impression on both men. Two years later, in 1928, Professor Glover was elected president of the Teachers Insurance and Annuity Association and he invited Menge to take his place teaching the courses in actuarial science at Michigan. Menge agreed, moved back to Ann Arbor, and had among his first students in advanced courses not only his older brother, Carlton, but the man who one day would succeed him as president of Lincoln National Life, Henry Rood. Menge recalls that he was

younger than many of his students and grew his trademark moustache in order to look older. Several years later when Glover returned to the University of Michigan to chair the entire Mathematics Department, he collaborated with Menge to produce what became the leading textbook in actuarial sciences, *An Introduction to the Mathematics of Life Insurance.*

Menge taught at Michigan for the next nine years. He also completed his Ph.D. and worked on occasion as a consultant for the Department of Insurance in Michigan; and it was during this time that he first worked for Lincoln National, taking a summer job in 1936 at the request of McAndless. Many years before this,

Who Said Actuaries Don't Have Fun?

Walter Menge recalls in his days as a professor of actuarial science at the University of Michigan a colleague named Harry Carver. Professor Carver was an excellent statistician and was co-author of a book on annuities and statistics tables. He was also a fine athlete and skilled in every sort of competition from track to billiards and chess. "It was his custom," Menge remembered, "to challenge some of his classes to a series of athletic contests, saying that if they were able to beat him in the majority of these contests, there would be no final examination. I can recall one class which decided to challenge him to a four-mile relay in which Carver would run all four laps himself. Even in that contest Carver managed to beat the class because one of the members of the class team was unable to finish his leg of the relay. In another contest Henry Southern, who later would be an underwriter at The Lincoln, was nominated by the class to play pool against Carver. Now Carver in his youth had been pool champion of New England and the contest was held in the Michigan Union before a large group of students. Carver refused to use the usual cue sticks that were furnished by the Union and instead walked down the hall to the broom closet and played pool with a boom stick, while Henry Southern had a normal pool cue. It was no contest, Carver won handily. To my knowledge over the many years that I knew Professor Carver he was never beaten and no class ever escaped his final examination."

Menge cuts the ribbon for the symbolic rededication of the company at its fiftieth anniversary. Looking on are (left) Bertha Imbody, the longest tenured employee, and Sue Plaskett, the newest employee.

however, Menge had formed a long-lasting friendship with McAndless, who in 1926 was the reinsurance contact man with Grange Life where Menge worked, and with Pete Kalmbach, who was McAndless's assistant. Through these associations and others, Menge came to know the leading people at Lincoln National quite well and was impressed with the company. Leaders of the company were impressed with Menge, too. When McAndless invited him to join the staff of Lincoln National in 1937, Menge readily agreed.

When he showed up on his first day, McAndless asked Menge where he wanted to work, in the actuarial or the underwriting department. Already highly skilled as an actuary, Menge chose to work in the underwriting area, the part of the insurance business about which he knew little. He became engrossed in issues touching on impairment underwriting and soon was offering revisions to the company's procedures. In 1940 he made a stir in the insurance industry when he pointed the way for reanalysis of risks in war-related occupations as international affairs threatened to pull the United States into the growing global conflict of World War II. In 1943 McAndless asked him to undertake a complete revision of the ratebook, and that same year Menge created the company's first fully developed Group Life and Accident line of business. Also in 1943 Menge was a principal assistant to McAndless in the development of the new tax formula for life insurance companies that came to be known as "The McAndless Plan." Menge moved quickly through the ranks of vice presidency by undertaking a wide variety of tasks throughout the company. When Kalmbach left Lincoln National in 1947, McAndless put Menge in charge of the reinsurance operation and saw him elected to the Board of Directors.

An important role Menge played in the company's behalf before he became president came in connection with the acquisition and merger of the Reliance Life Insurance Company of Pittsburgh. Menge knew this company well. In the mid-1940s the president of the Reliance had approached Menge with an offer to become an officer in that company. Although The Reliance

was a solid, well run operation, Menge turned down the invitation. In 1950, after McAndless had opened negotiations with the Reliance to purchase the company, Menge was brought in to resolve an impasse over reinsurance. When the stock transfer that signalled the acquisition was in fact finally successful in 1951, Menge was elected president of the Reliance. He chose as his second-in-command his former student, Henry Rood, whom he placed in charge of the Reliance home office operations. For Menge, the immediate challenge at the Reliance was to work with the field force to insure that as many agents as possible would not take their business elsewhere before the merger with Lincoln National was completed. One of his proudest accomplishments in this project was that almost the entire Reliance sales force remained and that Lincoln National lost only five or six of the hundreds of agents gained in the transaction. At the time, this was a record in life insurance mergers. Scarcely two years after the Reliance acquisition, McAndless died, and on January 29, 1954 Menge was elected president of Lincoln National.

Menge's more reserved management style recognized that Lincoln National was an immensely larger company than the days when McAndless became president. Menge firmly subscribed to the axiom that he should delegate himself out of his own job and that the officers below him should do the same. By doing this, each officer then would have greater opportunity to take on more and so cause the entire company to progress. In this, Menge harkened back to Hall's management philosophy that it was the duty of senior officers to train the junior officers to take their place and that the only way to do this effectively was to allow them the freedom to pursue their ideas.

Although there were several good executives at Lincoln National when McAndless died, it was clear from Menge's own experience that more attention had to be paid to the issue of succession. Accordingly, one of Menge's first directives as president was to instruct all management leaders to devise training for their successors. He would do the same.

In 1955 Menge was able to led the

celebration of the first half-century of the company. Employees and residents of Fort Wayne alike were justifiably proud of the extraordinary success of Lincoln National of the past fifty years. The previous year the company had joined the exclusive "billionaire club" when it became one of only 70 businesses in the United States to have assets in excess of $1 billion. With more than $7 billion of insurance in force, Lincoln National Life was the ninth largest life insurance company in America and the second largest life reinsurer in the world. Still, it was time for Lincoln National to grow some more. While the economy of the United States and western Europe was beginning to expand strongly in the early 1950s, direct sales of life insurance were down by almost 10% at Lincoln National. Menge's solution to the company's slipping behind the rest of the industry was to expand into new markets and seek new lines of business. In 1956, he launched an aggressive growth program that began with the first acquisition of a foreign life insurance company, the Dominion Life Assurance Company of Canada, located in Waterloo, Ontario. Canada, although a difficult market for a U.S. company, had promise as an important international presence for Lincoln National and a source of considerable revenue. This was the first measure taken to revitalize direct sales.

Reflecting the new levels of business already handled by the company, the home office was bursting at the seams. For many years Lincoln National had been purchasing property along Calhoun Street behind the home office. Since the Reliance merger, the company had had to purchase the entire 100,000 square feet available at the old Wayne Pump factory near the Coombs Street Bridge on Fort Wayne's east side. Menge decided, however, to build the first major new office complex in Fort Wayne since the Lincoln Bank and Trust Tower was constructed in 1930. Ground was broken in 1958 and the cornerstone laid in February 1959 for the building that would adjoin the home office on Harrison Street. The groundbreaking occurred on a bitterly cold day and when Menge announced that he would forego his speech for the occasion, the board members who were in

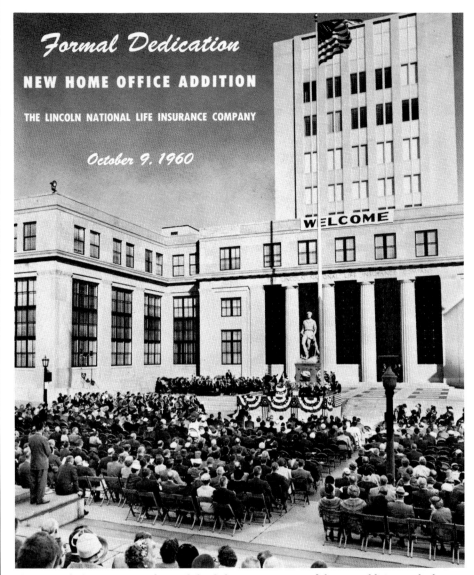

Formal Dedication

NEW HOME OFFICE ADDITION

THE LINCOLN NATIONAL LIFE INSURANCE COMPANY

October 9, 1960

WELCOME

The cover of *The Emancipator* featured the dedication ceremony of the new addition to the home office, October 9, 1960.

attendance cheered. At the same time, extensive remodeling of the original building also was completed, giving the company the entire square block with its proud electric sign facing the Pennsylvania Railroad tracks and the Baker Street Station proclaiming, "Home Office of The Lincoln National Life Insurance Company." Of special pride in the renovated north side of the old building was "The Electronics Room," which housed the new IBM 705 data processing system that brought Lincoln National into the age of computers.

Two notable projects that Menge launched in the early 1960s were the establishment of the Lincoln Life Insurance Company of New York in 1960 and the organization of CORE-

NA (Compagnie de Reassurance Nord-Atlantique) in 1963. Although these efforts eventually were abandoned, they were indicative of the aggressiveness of Lincoln National and its struggle toward expansion of the life insurance side of the business.

As a large population center, New York offered Lincoln National an opportunity for substantial levels of new business, but the difficulties and expenses confronting a new insurance company in that state were immense. In addition, there were many obstacles to a Midwestern- based company in competition with many old-line East Coast companies. Rood was assigned the task of working out the details. He asked another future CEO, Ian Rolland, having then just finished his

final actuarial exams, to assist him in determining how much capital ought to be invested in the new company to sustain it until it could earn a profit. The company was chartered on May 2, 1960, but never performed very well due, in part, to the strict New York regulations and competition. Similarly, Europe appeared potentially to be a lucrative market, but it, too, was tough to enter effectively. In Paris, in September 1963, CORENA was launched with a French president and an outstanding board of directors composed of leading insurance and other business figures in France. Like the New York venture, CORENA did fairly well and even offered some expansion into Africa and Asia. Yet, in the face of stiff competition from older established firms it never was very profitable and was sold to a French company in 1972.

Another acquisition undertaken by Menge led to the most important change in the company's history. The decision to enter the property and casualty insurance market was generated by the emerging concept of "one-stop salesmanship for all financial needs." For Menge it was only sensible to combine the two lines under one ownership and he began looking for a good property-casualty company. There were many available, but most were not very good prospects. Vice President Ed Auer, however, brought to Menge's attention the possibility of acquiring the American States Insurance Company of Indianapolis. The company was owned by two brothers, Dudley and Edward Gallahue, whom Auer, through his personal connections with the Gallahues, had reason to believe wanted to sell the company. Most importantly, American States was a very solid business, maintaining a good operating ratio and first-rate senior officers led by John Phelan. After more than two years of quiet negotiations, a deal was struck with the Gallahue brothers. Lincoln National Life Insurance Company could not simply take on a new line of business, however, because of the limitations set by Indiana investment laws for life insurance companies. The stockholders had to approve a resolution authorizing a change in the articles of incorporation so that the company to go into this line of business and then the Indiana State Insurance Department had to approve the merger. The arrangements were completed in 1962 and Auer became chairman of the American States board and Phelan became its president.

Menge first considered forming a holding company about 1960 amid the American States negotiations. The difficulties associated with a life insurance company acquiring a new line of business, such as a property-casualty insurer, led Menge to consider more effective and efficient techniques of organization. Creation of a holding company — one that would own all the other companies, including the life company — would allow Lincoln National to puruse any business activity unfettered by the extensive regulations governing life insurance companies. Menge as chairman of the board helped lay the groundwork with General Counsel Gordon Reeves and President Rood.

Throughout his presidency, Menge continued the high level of involvement in the insurance industry that marked his professorial days at the University of Michigan and his first years at Lincoln National. A ranking member of most of the industry's professional organizations, Menge took special pride in his standing as a Fellow in the Society of Actuaries. He was particularly honored, however, when he was elected president of the Life Insurance Association of America (which later merged with the Insitute of Life Insurance to form the American Council of Life Insurance), marking the first time a Midwestern company president had taken the lead in this professional organization.

Industry recognition of Menge and Lincoln National was due in large part to their leadership on matters of federal taxation. Menge had already been the seminal figure in the development of the 1943 McAndless Plan for assessing life insurance companies. Since this was largely a wartime measure, the issue of appropriate taxation for life insurance industry disappeared for nearly a decade. By the end of the 1950s, however, it was generally perceived that life insurance companies were not bearing their fair share, and the Treasury Department raised the issue again. Menge, like McAndless before him, served on the ALC committee on taxation and took the lead in developing a fair formula that could be applied to both stock and mutual companies.

Menge served on numerous Fort Wayne business associations and boards, most notably as a director of the Magnavox Corporation and American Electric Power. Although he did not become active in very many of the community's social issues, he took a notable interest in recruiting black employees for the home office well ahead of the mandates that would evolve from the modern Civil Rights movement in later years. As he once noted, "It simply was the right thing to do, and it was good for business." His speeches noted several times the need for business to function "without consideration of race, creed, or color." Working with Ronald Stagg, the vice president in charge of personnel in 1960, Menge directed that black graduates from the local Central High School be recruited and fully integrated into the work force. Not only was the conscious effort to integrate the company unusual in the financial services industry in general, but it was also completely at odds with the tenor of the Fort Wayne community where a segregated school system was the most obvious sign of open discrimination.

Many years earlier Menge had decided that he would significantly reduce his workload when he reached sixty, which happened in 1964. He had worked every year of his life since he was a child in grammar school and simply wanted time to enjoy life beyond work and spend more time with Elsie. His plan was to continue his leadership of Lincoln National through his role on the board but turn over the direct operation of the company to the president. For this job Menge turned to Rood, his old student and senior vice president, who was elected president in March 1964 and Menge became chairman of the board. In June 1965 Rood was made CEO, but three years later, Rood suffered a heart attack while returning to Fort Wayne from Jamaica. Rood would recover, but only after several months of rest and treatment. Menge suggested to the board that he serve as acting chief executive until Rood could return, assuring everyone that any long-range planning and decisions would be put on hold until Rood recovered. When Rood returned in May, Menge handed back the executive reins. Menge continued to work on plans for creating the holding company and when this was accomplished in January 1968, he was elected chairman of Lincoln National Corporation. He held this position for a brief time, at long last taking his retirement in October 1968. He left Fort Wayne with Elsie to enjoy his boat, "Aftermath." Menge did not sever his ties completely, however, for it was not until 1994 that he retired as chairman emeritus of the board of directors.

Henry F. Rood

HENRY F. ROOD
(1906 - 1994)

Henry F. Rood did not expect to become chief executive officer of Lincoln National. Because he was only two years younger than Walter Menge, Rood believed that he would be too old for the job when Menge retired. As it was, however, Menge had the firm intention to retire when he was sixty, and in December 1962 gave Rood his first indication that he might gain the top job. At that time Menge told Rood that he wanted to lighten his present load and share the responsibility of leadership. His plan was to suggest to the board that it elect Rood as executive vice president. After a trial period, Menge continued, "if things work out satisfactorily, I might make another recommendation." Menge then placed Rood in a number of new roles, such as membership on the important Finance Committee where he could participate in investment decisions. Early in 1963 Menge told Rood that he had discussed his plans with key board members and they agreed with his intention to recommend him for the presidency in 1964 when Menge would become chairman of the board. Accordingly, in March 1964 Menge stepped down as president and Rood was elected to take his place. The change was similar to that of 1939 when Arthur Hall relinquished the presidency to Alva McAndless so that Hall could be active in behalf of the company as chairman of the board, free of the day-to-day operation of the company. Menge, likewise, continued to be active as chairman, chairing board and shareholder meetings, but for executive operations, he made it clear that he would be there only to assist, and that "whatever Henry thought was appropriate was fine with me as well."

Rood had considerable personal strengths to draw upon: Untiring energy and devotion to tasks, enthusiasm for his profession, an upbeat attitude, and an unswerving love for the company and its values. In addition, he was a sharp, first-rate actuary. Rood was always quick to recall how much he had learned from the first three presidents of the Lincoln National. He never forgot, even many years after he retired, that special conversation with

Hall in the weeks before the first CEO died. Hall told him to work harder at being more understanding of the diversity of the people around him, that there is more gray than black and white when dealing with people. He was also deeply impressed by McAndless's stern common sense and solid values laced with good, sober humor. He was determined, however, also to follow the Menge example of delegating authority and monitoring with an eye on developing the rising generation of leaders who would take the company to its next level of growth.

Rood's early life prepared him for the tasks ahead. He was born in 1906 in Port Chester, New York, to parents who were both born in South Africa to Congregationalist missionaries. His father studied engineering at Yale College in 1877 as a classmate of the Lincoln National's first president, Samuel Foster. The elder Rood died while Henry was still a boy and the family moved to New Haven, Connecticut., where the young man was reared. He recalled these years with particular fondness, especially the dean of Yale, Henry Wright, who befriended him like a father, taking him to church father-son events and encouraging him in his studies throughout his school years. Among his admonishments for success, Wright frequently told young Rood, "Always seek to be highly proficient and an eminent authority in one subject." After high school Rood attended Oberlin College where he took his bachelor's degree in 1928. In the course of the next year he earned a master's degree in actuarial sciences at the University of Michigan where he was a student of Menge. Seeking to return to familiarity of the East, Rood joined the Travelers Insurance Company as an actuary, but stayed only a year and a half.

University of Michigan connections continued to serve Lincoln National when in 1930 Rood spent his summer vacation in Fort Wayne with his Michigan classmate, Henry Southern, who was working in Lincoln National's Underwriting Department. Rood told his friend of his interest in

finding a new job and Southern mentioned this to Pete Kalmbach, then in charge of the Reinsurance Department. Rood was offered a position in reinsurance at Lincoln National and arrived in March 1931 to begin a career that would last forty years.

In the next few years Rood completed his actuarial exams and served in a wide variety of functions in the company, particularly addressing issues touching on the acquisitions of Royal Union and Northern States in the early 1930s. Not long after the U.S. entered World War II, Rood joined the U.S. Navy, was commissioned as a lieutenant in the Naval Reserve, and was assigned to work in the office of Secretary of the Navy James Forrestal. As an investment banker, Forrestal understood the critical impact of the evident failure of the Navy to have good data about its logistical needs. Lack of accurate or organized data often meant that naval operations were over-supplied or were without sufficient mat‚riel to support their manpower needs. Forrestal turned to actuaries for help. Lieutenant Rood was assigned to the team charged to analyze the issue and develop a program for correcting the problem. Rood equated the problem with that of figuring premium rates and applied his actuarial skills to the procurement process of the U.S. Marine Corps. The team developed its statistics and procedures and first applied them fully in the preparation for the bloody battle of Tarawa in the Pacific Theater in 1943. As a result of these professional actuarial approaches to military procurement, costly duplications were avoided, necessary supplies were where they needed to be, and greater efficiency was brought to bear on campaign operations. In the last months of the war, Rood and his colleagues made similar plans for the invasion of the Japanese home islands, but these were made obsolete by the Japanese surrender in September 1945 after the atomic bombing of Hiroshima and Nagasaki. Rood left the service as a lieutenant commander and returned to his old position at Lincoln National in January 1946.

Lincoln National advertising in San Francisco, ca. 1935.

Rood played an important role in the acquisitin of the Reliance Life Insurance Company in 1951 when he served as one of McAndless's chief assistants throughout the process. When the deal was completed and Menge was made president of the Reliance, he had Rood named senior vice president of the Pittsburgh company and placed him in charge of the home office operations. In the arrangement, Rood would spend one day a week in Fort Wayne and four days in Pittsburgh, leaving on the Broadway Limited Sunday evening and returning on the Pennsylvania Flyer Thursday night every week for more than a year.

After Menge became CEO of Lincoln National, Rood continued to oversee the home office operations of the Reliance and, in 1954, its move to Fort Wayne. In the late 1950s he had the assignment of chairing the committee that investigated new data management technologies. This became a four-year study that resulted in the installation of the IBM 705, the

first electronic computer to be used by the company.

Rood also carried out exemplary work on federal taxation of life insurance companies in the years before he became president of Lincoln National. Recalling the advice of Dean Wright, his old boyhood mentor and surrogate father — to become proficient and known as an authority on one particular subject — Rood specialized in matters of federal taxation of life insurance companies. Because of this, Menge assigned Rood to assist the company's lobbying efforts in the "Tax War of 1959." In the wake of these events, the complicated tax legislation that resulted required a considerable amount of interpretation, and Rood was one of the five experts the Treasury Department called upon to form a committee to assist the government. It was a measure of the reputation of Lincoln National in taxation matters that Rood was chosen to be the chairman of the committee. Despite the sometimes acrimonious disputes that had arisen in the course

of the "Tax War," the five actuaries that made up the advisory committee developed a strong sense of comraderie. At the end of their chores, they came to call themselves, somewhat tongue-in-cheek, "The Five Wise Men."

Rood was particularly devoted to his profession. His most significant role was as a driving force in the formation of the American Academy of Actuaries, which was established in October 1965 to promote the need for national accreditation standards for actuaries. Rood was elected the body's first president. He also gave a great deal of time to development of the Society of Actuaries, which was formed in 1948 by the merger of the Actuarial Society of America and the American Insititute of Actuaries. Rood was elected the new organization's first secretary- treasurer. In addition, he also became heavily involved in the international actuarial organizations and in 1966 was elected vice president of the International Actuarial Association. In that capacity, he

In 1940 the Dern Month sales promotion also encouraged agents and employees to vote.

National's energetic growth appeared to be threatened when Rood suffered a heart attack. Again, the issue of leadership and succession was thrown into sharp focus. Menge came out of retirement to take the helm until Rood could recuperate. By late spring Rood was able to return to the office for short stays and by mid-year was fully in charge again. Clearly, however, Rood at age fifty-eight had to provide for the next generation of leadership for Lincoln National.

Menge and Rood were deeply concened about the next generation of leadership; most of the key men in the company in the mid-1960s had been key men for many years and there was little depth to the top management. The two conferred on the issue of the next president for Lincoln National and decided to take a bold step. Knowing that the company was to embark on a new direction and that one of the critical issues was lackluster sales, the two took a page from history. In the spirit of the company's founder, Arthur Hall, a consummate salesman and organizer, they chose Thomas Watson, the head of the Group Department, to be the next president. Accordingly, Rood was elected chairman of the Lincoln National Board in 1968 and retained the reins as chief executive officer. Watson was elected president and thereby put in a position to be Rood's successor upon his retirement.

With the succession thus secured, Rood led the company in its most significant organizational change since its founding more than six decades earlier. The vision had originally been Menge's, but Rood put the concept of a holding company into place, with the assistance of Chief Counsel Gordon C. Reeves. There was considerable controversy over the new direction. Opponents among the senior officers believed that the move was fundamentally unnecessary and might even mortally weaken the life insurance company upon which everything to date had been founded. But Menge and Rood firmly believed that the life company would be greatly strengthened by the move. The process was kept purposefully simple in order to alleviate any fears. The new shares were exchanged one-for-one for the old Lincoln National shares and in

presided over its 1968 Congress held in Munich.

When Rood became president of Lincoln National in 1964, he vowed to pursue aggressively Menge's vision "to create not just a great life insurance company, but a great financial services institution as well." Planning was an important part of Rood's approach to leadership of the company and the creation of a special planning group for Lincoln National was among the first actions he took as president. Rood continued Menge's attention to international markets. He moved quickly to create the Lincoln Philippine Life Company to protect the Lincoln National operations in the Philippines where nationalization of

U.S. companies was anticipated. The rapid expansion of the middle class in the United Kingdom promised to provide a strong new center of business, and Rood led Lincoln National's entry into the British marketplace with the formation of the Dominion-Lincoln Assurance Company, Ltd.. Then, in 1966, Rood began to explore the notion of extending the company's business into financial areas not traditionally associated with life insurance. Interested in establishing a variable annuity line of business, he assigned the job to Ian Rolland, a young actuary who had impressed Rood five years earlier extending the business into New York.

Early in 1967, however, Lincoln

this way the creation of Lincoln National Corporation in 1968 was accomplished without a new stock issue. As the holding company came into being, Menge was elected chairman and Rood was chosen to be president of the new corporation. Once Lincoln National Corporation was duly formed, though, Menge stepped down and Rood became chairman. Rood retained chairmanship of the Lincoln National Life board and Reeves was elected president of the corporation. Watson remained president of the life company. Now all the companies formerly tied to Lincoln National Life, such as American States Insurance and Dominion Life, were affiliates of the corporation. In 1969 LNC stock was traded publicly for the first time on the New York Stock Exchange and on the then-Midwest Stock Exchange.

Since it was not a life insurance company, Lincoln National Corporation could enjoy the flexibility to operate as freely as any other duly licensed corporation in Indiana, becoming involved in whatever enterprise it saw fit. It was Rood's intention, however, that future enterprises

The LINCS fashion contest of 1957 (left to right: Norma McMahon, Doris Minier, Ann Herman, Barbara Curie, Phyllis Raby, Sheila Bradley and Phyllis Boedeker).

would be closely associated with the insurance industry — a philosophy that has been held ever since. Still exercising considerable muscle founded upon a large surplus, the new corporation entered in the same year a different line of business when it acquired Chicago Title and Trust, the nation's second largest title insurance company, and its affiliates, including the investment management firm of Halsey, Stuart. Many Lincoln National officers were impressed in the first years with technology applications for records storage developed in the title insurance business at Chicago Title, and these were often deemed to be useful models for the Fort Wayne-based companies. Pursuing its development as a financial institution, the corporation also acquired Security Supervisors, a mutual fund management company, and formed numerous new financial companies, such as the

War Can be a Touchy Business for an Insurance Company

In 1941, as it became increasingly evident that the United States would be drawn into the widening global conflict of World War II, Henry Rood studied the issue of the impact on Lincoln National of disability, premium waiver and double indemnity provisions should its policyholders become involved in the war. In this concern he had been greatly influenced by the cautionary remarks made the previous year by Walter Menge to the Institute of Home Office Underwriters, that life insurance companies should closely consider the new and important problems that wartime conditions cause.

Although most policies provided that benefits would automatically become void if the policyholder enlisted in the military in time of war, there was serious concern that if the company did not take direct action and cancel or modify such benefits beforehand, it would be exceedingly difficult to deny claims made at a later date. Together with an actuarial student Rood reviewed these riders and consulted with the Law Department on the company's liabilities, rights and privileges in time of war. Rood was alarmed by the extent of Lincoln National's exposure these studies revealed.

On December 8, the day after the Japanese attacked Pearl Harbor and the day the United States declared war on Japan, most of the company's senior officers were in New York for a meeting of the Life Presidents Association. Back in Fort Wayne Rood, on his own, decided to put into motion the termination of numerous disability and double indemnity benefits. No one questioned the young executive's authority and preparations were made to send letters to all the affected policyholders and cut refund checks. As Rood recalled, "Everything was pretty well set to go when Mr. (Al) Dern arrived. He was the head of the Agency Department and one of the accountants asked if they should charge back the agent's commission on these cancelled riders. Dern hit the ceiling!" The immediate concern was the potentially devastating public relations impact such cancellations would have had if handled this way, no matter how prudent they might be. Nothing, fortunately, had been mailed as yet.

The management committee that dealt with operating issues met under the direction of McAndless who, sitting at one end of the board room table, argued with junior officer Rood who sat at the other end. The senior executives in between sat quietly, heads moving in unison from one side to the next as if witnessing a tennis match while the arguments intensified. In the end, Rood stood his ground for what he believed was right for the company. The cancellations were to go out, but only for the duration of the war. There would be an intensive reinstatement effort after the war. In a scene familiar to other top executives who have had to stand their ground in the face of opposition by superiors, Rood remembered on the way out of the meeting, "Joe Frank (general counsel) patted me on the back and said 'I agreed with you right down the line, Henry.' And I replied, 'Well, why didn't you speak up and help me then?'" Rood gained a great deal of respect that day.

Rood at the height of his career.

Lincoln National Development Company and Lincoln National Investment Advisory Corporation, so that by 1971 there were 40 major companies under the umbrella of the Lincoln National Corporation.

Having reached age sixty-five, Rood had to step down in 1971. He was the last chief executive officer of Lincoln National to have known all of his predecessors in the office. Rood never really left the company, though. Just as he had done in the nearly half-century since he joined Lincoln National, he continued to participate in whatever way he could. During his years as an officer, he came to be one of the best loved home office figures among the field force. Old Reliance agents still remember with fondness the obvious joy with which Rood approached

his dealings with the agencies. He always had a ready ear to their problems, a solution to their difficulties, and pats on the back for jobs well done. Every year after his retirement he studied the board materials sent to his home and he faithfully attended every annual shareholders meeting. Even in the year of his death, 1994, old insurance agents' faces would light up at his mention as they recalled the first time they worked with him in the 1940s or the 1950s. Rood was the consummate company man. He devoted himself, as did Hall before him, so completely that he even subsumed his marriage and family life into the com-

pany. One of his children, Doug Rood, recalls with great fondness how his father involved all of the family members in Lincoln National business. For her part, Ruth Rood understood and gladly accepted that she would be his partner at all the conventions. She, too, remembers fondly the hundreds of agents and their spouses she befriended over the years. This was a rich time for her, as it was for her husband. One family member noted that just hours before he died at home Rood spent the afternoon skimming through one of his many scrapbooks on the company with a broad smile filling his face.

The leadership of Lincoln National on the eve of Rood's retirement (left to right) Allen Steere, Thomas Watson, Rood, Walter Menge and Gathings Stewart.

"Behind the Succession Crisis of 1967"

When Henry Rood had a heart attack in January 1967, he was in the Miami International Airport on his way back to Fort Wayne from Jamaica. Medics took him to a hospital in Hialeah and it was there that Walter Menge went to visit him to get a first-hand impression of the situation. Rood, like Menge before him, had been concerned about the issue of succession and had already compiled a list of potential advancements in the company, locking it away in the top drawer of his desk. Lying in his hospital bed, he was concerned that this list might get out, knowing full well what damage this might do in view of the nature of company politics. Menge assured him that he would attend to that issue and insure its secrecy.

When doctors advised the board that Rood would need several months to recuperate, discussion quickly surfaced around the suggestion by William B. Hall, the founder's son, that perhaps Edward Auer, a senior vice president and chief investment officer, would be the best substitute for Rood because he was the oldest of the officers. A long and forthright discussion then followed about Auer who, while a good financial officer, was perceived as too involved in numerous personality conflicts, not least of which was his long-standing feud with another investment officer, Fergus McDiarmid. Menge spoke out against the senior officers, saying that "putting [any of these men] in charge in Henry's job as an active chief executive officer would do The Lincoln no good because of the antagonisms this would cause."

Menge then told the board that "the best thing would be if I came back on a temporary basis until Henry recovers. I can sit on the lid here for three or four months and no one will think I'm trying to get my job back because I already had given it up." The board agreed to make Menge acting CEO, and in due course Rood resumed his office.

Thomas A. Watson

THOMAS A. WATSON
(1916 -)

Thomas Watson's elevation to the top position at Lincoln National on September 30, 1971, was revolutionary. The transition was smooth, however, for Henry Rood had prepared matters for the change. There were five or six disappointed hopefuls and there were numerous raised eyebrows at the new CEO's lack of actuarial credentials. Those involved in sales, however, were delighted that a person with an outstanding record in marketing would be running the company. The concern of the senior management was not to maintain a tradition but rather to place the company in the hands of a good administrator who would bolster sales. The company had grown in dramatic ways, but largely through acquisitions. Sales growth needed to be the new focus.

Throughout his life, Watson has been a man who stands firmly by matters in which he believes deeply and once committed to action does not retreat. To very large extent he inherited this determination from his father, Ralph, an evangelical minister from Winona Lake, Indiana. Watson remembers the time when he was very young and the Ku Klux Klan was scheduled to come to nearby Wabash for a parade. Ralph Watson hated the Klan and all that it stood for. He was an imposing man physically, standing six-foot-four inches tall, and unafraid to preach against the Klan across the northern Indiana region that was a hotbed of racial hatred. He had received so many threats that he often travelled with a bodyguard. When he learned of the Klan parade in Warsaw he wanted to go, but he could not drive. Only Tom's sisters could drive. Mrs. Watson begged her sometimes fiery husband to promise to stay in the car and not get involved. He agreed and the entire family went to Wabash. Tom, who was about six years old, was just tall enough to stand on the floor of the car and look out the window. The Klan parade was large and led by a pompous character on horseback. On seeing this proud symbol of hatred and bigotry, Watson's father could stand it no longer. He jumped from the car, raced to the hooded figure, dragged him from the saddle,

threw him into the street and tore off his hood. Young Tom saw this and raced to his father's side just as several Klansmen fell on Mr. Watson and beat him with their fists. His sister spirited the boy away and later that night his father returned home badly beaten, but he had soundly thrashed the lead Klansman first. This sort of bravery and the principles it represented deeply impressed the young Watson.

Watson, who was born in 1916, grew up in the wonderful atmosphere of Winona Lake when it was on the Chautauqua circuit. As a child, Watson talked with Will Rogers, walked with Admiral Byrd, listened to John Phillip Sousa and met Harry Houdini. The summers were almost magical as he remembers seeing just about every play Shakespeare wrote. His father was compassionate as well as brave: in addition to preaching, he worked for a leper's mission in India and for a tuberculosis hospital in Kentucky. The Watsons suffered the economic effects of the Great Depression deeply when Ralph Watson died. At seventeen the young Watson was ready to go to college. He had worked since he was eight years old selling magazine subscriptions, however, and worked his way through college . He enrolled in Purdue University to study architecture, but transferred to Indiana University where he pursued the pre-law program, graduating in 1939.

After college he married and worked for several finance companies. Today, he still vividly recalls the news of the Japanese attack on Pearl Harbor in 1941 and his determination to join the U.S. Army Air Corps. He eventually served as a pilot of a B-24 Liberator bomber in Africa and then Italy. The Air Corps tradition at that time was that a crew that had flown more than forty- five missions could choose its next bombing run, unless it was a "maximum" target. Watson's crew had flown forty-seven missions, but number forty-eight was the "maximum" target of the Romanian oil fields at Ploesti in July 1944. Over Ploesti Capt.Watson's plane was struck by German anti-aircraft fire and he was severely wounded. The co-pilot man-

aged to get the plane five hundred miles back to the base in Italy, but Watson had to have part of his hand amputated.

While recuperating in Fort Wayne, he happened to have his car serviced at a station on Fairfield Avenue in Fort Wayne where an acquaintance asked him what he intended to do now that he was out of the war. Feeling especially self-conscious about his disfigured hand, he answered, "Just about anything where I can sit in the back and not meet people." The friend then advised that he check with Lincoln National Life. "It is," he said, "the ideal place for such a job." Watson contacted Don Crouse, a friend in the company, who put him in touch with the head of the newly formed Group Life and Accident Department, Arthur Rogers. It happened that Rogers was indeed looking for someone to take the inside job so that his three trained men could go into the field. Watson remembers that on the application form the question was asked, "Where do you intend to go in the company, if hired?" Watson answered, "President." "It was," he recalls with his characteristically broad grin, "the only really accurate prediction I ever made." Rogers and others, such as then-Vice President Walter Menge, liked the potential in the man.

Since Watson didn't know anything about insurance, Rogers gave him all the literature on the Group line and told him to report to work in three months after he had completed his last rehabilitation for his injured hand. During this convalescence Watson consumed all the materials and reported in May 1945. He was troubled, however, that he had found numerous errors in the written material and was unsure how a new employee could raise the issue. Encouraged to take the errors directly to Menge who had oversight of the area, Watson was relieved to learn that Menge was not at all imperious, but was impressed with Watson's abilities and forthrightness.

As it happened, Rogers decided that Watson would be best used in the field and not in the home office, notwithstanding the veteran's shyness about his injury. He sent a reluctant Watson to Chicago to develop the field office. Over the next three years, Watson overcame both his ignorance about group insurance and his uneasiness in front of people and quickly drew the attention of his superiors as a good administrator who could produce consistently improved results. He returned to Fort Wayne in 1949 and immediately became involved in a disagreement with senior staff. Typically, the dispute centered on his defense of agents. Drawing on his earlier experiences with matters that he felt deeply about, he held firm in his opposition to a group insurance case sold by the home office staff. It was the largest group case yet written at the Lincoln National and it involved direct negotiations with Walter Reuther, the head of the United Auto Workers. The deal was structured to eliminate the agents' commissions and Watson refused to sanction it. When he returned to his office from this meeting he remembered thinking, "What have I done to myself and my future?" Cecil Cross, the head of the Agency Department, came to Watson and said, "I suppose you don't feel very good about anything right now, do you?" Watson replied that indeed he did not feel very well and Cross told him, "Well, I thought you'd be interested to know that Mr. McAndless was quite pleased that you said exactly what you thought rather than trying to second guess what maybe somebody else in the room who completely controlled our future might think. When you left, McAndless said, 'Thank God we have at least one guy around here who stands up for what he believes.' "

During the next several years in the Group Department, Watson rose to become sales manager and finally department head. The Group area grew so fast in the early 1950s that Watson led the move of the Department into the old Wayne Pump building, which was renovated in 1953. In 1956 Group Life and Health reached the mark of $1 billion of insurance in force and within a decade would reach $5 billion level. In 1960 the department moved into the entire fourth floor of the new extension of the Harrison Street building. During these years Watson enhanced his rep-

Watson as the head of the Group Department.

utation as a strong agency leader and a fiscally conservative administrator, qualities that Menge and Rood sought in the mid-1960s when they turned their attention to matters of succession and the future of the company. Accordingly, Watson was elected president of Lincoln National Life in 1968 and in 1971 he became the corporation's chief executive officer. Watson recognized the need for actuarial skills in running the company and Gathings Stewart, an actuary, was elected president of the Lincoln National Life Insurance Company.

Watson does not recall having a grand vision for the company when he assumed the presidency of the corporation. He does recall vividly, however, that the company faced two serious issues that he believed retarded its growth: high expenses and the need to improve sales and marketing. The first problem would be solved, in part, by a retreat from direct sales in overseas markets. Watson viewed the operations in Great Britain and France to be too expensive for their return and these companies were sold in the first three years of his administration. In the Philippines, the possibility of nationalization of foreign companies was well advanced and this moved Watson to divest the Lincoln

Philippine Life Company. Also sold was the brokerage firm of Halsey, Stuart and Co., an affiliate of Chicago Title and Trust, deemed to be too expensive to maintain. In the campaign to reduce expenses, Watson instituted an executive committee to assist him in reviewing a variety of difficult issues in the company's operations, and among the problems identified was the continuation of several high-ranking officers whose functions were no longer clear. In one swift stroke in 1972, a "Black Monday," as it came to be called, he let seven officers go, among them some very senior men. It was a move that shocked not only the company, but also the Fort Wayne community, which in six decades had never seen so many Lincoln National executives dismissed at one time. What was occurring was the replacement of the "old guard" so a new generation of executives could carry forward new initiatives in a changing business world.

The other paramount difficulty for the corporation in Watson's view was the serious attention needed in sales and marketing. The central issue remained direct sales and Watson saw this as a simple equation: the sales force brought in money and yet it was the weakest part of the corporation. This, Watson believed, was because actuaries had little understanding of sales and yet controlled the process and often were not sensitive to marketing issues. At the same time, more than mere leadership was involved here. A wide array of new products was beginning to appear in addition to the principal lines of individual life, group life and health and annuities. The life company now could offer computerized estate management, pensions and various business insurance plans. Other variable products were on the horizon. Clearly, in

Watson (left), the newly appointed head of the Group Department, with the McAndlesses at a Reliance convention in Atlantic City, 1952.

Watson's mind, more training, expertise, expanded facilities and additional home office support were required for the agents to compete effectively and improve sales. Something revolutionary had to be done to reinvigorate the agency system. His solution was the formation of the Lincoln National Sales Corporation (LNSC), an innovative concept that would be the marketing arm of Lincoln National Life.

The vision of LNSC was to create a corporate agency system. Each regional office and each agency would become a small corporation — a subsidiary of LNSC — complete with corporate titles and a corporate image that would be attractive to bright young agents. The home office would provide greater support facilities for the agencies, more financial suport for agency development and more specialized support for the agents, especially in the areas of financial planning and new products. As a result of greatly increased funding for agency development, the home office was soon host

to hundreds of new agents recruited by the regional and agency offices. Sales increased dramatically, but so did expenses, reducing the margin of return to seriously low levels. The lower quality of some agents in the enlarged field force also raised concerns as an unwelcome by-product of mass recruitment and training. These and other issues vexed the LNSC system through the mid-1970s and would continue to trouble the administration of Watson's successor. Yet the program clearly achieved its goals of reinvigorating the agency system and proved an effective vehicle for transforming the agents into a more sophisticated sales force.

Another far-sighted undertaking by Watson was the organization in December 1973 of the Lincoln National Investment Management Company (LNIMC). Although the original purpose of LNIMC was simply to consolidate management of several mutual funds owned directly by Lincoln National Corporation and

"The Educated Watson"

Minority recruitment to the company had been a difficulty since the days of Walter Menge. During Menge's tenure a program to hire young black office workers began with the employment of a part-time Fort Wayne Community School administrator named Bill Watson. It was his job to smooth the transition and prepare the young people for a place where in an earlier time they typically had not been welcome. Bill Watson held a master's degree in education and was a highly respected figure both in the area schools and in the halls of Lincoln National. Tom Watson used frequently to get Bill Watson's telephone calls; his usual answer to the calling party was "No, I'm afraid you want the educated Watson, not me" when he realized that it was the other Watson who was being sought.

serve as the investment advisor to the affiliate companies of LNC, the role of investment management grew dramatically from the early 1980s. By the 1990s investment management had emerged as one of the most important lines of growth for Lincoln National.

Watson's attention was also turned to the internal well being of the company during his administration in ways that his predecessors had not addressed fully. Equal opportunity for minorities and women in Lincoln National had begun to emerge with Menge's leadership. The company had always been ahead of its industry competitors in the area of minority employment; yet even under Watson, who was a social activist, there were still no formal programs for the advancement of women in business. He was opposed generally to any kind of discrimination and demonstrated in the staffing of his own office the broadest approach to equality issues. Below his level, however, there continued to exist widespread opposition to the advancement of racial minorities and women into the upper echelons of the company.

Watson personally had been deeply involved with area minority issues. He served for many years on the board of the Fort Wayne Urban League and was its president for four years during his time as CEO of Lincoln National. By Watson's own reckoning, despite

the CEO's directives against discrimination, once the personnel office had hired a black individual, there was often someone who was just as determined to see the individual fired on some pretense. This would happen regularly until Watson could identify and eliminate all these open racists from the company.

Attention to the social responsibility of the corporation became a notable characteristic of Watson's tenure, an attitude he signalled just the year before he became CEO when he remarked that the most important development of the 1960s was "increased social consciousness, particularly the concern for the poor, both in the U.S. and in the world." He predicted in 1970 that focus for the new decade would be "an increased dedication to the reduction of poverty and a solution to the incidence of crime." Watson's determination to act upon these ideas was reflected in his principal contribution to social change, the creation of the Lincoln Life Improved Housing Corporation (LLIH). Watson counts this program as one of his proudest achievements at the company. For years the company had given generously to various causes in the community of Fort Wayne, but there was little focus for the giving and still less sense that anything truly substantial and measurable was happening. Concerned about this, Watson instructed the charitable giv-

Howard Steele was placed in charge of the Lincoln National Sales Corporation (LNSC) in 1974.

ing committee to re-evaluate its recommendations with an eye toward programs that would demonstrate a substantial impact, rather than simply giving away dollars. Thanks to the efforts of several junior officers, such as John Mascotte who did the tax

Watson's Senior Staff Committee in 1975: (left to right) William E. Lewis, Gathings Stewart, Nancy Peden, Watson, Ian Rolland, David Silletto and Howard Steele.

studies, and Rolland, who applied his experience and strong sense of social commitment, the concept of using Lincoln National funds to call attention to the deteriorating housing stock in the center of the city and to rehabilitate low-income housing was launched in 1973. Through the help of the city and major lenders, this program has been able to acquire run-down houses, rehabilitate them, and lease them to low income families for five years. At the end of that time, the family may assume the low- interest mortgage. The result is that the family is able to purchase a fully rehabilitated home for less than half the original cost.

Like Menge, Watson wanted to enjoy retirement and was determined to step down by age sixty. Watson gave considerable thought to the choice of his replacement, which he had to settle upon by 1975 or 1976 at the latest. Watson, like Rood before him, had noticed Ian Rolland since his first year with the company as a man who could understand complicated issues and develop solutions effectively and humanely. Watson was especially impressed with Rolland early when Rolland was assigned as a "rotating actuary" to the Group Department. An issue arose touching on the opening of a position in the Group Department that required some mathematic expertise. The actuaries working in Group strongly believed that only another actuary could fill this position, but Rolland disagreed with his colleagues and boldly stood against them, something with which Watson was very familiar. When Watson had earlier stood his ground, he gained respect and now Rolland obtained and held the everlasting respect of Tom Watson. This sort of character trait was most important to Watson when he finally decided to name Rolland as his successor in 1975.

A little more than a year later, in 1976, personal issues facing Watson came to a head and he had to announce his impending divorce. He had already confided in Rolland and when the announcement came it was not long followed by the announcement that Tom Watson would take an early retirement along with Gathings Stewart in the first half of 1977.

Watson on the eve of his retirement in 1977.

Ian M. Rolland

IAN M. ROLLAND
(1933 -)

When Ian Rolland became CEO of Lincoln National on May 8, 1977, it was a critical moment for the company. Although Rolland had been the recognized successor since December 1975 by virtue of being elected president of the corporation, the announcement of Watson's retirement only one year later, in December 1976, came as a surprise. Further, Rolland felt singularly unprepared for the new job — not for want of self confidence, but rather because he had been brought into the inner circle of decision-making only recently and had not been groomed for the top position for very long.

Rolland viewed the challenge as a welcome opportunity, as he had done with previous assignments in the company. But when Watson retired at the end of June 1977, Rolland was struck by the breadth of his responsibilities. "I had the job, but if I were a Lincoln stockholder and knew how little I knew about the job, I would be really worried. Then, I watched out the window of the Harrison Street building the western sky grow really black as a huge thunderstorm came through Fort Wayne. I wondered if this was an omen of the future."

Colleagues who know him well describe Rolland as an intensely proud but self-effacing man. He is recognized as a man of profound intelligence and extraordinary powers of concentration, possessing a notable ability to focus on the issues before him without losing the larger picture. Indeed, he is unique among corporate leaders in that he views the corporation and its business in the larger context of the community and sees them as inseparable. This occasionally leads him into controversy, his colleagues concede, which he meets with confidence. He is a compassionate man who comes to a decision cautiously, with a thoroughness of analysis some judge a fault. That caution stems from a deep sense of respect for other views, though he does not suffer fools easily, and for a willingness to allow others the fullest opportunity to accomplish. Once a decision is reached, however, his self confidence is revealed by his singular ability to

view often immensely complicated issues with clarity, see the common sense solution, and then never waver from the implementation of the task.

Rolland was born in 1933 to a rather typical Fort Wayne family. His parents were Scottish immigrants who provided a comfortable home even during the Depression. His father, an electrician, was able to manage a successful electrical contracting business and the Rollands were content as members of the Crescent Avenue Evangelical Church. In these early years the boy grew with views very similar to those of his peers in conservative Fort Wayne of the World War II era. Yet, his increasingly frequent arguments in behalf of liberal issues within his conservative congregation, which had become the Evangelical United Brethren Church, helped him to form his own values about society. Rolland became the head of the Social Concerns Committee and with Pastor A. Hunter Colpitts developed the ministry idea that became the East Wayne Street Center, a non-profit organization dedicated to helping residents of the inner city. Rolland and Colpitts persuaded the church and denomination boards to fund the purchase of the old Turner Chapel of the African Methodist Episcopal Church, which became the home of the Center in 1965.

A good student at North Side High School, Rolland went on to attend DePauw University and worked summers at Lincoln Life (1953-1955). He didn't set out to be an actuary. As he recalls it, "I started out my college career majoring in chemistry and decided as a freshman that I didn't like the lab work. I thought mathematics was a pretty good alternative, so I majored in math and economics at DePauw. Then I had to decide what to do with a degree in mathematics. I could have taught, but I wasn't sure that was for me. It was then that I was introduced to the actuarial program, and that summer to Lincoln National Life." In order to get the summer job at Lincoln National, Rolland's father helped him get an interview with Ed Auer, then in charge of investments, and Auer arranged an interview with

the one of the company's actuaries, Sam Adams. Evidently encouraged by his summer experiences, Rolland's academic career shone at the University of Michigan where he graduated with high honors and a master's in actuarial sciences in 1956. Returning to Lincoln National that same year as a technical assistant in Group-Administration, he began a process of rotation throughout the company familiar to all the young actuaries who arrived in Fort Wayne. "My prime goal in life when I started work here," Rolland remembers, "was to get through the actuarial exams, and after that I just wanted to be an actuary. That was about as far into the future as I was looking. I can also remember one of my principal goals was to make $10,000 a year. I figured that would give me all the money I'd ever want to have." For the next four years he worked in Group Health, Individual Health, and the Actuarial Department. Having spent time in various areas of the company, Rolland was ready to settle down to do something substantive.

The chance came in 1961, on the very Friday he completed the last of the gruelling actuarial exams. Then-Vice President Henry Rood not only congratulated him, but also gave him an assignment that was due by Monday: Establish the amount of capital necessary for setting up a Lincoln National Life company in New York in order for it to operate before it could earn a profit. Rolland continued to work on the Lincoln of New York's actuarial problems as that company struggled to survive in the tough New York market. He liked working with Fred Clark, the president of Lincoln of New York. Stationed in the home office as assistant actuary under the leadership of Chief Actuary Adams, Rolland tended to both parent company and New York actuarial problems. Although later this New York company did not succeed, it was Rolland's first important assignment and gave him the opportunity to see the corporation in its entirety.

In 1966 Rood asked Rolland, then an associate actuary, to develop a variable annuity product. He was promoted to second vice president and manager of the Equities Department. Then, starting from scratch and working at a furious pace, the members of the team Rolland assembled threw themselves into the project, excited about creating something new not only for the company, but also in the industry. The pace kept up even after the first case was written. The field force had to be sold on the idea and training expanded beyond the agents to the personnel and clients of reinsurance. The reinsurance experience put Rolland into his first sustained significant contact with other insurance leaders, a level of personal relationship within the industry that con-

tinues to serve him well. And this experience would serve Lincoln National well also when he went to reinsurance in 1970.

Rolland did not set out to be CEO. The philosophy that he consistently followed is evident in scores of interviews about his career advancements. "I have thoroughly enjoyed every job I have had," he said in 1976, believing that "the best approach would be to do those jobs in the best way I knew and let the future take care of itself. I didn't spend time worrying about what others were doing. In fact, I always thought other guys had a better shot, like Jake Mascotte (who later became CEO of Continental

Corporation, a large property-casualty insurance company). Working on variable annuities, Rolland said, "was hugely enjoyable to me. I could have done that for the rest of my career. We had such good teamwork in that project." Being part of a team whose members are competent and respect one another as they work for a common goal is of the greatest importance to Rolland. His success, he insists, is due to a strong commitment to work for the team, "combined with good timing and a great deal of good fortune." Rolland continued to direct the equities department until 1970, when Watson moved him to manage sales in reinsurance. The most diffi-

Burgeoning Community Commitment

In the mid-1960s Rolland became involved for the first time in inner city issues. Drawn to an outreach concept developed by his pastor, A. Hunter Colpitts at the Evangelical United Brethren Church, Rolland became the first president of the East Wayne Street Center, a neighborhood based self-help program, in 1965. The creed of the center was "to expand the experience of human love through involvement of the entire community in actions which solve its human problems." As he remembered it, "this was the first exposure I had to inner city problems, since I came from a typical white suburban environment." The East Wayne Street Center experience was "a threshhold event" for Rolland, for this was "the first time I learned about what blacks had to put up with — and what it was like to be poor — it was revolting. It just wasn't right." He traces his commitment to being involved in community issues to these early years helping to develop programs on Fort Wayne's impoverished east side. One of the first projects he helped to organize was a nursery school that anticipated the Head Start Program.

He was also sensitized by these experiences to the idea that business had a responsibility to the community. Under Henry Rood and especially Tom Watson, who himself was particularly sensitive to social issues and the concept of corporate responsibility, Rolland enjoyed management's support and even garnered some financial help from the company. As a founding officer in 1970 of the East

Assistant Treasurer Marilyn Vachon in 1970 presents a LINCS check to Rolland, then Manager of the Equities Department, for the East Wayne Street Center.

Central Improvement Corporation, for example, Rolland was able to gain a substantial corporate grant of $100,000 for a housing improvement project that was a forerunner of the nationally recognized housing effort he later participated in designing, Lincoln Life Improved Housing. In 1970 he became chairman of the Chamber of Commerce's Human Development Department and launched several aggressive programs aimed at addressing a variety of social problems, including "Help-A-Kid," a program that assisted 250 underprivileged children attend summer camp, community seminars on racial understanding and crime prevention; and a cooperative venture with the National Alliance of Business to provide jobs for inner-city youths, again anticipating a later Lincoln National program known as B.A.S.E. (Business Assisted Summer Employment).

While Rolland was careful not to embarrass the company, he did not hesitate to be openly supportive of social change. When the local school administration would not respond to his call for desegregation, he became involved in school boycotts and alternative classrooms known as "freedom schools" held at the East Wayne Street Center. His community activity was a family affair, too. On one occasion early in the early 1970s Rolland's wife, Mimi, who is also an activist, was picketing a local real estate office in which a former senior officer of the company had an major interest. The realty firm was thought to be engaging in widespread "redlining" practices, effectively segregating neighborhoods. When the officer reported Mimi's actions to Watson, the CEO visited Rolland's office and asked, "Do you have any idea what your wife was doing today?" to which Rolland replied, "I don't have the faintest idea what my wife is doing," making clear that Mimi's activities were not a company concern nor was he her custodian. Watson understood perfectly and that was an end to it.

cult part of this assignment was to prepare the way for Watson to make major changes in top management. When "Black Monday" came in 1971 and Watson removed several top officers, including Walt Steffen, the senior vice president managing reinsurance, Rolland assisted the CEO with the severance details and was put in charge of reinsurance with a promotion to vice president. In 1973 Rolland was again promoted, this time to senior vice president of Lincoln National Life Insurance, and he continued to direct reinsurance until 1975.

"The first time I had any inkling I might follow Tom (Watson) as CEO was the day in 1975 when he asked me to spend the afternoon with him at Lake George and he explained what he had in mind. It was a big surprise to me. I think I then had enough sense in the succeeding months not to overplay the situation and so no one knew for a long time I had been tagged." Turning to his young senior vice president was a bold step for Watson, for by so doing he was skipping the generation that normally would have ascended to the top of the company. Watson simply did not see the leadership he felt the corporation would require in this group of senior managers. In an effort to position Rolland for succession, Watson sought to have him elected president of the corporation in 1975. As Rolland remembered it, "Tom came to my office and told me that he thought he had enough votes on the board to have me elected president; I said 'OK, just tell me what to do.' On the day the board met at our offices at Chicago Title & Trust, Tom told me to wait outside the room while he took care of things. I waited and waited, and waited some more. And I couldn't figure what went wrong. I said to myself that there must be one helluva debate going on in there to take this long. Is someone that opposed to me?'" When Watson returned to the hallway where Rolland was sitting by himself, he explained that he indeed had enough votes to elect Rolland president; however, the corporation's general counsel, Gordon Reeves, noted that before that Rolland had to be a member of the board before he could be elected president and that

Students cited for passing actuarial exams in mid-1957 gathered with Vice President and Actuary Henry Rood. They are, from left, seated: John Glass, Don Fackler, John Williams, Charles Barnaby and Ian Rolland; standing, 2VP Carl Ashman, Jim Lewis, Bill Easterly, Rood, Ken Clark, Don Edwards, Lloyd Grever and Actuary Gatherings Stewart.

there were no seats vacant at the time. The debate centered on how to expand the board to make Rolland's election possible. The election, when it finally occurred, was the first time the entire company knew Rolland was the designated successor to Watson.

The most important assignment given to Rolland by Watson in 1975 was to chair the corporation's first long-range planning committee. This "blue-ribbon" group of the rising management leaders — Jack Hunter, Dave Silletto and Howard Steele of Lincoln Life and the senior officers of the major affiliates, Ed Goss and William Miller of American States Insurance, Jack Jensen and Robert Bates of Chicago Title and Trust and Gordon Coyne and Derek Eckersley of Dominion Life Assurance — met in Chicago to get their work done. This was the first time the senior management had come together as a formal long-range planning group. Interestingly, the planning committee did not include the CEO or other older leaders, although it did contain those who would lead the company in the coming decades.

The vision for the corporation that Rolland articulated in 1977, on the eve of his promotion to chief executive officer, was deeply influenced by this first LNC Corporate Planning Committee work, as well as by his different roles in the company and his community involvement. Rolland

believed that the company had to be innovative rather than reactive in order to cope with the difficult issues it faced in the late 1970s. Paramount in his vision was the need for regular, formal strategic planning. The company, he noted, "would need to do a better job of corporate planning if it were to survive in the rapidly changing business environment of the late 1970s and the coming decade of the '80s." He also expressed a continued commitment to the growth of the career agency system, but this meant facing the pressing challenge of reorganizing LNSC, which was suffering considerable difficulty by 1977. Mindful of a chief duty to the shareholders, profitability for every aspect of the company would be a guidepost. At the heart of this determination, was a new vision of company employees. It would be one of Rolland's important goals to create an atmosphere in which everyone would seek to increase his productivity as a personal matter, to make this a way of life, rather than as the result of orders from superiors. If successful, this would be the principal means for increasing profitability in the face of the pressures of continuing high inflation, rather than cutting costs through layoffs. Improved communications would also be a constant and critical challenge for the company, as would more extensive cooperation among the corporate affiliates. In both cases,

"More Cheeseburgers Than I Care To Remember" Creating The Variable Annuity Department

"It was one of the neatest things I had done in my entire career; it was an opportunity to build something. It was fun," Ian Rolland remembered nearly three decades later. "I'll never forget the morning Henry Rood called me to his office and said, 'We want to get into the variable annuity business, and we want you to put us into that business.' All I knew was generally what variable annuities were; other than that, I had no idea."

In 1966, only one or two companies were in the business of variable annuities and these companies were viewed as mavericks. Most of the traditional companies looked down on any non-guaranteed product as being unworthy of an insurance company's line of business. Any effort at the Lincoln National, therefore, would essentially be breaking new ground. The sensible thing to do, Rolland decided, was to get the help of a consultant, and he turned to Arthur Blakesley, who had worked for the company started by John Marsh, a Lincoln National general agent in Washington, D.C., that developed Variable Annuity Life Insurance (VALIC), one of the major present-day companies in the business.

Everything had to be set up from scratch. "We were flying by the seat of our pants," Rolland recalled, "that's what made it so exciting — that and the people who worked so hard together as a team to get the job done." Lincoln National was a pioneer. "We had to set up all the mechanisms: the forms, the internal administration, security registration with the SEC and each of the states in which we did business, the pricing, and find the investment advisor to manage the funds — everything."

"The esprit de corps of the people working in this was outstanding and exciting," Rolland said, "because everyone was in a new business, with new opportunities and new challenges." There were a couple of attorneys and in sales there was Bill Sanders and Don Gifford, with Wayne Bock handling the administrative side. Jane Esterlein was in charge of new business and Ina Napier handled masterfully the intricate licensing processes. All was under the overall direction of Gathings Stewart, president of Lincoln National Life Insurance. The crew occupied the second floor of the Harrison Street building when they could come and go by the south door. They quickly gained a reputation in the company for putting in exceptionally long hours. CEO Tom Watson said that "once when I came in on a Sunday morning, and thought: I'll bet this is one time no one will be working in the variable annuity sector on second floor. By God, there was Bill Sanders working on a sales idea."

The project required many trips to Washington or to New York and Rolland remembers "riding the train more times than I care to think about. You see, one of our attorneys didn't like to fly, so we rode the Broadway Limited or the Capital Limited literally day and night sometimes. We consumed more cheeseburgers than I care to remember — and at New York prices."

"Because we were breaking new ground," Rolland said, "we did a lot of things without much research, but simply because they felt right, because they seemed to be the right thing to do." The haste was prompted by the news that the Chicago Public School Teachers' case was coming up for bid and the Lincoln National people wanted to be there with a competitive prospectus and the product in place. According to Rolland, "we got everything registered on time and we did it in an amazingly short period of time; other companies would have a much tougher time of it later." As it turned out, the Lincoln did not get the Chicago Teachers' case, but did land as its first the California state college system.

All these early sales relationships were intensely personal. As Rolland remembers, "we knew all our policyholders by name — there were so few of them. We were so excited about all this that we eagerly opened the mail each day to see if any applications had come in." One of the early big cases was the Texas A&M University Optional Retirement Plan (ORP). Rolland recalls that when he went to College Station, Texas, to bid on the case, the man he met had already known about Lincoln National through an experience with reinsurance and "had a good feeling about us. That became the basis for a lot of business in Texas."

The new department also had to introduce the sales force to the new product, and this, as it turned out, was not easy. Don Gifford had the job of making the presentation to the sales force at a large meeting in Los Angeles (in order to be in California, where the first case was written). Gifford assembled a large number of agents for the presentation, which he made with all the expertise he could muster. Everyone was duly impressed. Then he got to the part about compensation. When he explained that agents did not receive nearly as much in the first year as they did selling traditional products, and that, in fact, with first products there were virtually no renewal commissions, there was deep silence. Then Gifford announced the commission scales. Almost every agent in the room got up and walked out. Gifford called Rolland and pleaded, "What do I do?" and Rolland responded that they simply had to start over and do a better job of showing that income would be earned through volume, not individual sales. Better yet, they had to get a few agents convinced and help them become successful, then the rest would follow. So the variable annuities team launched an all-out campaign with the sales force, holding seminars with the goal of getting them licensed. The first individual variable annuity contract was sold in October 1967 by an agent of the E.B. Bingham and Associates agency in Fort Wayne. Although the business was slow to grow at first, it gradually began to build and become successful, laying the foundations for the great explosion in the annuities business of the 1990s.

The work of the department did not end with the direct sales force, but extended to reinsurance as well. As the success of the product became known in 1966 and 1967, clients of reinsurance began asking how they could get into this new line of business. Typical of the unique relationship of departments within the Lincoln National, the variable annuities staff, who were a part of the Lincoln National Life Insurance Company, came over to reinsurance and began to hold seminars for their customers, who were also the competitors of LNL. And this seems to have been done without undue stress or anxiety. Rolland and one of the attorneys held a seminar a month for hundreds of personnel from other companies. As for direct sales side, reliance was placed upon confidence in being able simply to stay one step ahead of the competition. For Rolland personally, all this contact with representatives of the insurance world through the seminars at reinsurance held him in good stead when he had to direct the reinsurance division himself and continues to the present in the numerous leadership roles he undertakes in the industry's various professional organizations.

Lincoln National would have to improve dramatically if it were to survive, much less prosper, in the future. These broad, overlaying visions still direct the CEO. In reflection, what was missing in Rolland's view of the future for the company was the role of the investment operation. In 1977, however, no one had any idea that this area of corporate activity would explode with opportunity and challenge in the next decade and a half.

Rolland's first eighteen months in charge of Lincoln National was a time of planning and setting a new course for the company in the midst of a rapidly changing business environment. The company had some serious difficulties to overcome and there was little room for error. The economic environment of the late 1970s was volatile. Inflation skyrocketed above 13%, unemployment rose to painful levels, mortgage rates soared beyond 15%, the dollar was at an all- time low on the international market, and the federal deficit began to explode. Efforts by the Federal Reserve Board to slow the economy threw the nation into a full-blown recession by 1980. Confronted by these economic hurdles and the internal difficulties posed by the run-away expenses of LNSC, Rolland sought a clearer view of the company's options through an analysis by an outside consulting firm. This approach had served him well in developing the variable annuity operation and he invited McKinsey & Co., highly respected corporate consultants, to study the corporation and advise him on a course of action. As a result, Rolland decided to curb the expenses of LNSC in a way that would increase profitability and control of the operation without harming the dynamics of the concept. Thus, beginning in 1979 he implemented a steady process of reducing the number of corporate agencies in the field from seventy-eight to only thirty-six. By doing this, he would increase the profitability of direct sales, enhance the effectiveness of the sales force, and ensure that the image and reputation of Lincoln National was well guarded. The struggle to mold the field force in a new sales environment in which agents increasingly offered a wider array of financial products while maintaining the integrity of the com-

pany would remain a major concern.

Closely tied to this, a second concept Rolland initiated that arose from his work with the McKinsey group was the reorganization of the corporation into Strategic Business Units (SBUs). Recognizing that each line of business had its own customers, with distinct distribution systems and marketing needs, it was decided that business lines ought to be geared to the way the products were sold and have direct control of those functions necessary to become more effective, such as marketing and product development. This new structure for the corporation had the greatest effect on the life insurance company, which witnessed its areas of Group Life and Health, Individual Products, Pensions, and Savings Products become, in effect, separate companies.

A third early decision emerged from Rolland's determination to make a fundamental change in the way in which the corporation functioned with the program called "Quality Commitment," which was launched in 1978. Rather than submit, as other companies were doing at the time, to short-term cost-cutting measures, Rolland chose to develop a long-term program that would transcend mere cost control efforts and position the company to be more competitive when "stagflation" finally ended. The goal of "QC," as it was called, was to increase productivity through greater efficiency. The plan envisioned that increased productivity would be realized by fostering a new attitude about work, one that was based on a willing-

ness to make changes and adaptations and a belief that all work could be done better through improved work procedures and improved quality of work life, concepts that would have very broad ramifications for the culture within Lincoln National Corporation. By 1979 these new policies and the slowdown in the national economy marked the end of the 10%-15% increases in staff common in the previous decade. There were no staff cutbacks, however.

In order to push for a highly competitive level of profitability, the CEO early established as a goal 15% return on equity. Although there was no effort to create a standing corporate planning committe or department as yet, each of the major Strategic Business Units developed its own long-range plan. American States Insurance, which had had the longest experience in doing sophisticated planning, provided an example for the other SBUs.

Concern for future developments led Rolland to seek greater diversification in the early 1980s. Anticipating the spurt of growth the company would experience in the mid-1980s, Lincoln National acquired Security Connecticut Life Insurance Company of Avon, Connecticut, in 1979. This was a well managed company that marketed its products through independent agents and brokers, and Rolland believed that it would be wise to have the added strength of an established brokerage business on its team. Lincoln National, at the time the fifth largest writer of individual

Seminars and training courses for employee improvement programs became common at Lincoln National beginning in the 1970s.

The Lincoln Attracts Suitors

Successful companies are often the object of unwanted interest by other companies. Such unsought interest in Lincoln National first occurred in 1931 when the American Founders Corporation of New York, an investment company, purchased a substantial amount of Lincoln National stock and had its vice president, George E. Devendorf, elected to the board. Later that year more stock was purchased by American Founders and another officer of the company was placed on Lincoln National's board. American Founders wanted Lincoln National to make increased invest-

Rolland confers with General Counsel Jack Hunter in 1979.

ments in common stocks. In this case, these outside pressures were soon abandoned in the face of the Great Depression and American Founders sold its shares in Lincoln National.

In 1979, shortly after Rolland became CEO, another threat developed. Management had watched with growing interest as American General Insurance Company and its affiliates began to accumulate LNC stock. The ante was raised when Lincoln National personnel learned that American General had filed a Schedule 13 D signalling that they had taken 5% of the company's stock. This set off alarm bells for American General had a reputation for being aggressive with other companies. American General continued to buy and moved up to a position just short of 10%; although it was exceptionally difficult to acquire an insurance company in a hostile bid, aggressive raiders of the late 1970s were beginning to make inroads. Lincoln National continued to tune up its defenses as a precaution.

The chief investment officer for American General called Rolland to ask if Lincoln National would like to buy back its stock. "We saw this as a golden opportunity for us," Rolland remembered, "So we pursued that; we knew that if they continued, then it would become a real threat." A deal was worked out to buy back Lincoln National stock at a price over market value but under book with no cash up front; Lincoln National would issue a fifteen-year note at 9 3/4%, but would not begin payment on the principal until 1985. "This looked good financially," said Rolland, "although we were paying a higher price. So, I thought the deal was all set, except a few details to be worked out by the attorneys, and left for a sales meeting in Durango, Colorado."

Murphy's Law prevailed and things did not go as planned. "I remember getting up that morning in Colorado and went out to run," Rolland recalled, "I fell and hurt my shoulder and so was not in a very good mood when I came back to my room. No sooner did I get in than I got a call from Harold Hook, the CEO at American General. He was madder than hell, saying 'What are you guys up to? Your lawyers are ready to sue us and everything is coming unravelled. Don't you want this deal?' I said 'What are you talking about, I thought the deal was all done.'" Hook assured Rolland that lawyers were ready to go to court and so, Rolland remembered: "I called Jack (Hunter) back in Fort Wayne and he went over the issue that the lawyers had gotten into a tussle over. I thought was pretty trivial, but the lawyers thought was a matter of life or death." Rolland finally exploded: "Jack, who is running this company, you or me?" Hunter gave the obvious answer and Rolland told him "to put this thing back on track and get it fixed. I remember spending the rest of the day with a sore shoulder on the telephone between Colorado, Texas and Fort Wayne. By night, it was all back on track. Jack and I have a big laugh over all that now."

As for the Board of Directors in all of this, a cautionary objection was raised by Robert Efroymson. While management had proposed seeking approval of a majority of shareholders — an action not required under Indiana law or Lincoln National's by-laws — Efroymson convinced the board that it should set for itself a requirement for a two-thirds majority vote to approve, and a special meeting of the shareholders was called. Proxies were sent out and Rolland spent "a considerable amount of his time" with the major stockholders explaining the Lincoln National's position. Rolland proudly recalls that "we got a 95% approval vote; it was a testimony of good faith by our shareholders, which at this time did not include very many institutions."

In the early 1980s, another rumbling of possible takeover trouble occurred when a well known stock raider suddenly bought nearly 5% of Lincoln National stock after being frustrated in his efforts to acquire a Lincoln National subsidiary. Big red flags went up and the company's takeover defense team readied themselves for a fight. Lincoln National was soon contacted for a meeting. Rolland's memory of that event is vivid. "We met at the Teeterboro, New Jersey, airport. He talked about what a great company The Lincoln was and looked forward to working with us, etc.. I said, 'Look, we don't need your help. We're perfectly capable of running the business on our own and we really don't want you as a shareholder. So, we'd like to buy back our stock.' " The raider at last agreed to sell and evidently was unabashed by forthright views, for he quoted a price that was close to the market value and fears of "greenmail" were mitigated. In this case, Rolland and the board decided against going to the stockholders since the company was in the midst of a stock buy-back, which had been authorized by the board of directors.

life insurance in the nation, entered the new decade prepared for change.

The 1980s opened in a recession. Although direct sales remained strong and LNSC agencies by 1981 were reduced to about half their number from their 1976 high, expenses in Rolland's view continued to be "exorbitant." The depressed housing market, said to be worst since the Great Depression, was disastrous for Chicago Title & Trust. Natural catastrophies kept American States in a difficult position, experiencing in 1984 its first overall loss in its history. Lincoln National Life briefly experimented with mass marketing of insurance products with the partial acquisition of Associated Madison Company, but did not feel comfortable with this approach and exited the business in 1982.

The early 1980s witnessed a growing array of investment options and individuals acquiring a heightened financial awareness. People increasingly sought investment products which would outstrip inflation, provide flexibility and offer tax advantages, features not available in many traditional insurance products. To meet these new challenges, Rolland put Lincoln National into a new line of business: universal life. In order to get the company into the business as quickly as possible, Lincoln National acquired First Penn-Pacific Life Insurance Company, of Oakbrook Terrace, Illinois, in 1981. This company was a pioneer in the field of universal life and, as the first company to computerize universal life proposals, had one of the best administration systems for this product. With this addition to the corporation, Lincoln National became the first major life insurance company to enter the universal life market.

Universal life was hailed when it was introduced for its flexibility and because it responded to a perceived market need. Universal life policies provided insurance elements and savings elements, with the latter usually carrying a current interest crediting rate with a guaranteed minimum. Additional innovations have been introduced, such as allowing policyholders to increase, decrease or stop paying premiums.

Rolland also turned to a familiar tool, the strategic plan, to fight the tough economic pressures of the early 1980s when he launched a new plan in 1982. In this early era of deregulation, the barriers between insurance and banking began coming down and Lincoln National increasingly sought other ways of distributing its products, whether through Security-Connecticut's brokers or Richard Leahy's mass marketing. In this way, Lincoln National identified several targets for the corporation's activities for the next decade. Key among these was the goal of achieving a leadership position all areas of business. At the same time, it was decided that where leadership could not be achieved, the company would withdraw. In a matter close to Rolland's personal interest, the strategy also called for maintenance of the highest degree of integrity in dealing with all constituencies. The 1982 plan was also the first to emphasize the importance of corporate community involvement and to address the impending technological explosion.

Accordingly, it was determined that neither Dominion Assurance in Canada nor Chicago Title & Trust would fit the strategic plan and they were divested in 1985. LNSC was further reduced to the level of the pre-

sent-day thirty-eight agencies and expenses were greatly controlled. The agents, however, increasingly focused their sales efforts on "the total financial needs and programs of his or her clients" and the agencies increasingly functioned as "one-stop" shops for a variety of asset accumulation and insurance products. With the blossoming of technology early in the decade, the company installed the Automated Office Systems (AOS) in 1982 and Rolland championed its use throughout the company. Several years later, Lincoln National was recognized for its use of AOS for electronic mail, performance monitoring and word processing. AOS was marketed by Lincoln National Information Systems and was used in large organizations such as the U.S. Senate and the House of Representatives. Consistently upgraded to meet new needs, the system became known as OPN (Office Productivity Network) by the end of the decade.

In retrospect, the single most difficult issue for Rolland in the 1980s concerned the health insurance business. A major element of Lincoln National's operations since 1943, the Group business faced challenges associated with skyrockiting health care costs, challenges which had their roots in the creation of Medicare in 1965 and the Employee Retirement Income Security Act (ERISA) in 1974. In a 1991 interview Rolland reflected on the changes of the previous decade, noting that when it started health insurers were expected to process claims, quickly and efficiently, for employees of businesses contracting for the service. The relatively low cost of health care in the period of economic growth of the 1950s and 1960s meant employees could have "first-

The Lincoln Tries Its Hand At A Takeover

Lincoln National itself attempted what might have become a hostile takeover of another insurance company, although it did not start out that way. In 1978 Rolland got some feelers from the investment bankers of Lazar-Freres in New York that American Re might be acquired. This would have been the first acquisition since the tenure of Tom Watson, an opportunity which was appealing since American Re was a well managed reinsurance company. "We visited the American Re people," Rolland recalled, "and they made it appear as if they would be receptive to an offer. So we put together an offer and we thought this would go through in a friendly manner." As it turned out, however, the American Re investment bankers of Goldman Sachs apparently advised the company to seek a "White Knight" to take the company (and increase the price). "We hung in there for a while," Rolland said, "but our board, and especially Bob Efroymson, became nervous about getting into a bidding contest and was reluctant to pursue them in a hostile fashion." Once it was discovered that the principal bidder was the Aetna, "We said to hell with it, and dropped out," remembers Rolland, "but I still don't know what happened to make it turn hostile."

dollar" coverage, meaning all of their medical bills would be paid through insurance. "If actuaries could predict claims trends over the next twelve months, you could price the product so you have a little profit left over at the end of the year," Rolland said.

But spiralling health care costs changed all that. Between 1980 and 1989, health care costs rose from nine percent of gross national product to almost thirteen percent — almost three times greater than domestic inflation. Businesses that once wanted only a provider of benefits now wanted a manager of benefits to help control costs. The answer to double-digit inflation seemed to lie in managing care through the building of networks of contracted health care providers.

Lincoln National, like many other health insurers, acquired health maintenance organizations (HMOs). Also established were preferred provider organizations (PPOs). It became evident that only the largest players would be successful and very substantial investments in systems and operations would be necessary for Lincoln National, even with its emphasis on the small- and medium-sized employers market.

In 1991 Rolland reached the conclusion that further investment in managed care would be to the detriment of other, more profitable lines of business. In particular, the Managed Health Care Group needed a very sizable investment for further development of a mammoth relational data-

base known as the System for Managed Care (SMC), as well as expanded HMO networks. It was also evident that the health care arena was destined for further upheaval. The enormous implications of an aging population and unrelenting consumer demand for the latest medical technology, regardless of cost, gave little hope for profitable growth in the business. In addition, the issue of millions of uninsured Americans was becoming a political issue well in advance of the presidential election, casting another shadow over the managed care business.

In January 1992, Lincoln National announced it was exiting the managed care business by selling HMOs and PPOs to TakeCare, Inc., a California-

The Ian M. Rolland Community Service Award

In 1987 Lincoln National's department of Corporate Public Involvement (CPI) created the Ian Rolland Award to recognize exemplary volunteer service given by Lincoln National employees. Named in honor of the CEO because of his extensive record of local and national volunteer work, the award originally was given to two employees each year, one in the home office and one in a field office. In 1995 the award was expanded to three recipients, to be chosen from any part of the Lincoln National operation.

The award has special importance for Rolland who holds volunteering as a unique American concept. As he noted in 1987 when the program was announced, "Nowhere else in the world do so many millions of people offer to work for community organizations without expecting any financial reward. People volunteer because they have a strong commitment to meet the needs which exist in their community and because of the good feelings they derive from the experience."

Recipients over the past eight years have been:

	HOME OFFICE	FIELD OFFICES
1987	Lowell Tillman	Leon McClaflin
1988	Felisha R Curry	V. Scott Gantt
	Donald Crumpacker	
1989	Merit Smith	Molly Smith
1990	Vancha Collins	George Bryce
1991	Julie Applegate	Jeffrey Horstman
1992	Darlene Bush	Tim Owen
		Greg O'Quin
1993	V. Scott Kingdon	Gary Kuzmich
		Joseph Dekat
1994	Scott M. Bushnell	Tony Fusco
	Leonard Helfrich	Jack Field Jr.

A typical recipient is Leonard Helfrich, an associate counsel in the Law Division recognized in 1994 for his extensive work as one of the founders and leaders of the Fort Wayne AIDS Task Force and the Indiana Youth Group, a statewide gay and lesbian organization for young people seeking information, assistance and mutual support. In addition, Helfrich has given considerable pro bono legal assistance to the gay community, led in fund-raising campaigns for AIDS-related issues and has been an organizer of the Gay and Lesbian Community Center in Fort Wayne.

The award to Helfrich is seen as a special example of Rolland's and Lincoln National's willingness to treat all people with respect. For Rolland this has been particularly important in the face of the AIDS epidemic and the need to overcome fear with a rational understanding of issues both among employees and in the field force. The advance of this notion into the corporate culture received formal blessing when in December 1991 the provision forbidding discrimination because of sexual orientation became a part of official Lincoln National policy and the employee handbook.

based HMO company. The group life and health business was sold to Great-West Life and Annuity of Colorado. In addition, the third- party administrators — firms that provided insurance services to companies that self-funded their employee benefits — were sold to a management team. All that remained was Employers Health Insurance Company of Green Bay, Wisconsin, one of the nation's leading providers of health insurance to small businesses. That company was spun off as an independent business in 1994 with Lincoln National holding approximately thirty percent of the new company's stock.

Rolland is unique among CEOs for the level of his activism in the community in which his business makes its home. The active participation in community affairs that he displayed in his early years continues during his tenure as CEO, and he has not hesitated to use corporate resources in the effort. Likewise, he has fostered programs in the company which instills in the employees a similar sense of community responsibility through volunteering and giving. Again, this was conceived in an all encompassing way; this sort of activity by all employees, including himself, is viewed as good for business. It is an integral part of life at Lincoln National and another way of expressing the inherent value of the company.

Among the first changes he made in the corporation was to increase the pre-tax contributions to charitable organizations from 0.5% to 2% of pre-tax net income, placing Lincoln National among the top companies in the industry in corporate giving. Like Arthur Hall half a century earlier, Rolland became a leader in the Chamber of Commerce, helping to reorganize its economic redevelopment efforts and leading in the record-breaking fund drive to revitalize the Chamber. Impressed by the organization of the Indianapolis Corporate Community Council, that he encountered while visiting the American States operation in 1980, he thought "this would be great for Fort Wayne." He got Tom Binford of the Indianapolis Council to join him and Doug Fleming, then-CEO of Central Soya Corporation, to create the informal group known as the Fort Wayne

Corporate Council. Composed of the corporate leaders in the city, the Council met from time to time to set priorities for fund raising and discuss the role business might play in critical community matters. Rolland was responsible for convincing the Council to support the creation of the Fort Wayne Local Education Fund, which was established in 1989 with Lincoln National assistance for the purposes of expanding support and expectations for quality, innovative public education programs. He also joined the vice chancellor of Indiana University-Purdue University at Fort Wayne, Ed Nicholson, in the creation of Leadership Fort Wayne, an innovative program that brings together each year a class of rising leaders in the community and introduces them to the leaders, issues, institutions and mechanisms for change. One of the most creative community assistance programs carried out under Rolland's leadership was the Arts United of Greater Fort Wayne "Renaissance Campaign," which raised enough money in the Fort Wayne area to address the capital needs of the city's arts organizations. In addition, it created a special endowment, the earnings of which would be used for the maintenance of the arts infrastructure, thereby eliminating the need for future capital fund drives from this sector.

Since his days at the East Wayne Street Center, Rolland has been an advocate for integration and racial balance in the community schools. Fort Wayne experienced segregation throughout its history and was slow to change. "This is a community," Rolland notes, "in which people don't rock the boat. Many do support projects generously, if you can get their attention. Sometimes I just despair of the timidness of the business community. There just is not much activism." In the face of little support in the mid-1980s, Rolland decided, "It's the right thing to do, and I really don't care what people think about it," and so he pursued the issue of integration within Fort Wayne's elementary schools. Infuriated at the lack of response to calls for improved racial balance in 1984, Rolland supported a parents group in a landmark class-action lawsuit against the Fort Wayne

Community Schools and the state of Indiana. Known as the PQEI (Parents for Quality Education through Integration) suit, the issue dragged on for years in the courts. It was finally resolved in 1994 as a landmark victory for minority and low-income students in Fort Wayne.

Respected by other insurance professionals and the Black Caucus on Capitol Hill for his leadership in bringing greater minority representation to the industry and his community, Rolland has taken the company well beyond the federal mandates of Affirmative Action and Equal Opportunity Employment regulations. Racial Awareness Seminars and a wide variety of career development programs have been developed. Most recently, in 1994 the black employees of Lincoln National have formed the Black Officers Network and the African-American Group as a means of working with the company to identify and resolve minority issues. Rolland acknowledges that Lincoln National still has a long way to go in achieving racial parity and that the company must face tough challenges, such as the highly competitive employment market for minority actuaries, attorneys, investment analysts, publicists, and other professionals. It is also a challenge to attract either rising or established professionals to Fort Wayne.

Lincoln National's support of the arts in Fort Wayne and the communities of its affiliates became an important part of the company's public involvement program from the late 1970s.

Rolland has also addressed the issues of gender equality in the workplace and in community organizations. Beginning with Watson's tenure as CEO, there has been a steady improvement in the role women play in the company. Many now hold senior level responsibilities and with the appearance of women among the directors of the corporation and its affiliates women's issues have received still further attention. One outgrowth has been the formation of a networking organization in the Fort Wayne-based companies known as Women Executives, or the WE group. In 1992 a major effort to study the place of women in the corporation was initiated by Rolland as the Women At Work Task Force. Largely in response to issues raised by the Women At Work Task Force concerning the special needs of single parents and of working couples, for example, the company opened a Child Care Center in 1994.

Throughout his nearly two decades as CEO of Lincoln National, Rolland has been a leader in significant ways in the insurance industry. One significant recognition of his leadership in the industry is the fact that he has served for many years as chairman of the Nominating Committee of the

The Marathon Man

An important measure of the character of Ian Rolland is his devotion to running. Although an ardent runner today, he only started in the late-1970s. While at an agency convention in San Francisco, Rolland recalls, someone talked his wife, Mimi, into jogging in the city. "I thought that would be too boring," he said, "so I didn't join her." After they returned to Fort Wayne, however, Mimi took up running in earnest and kept urging him to join her. Rolland remembers that one day "he just started running, two blocks at first, then longer and longer. Finally, one Fourth of July, I entered the Fort Wayne 'Firecracker Four,' a four-mile run. Things really picked up from there and there was great satisfaction in doing better and achieving."

The discipline was attractive, too, as he made sure always to work his regular running into his schedule — every day but Tuesday and Friday — no matter where he is or what the weather. The benefits, he found, were not only physical, but mental as well.

Rolland entered his first marathon — a twenty-six-mile run — in 1980. It began when his son-in-law, who also is a runner, stayed with the Rollands with some of his running friends. The marathoners talked Rolland into entering an upcoming race. As Rolland remembers, "Up to that time, I had never run more than nine miles. I just figured I start out in the marathon and just stop when I get too tired. So, I asked Mimi to wait for me at the 13-mile mark, which is about as far as I thought I could get." As it turned out, he was still feeling strong at thirteen miles and asked Mimi to meet him at the 15-mile mark. "By then," he said, "I was beginning to hurt, but I thought to go just a few more miles. Soon, I was really hurting, but asked Mimi to meet me at the 20-mile mark. By the time I got that far, I thought to myself, 'No matter the pain at this point, I'm going to finish.' And I did, in a less-than-world-class time of a little over four hours. But what a thrill it was to finish. I had to be helped into my home and the next day I couldn't walk, but I was hooked." Since that first race, Rolland has run fifteen marathons, including several well-known ones in New York and Boston.

American Council of Life Insurance (ACLI), the leading life insurance industry trade association. This position is voted upon each year by the members of the ACLI, and is the only ACLI committee chairmanship to be treated this way. He has served on the board of the ACLI longer than any other industry CEO and has been in the middle of the profession's responses to the major issues of the past decade and a half — from the Unisex proposal of 1983 and the advent of AIDS to present-day concerns over sales practices and the taxation of annuities.

Rolland has served once as chairman of the ACLI, twice as chairman of the Health Insurance Association of America, and in 1988-1989 he was president of the Society of Actuaries. During his ACLI chairmanship in 1984, however, he had to preside over the enormous difficulties presented by the collapse of the Baldwin-United Company and the threat that that debacle presented to the insurance industry's guaranty system and its image of caring for the policyholders. As chair of the trade association, Rolland took responsibility for settling the situation and negotiated arrangements within the industry to resolve outstanding obligations. "We at the Lincoln," Rolland recalled,"were prepared to be the lead company in the Baldwin rehabilitation, but the people in Fort Wayne were really nervous

whether LNC could pull off something as enormous as this." As it turned out, the Rolland was able to convince the Metropoliltan Life Insurance Company to step forward and take the lead with the Lincoln National working behind the scenes and sometimes "shoulder-to-shoulder with them." "The Met was great," Rolland remembered, "they had the size and the depth of personnel to cope with this mess." Rolland's part in this potential industry disaster enhanced the reputation of Lincoln National as a force of mediation. Later, when a few insurers ran into problmes, Rolland became the ACLI's chairman of its new CEO-level Solvency Committee.

Rolland's reputation in the industry for fairness and balanced judgment placed him in the middle of a host of issues, not least of all the manner in which insurance companies would be taxed. Standing on the long tradition of Lincoln National leadership in the area of federal taxation, Rolland is recognized for his technical knowledge and has been at the center of each debate and a key industry person in the resolution of conflict. Rolland has been, in fact, one consistent voice of reason in the on-going tension within the industry over taxation, known in some circles as the "stocks-mutuals wars." Although a leader on the stock side of the issue, Rolland's reputation for understanding the totality of the

Robert Anker, president and chief operating officer of Lincoln National Corporation, 1991.

issue and his reputation for fairness has placed him in the role of mediator in what has sometimes become a bitterly acrimonious dispute between the stock companies and mutual companies.

Matters of corporate organization and strategic planning, however, continued to demand Rolland's attention. By the end of the 1980s it was clear that the broad diversification that served the company well in the late 1970s and early 1980s needed to be reassessed. The face of the industry was changing, resulting in increased competitive pressures. On the one hand, deregulation of banks put them on a collision course with insurance companies, while mutual funds and securities firms began to have a greater impact in the marketplace. On another, regulations to protect insurance consumers dramatically increased. Lastly, demographic changes, new technology and global economic issues made it clear to Rolland that his primary goal for the 1990s had to be to position the company so it could respond to rapid change. As he recalled in 1994, "We'd been an average performer, better than the other multi-lines, but not one of the top companies. I was not content with this, [and so] we started to rachet up our performance." To do this, Rolland and senior management,

Rolland's interest in education became a hallmark of his tenure.

assisted by the consultants from McKinsey & Co., conceived a program designed to create a plan for the orderly redirection of Lincoln National known as Project Compass. It stressed corporate goals above all, Rolland told officers, in order "to maximize long-term shareholder value through superior operating performance and return: 15% annual return on equity and 9% growth in book value." The CEO recalled later, the effort "gave rise to a major strategic re-evaluation of the organization [as] we determined that we would only be in businesses where we had the skills to be a leading competitor." This marked the beginning of the final push by Rolland to change the old insurance holding company he inherited into a true corporate management company.

By the time it was completed in August 1992, Project Compass had clarified several key strategies for Lincoln National to follow in the last decade of the century: To narrow the focus of the corporation's operations in order to remain competitive; to delineate clearly the corporate center and its services to the lines of business; and to establish a broader structure for top-level decisions to enhance risk management and response to new opportunities. The decision to exit the health insurance business was the first major decision in refocusing the corporation. Further, in order to delineate clearly the separate, managerial role of the holding company, a new corporate center (LNCC) was defined in 1991 and located in a renovated departement store known as "Renaissance Square."

Simultaneously, Rolland announced the principal strategic personnel change on December 3, 1991, when Robert Anker, CEO of American States, was named president and chief operating officer of Lincoln National Corporation, as well as president and COO of Lincoln National Life Insurance Company. This marked the first time the corporation had a COO and denoted a new structural change. Anker, a property-casualty actuary, had joined American States in 1974 and became its president in 1988 and chairman in 1991. When he was brought to corporate headquarters he was charged with overseeing the daily operations of the corporation. For the first eighteen months, however, he devoted most of his attention to the direct life insurance and annuities operations. By placing a property-casualty actuary over the life insurance company, Rolland broke from the tradition. He clearly indicated he wanted the best management skills available to help prepare Lincoln Life for the comprehensive revitalization program that began in 1994.

In addition to these top-level adjustments in the organization, Rolland also instructed Senior Vice President Reed Miller to organize an effort to capture as many savings as possible in the wake of the divestiture of the Managed Health Care Group. This marked the beginning of Project CORE in the summer of 1992. When Managed Health Care was sold, the impact on corporate operations was serious; as much as 40 percent of corporate overhead expenses, for instance, were supported by the Managed Health Care Group. With its sale, therefore, a 40 percent savings at the corporate center had to be found. More than cost-cutting and improving staff efficiency, however, CORE also was an additional tool for more clearly defining the holding company and its relationship to the subsidiaries. Simultaneous with Project CORE, Vice President Carl Baker led a project known as Workforce '92, which

sought to retain as many of the excellent employees from the Managed Health Care Group as possible. Many of the key staff from the divested operation have gone on to make significant contributions in the corporation, foremost of whom has been Richard Vaughan, executive vice president and chief financial officer.

With the completion of these major reorganizational projects by the end of 1992, Rolland began to focus on implementing the strategies for taking the company to the end of the century. This meant setting Lincoln National in a new direction, one which fulfilled in large part the visions of Menge, Rood and Watson and the dreams of Hall and McAndless. Under the umbrella of three strategic imperatives identified in the corporate strategic plan — top-tier performance for all businesses, substantial value creation for each business, and risk management — Rolland undertook several key initiatives in 1994. Having pared the company to its core strengths, given the holding company clear definition as the managerial head of the corporation and started, under Anker's leadership, the revitalization of the life insurance company, he turned his attention to finding opportunities for further performance improvement and growth. Thus, he soon took a major step toward expanding Lincoln National's role in the business of

In keeping with his commitment to taking a personal part in community affairs, Rolland, as Chair of the Fort Wayne Leadership Roundtable, appears with Vice-Chair Rosetta Moses-Hill in a discussion of the issue of youth and violence. Aired in 1995 on WFWA with Primetime 39 moderator Vince Robinson.

Rolland in the 1989 Corporate Public Involvement report.

tion in the history of Lincoln National. Furthermore, this was also a significant step toward creating a fourth major line of business — investment management — to add to those of property-casualty, life insurance and annuities, and reinsurance.

Although Lincoln National has had an international presence since 1934, with reinsurance operations playing the strongest role, international operations have also received renewed attention in the latest strategic plans. Already well established is the most rapidly growing overseas business, Lincoln National (UK) PLC. In the wake of the recent acquisitions of Citibank's British life insurance business, the Liberty Life Assurance Company and the Laurentian Financial Group, Lincoln National (UK) has become the twelfth largest life insurer in the United Kingdom based on unit-linked assets. In addition, three other nations have been identified as attractive marketplaces: China, Mexico and India. Lincoln National opened a liaison office in Beijing in 1994 with the goal of assessing the opportunities of selling life insurance in the People's Republic of China, and there is an expectation to open an additional office in Shanghai. Joint venture partnerships are envisioned in Mexico and, at a later time, in India.

The commanding philosophy of the company as it entered this new phase of its life was that of Shared Values: integrity, commitment to excellence, responsibility, respect, fairness, diversity and employee ownership. Developed throughout the corporation in a study program led by LNC General Counsel Jack Hunter in 1993, the Shared Values concept articulates the spiritual cement that bound the entire corporation in its recent dramatic changes, but it also draws heavily on the core heritage of the company. Although published as Shared Values for the first time in 1994, each of these are the values that Lincoln National, in fact, had maintained as the company philosophy of the previous 90 years. The stability reflected in these values is a fitting capstone to the career of Rolland, who has overseen some of the most dramatic changes in the history of Lincoln National.

financial services with the acquisition of Delaware Management Holdings, Inc. for $510 million. One of the nation's oldest and largest investment advisors, Delaware Management Holdings was also the largest acquisi-

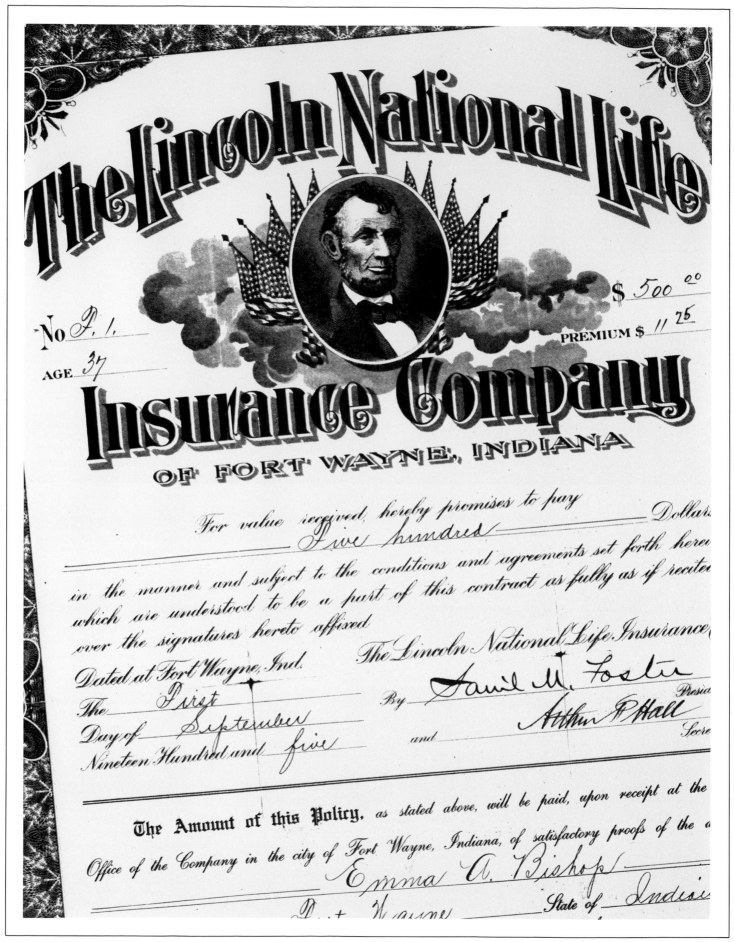

CHAPTER II
CORPORATE GROWTH

The growth of Lincoln National as a corporation has been extraordinary. In the ninety years since it was organized, the company has expanded even in times of adverse global economic conditions. Lincoln National had its beginnings and grew as a life insurance company, with a core strength as a life reinsurance company. It consistently nurtured a strong capital foundation for growth, and did not shy from pursuing new opportunities and ventures. In its first half-century no other insurance company matched the explosive expansion of "the little company over the grocery store" to the then-ninth largest life insurance company in the United States and the largest life reinsurer in the world. In many ways, the last three decades have been the most dramatic. In that time Lincoln National transformed itself from an insurance company to a nationally important financial services corporation. Since the 1960s, the company successfully branched into the property-casualty business and made a powerful impact in several important niche markets through unique distribution systems. Apart from the struggles to remain in the tumultuous group life and health business and the painful divestiture of that part of the business, perhaps the most exciting aspect of the company's growth in the last decade was the company's emergence as an insurance industry leader in the field of invest-ment management.

Above all, Lincoln National's growth since its beginnings has been spurred by personnel operating in a corporate culture that by and large rewards creativity and venture, a culture that still gives opportunity a chance and believes that success is derived from the diverse workforce. While the general direction of the company can be seen from the perspective of its top-most leadership, the reasons behind Lincoln National's growth are more comprehensible when the company's story is examined in terms of the evolution of lines of business that were created, molded and implemented by the thousands of people behind the leadership.

THE FIRST HALF-CENTURY

Lincoln National went into business in September 1905 and like any new enterprise struggled in its first years. The foundations of the company were laid with a $100,000 stock subscription, which was raised entirely by Arthur F. Hall, the company secretary, and by the requisite sale of $200,000 in life insurance policies, which was completed by the company's three agents, William Paul, Max Blitz and Hall. Once these goals were achieved, Lincoln National Life was duly incorporated to do business in Indiana. While it was very clear that, as Hall later noted in a speech, "Choosing a name didn't establish a life insurance company;" choosing the name of Lincoln did give the company an important beacon for defining its own character. At the end of 1905 (i.e., after four months in operation), Lincoln National had just over $500,000 of insurance in force, almost $21,000 in premium income and $116,007 in assets. During the next five years the growth of the company accelerated. In 1911 Lincoln National boasted $6.5 million of insurance in force, a quarter of a million dollars in premium income and nearly three-quarters of a million in assets. This was an impressive growth record for a small Midwestern company, made more impressive by the fact that it was the work of a small sales force marketing one product in a limited region.

In 1911 Hall hired Franklin B. Mead to be the company actuary and secretary. This proved to be a critical event in the life of the company, for Mead not only was the first insurance professional to join Lincoln National, but also a creative and daring businessman who developed reinsurance as a new line of business. Not long after Mead's arrival in Fort Wayne, the company began to write reinsurance contracts and premium income rose. Buoyed by rapidly increasing sales and by the growth of reinsurance, Lincoln National was ready to expand dramatically in the marketplace.

The possibility of purchasing Michigan State Life, a young, dynamic company in Detroit, offered an opportunity that would set the tenor for growth for the next four decades. Mead had worked for Michigan State before coming to Lincoln National and knew a great deal about the value of the company. Particularly attractive was the aggressive field force in the lucrative Detroit market that had rocketed Michigan State Life from its founding in 1907 to a company with $8 million of insurance in force, a rate of growth almost as vigorous as that of Lincoln National's. The founder and owner of the company, Frederick L. Apps, was a shady character from Missouri who had been involved in a number of stock schemes throughout the Midwest. As a result of his stock juggling, all of his other companies

Lincoln National's first financial statement, 1905.

and projects failed because their funds had flowed into Michigan State Life, which in 1913 was the only Apps enterprise on solid footing. Always one step ahead of his bursting bubbles, Apps was eager to sell and Mead knew this. He believed Lincoln National had sufficient surplus to acquire a majority of the stock and, more importantly, run the company professionally. As it turned out, though, the deal hinged on Hall's creativity in the face of adversity.

Although Hall purchased seventy percent of the Michigan State Life stock from Apps and believed he had won control of the company, the Michigan insurance commissioner and the state's attorney general would not allow the deal because they lacked precedent to regulate the takeover of a solvent insurance company. Michigan law only covered takeover of an insolvent insurer. They therefore insisted that before Lincoln National could presume ownership, it had to own one hundred percent of the stock. When Hall offered to purchase the outstanding thirty percent, however, he found that there was a block of stockholders, or voting trust, which had made a pact not to sell, saying they were determined to keep Michigan State Life in Michigan. For fifteen months Hall lived in Detroit five days a week to establish legal residence and to manage Michigan State Life, during which time he increased the surplus of the company from $100,000 to $146,000. Pressed by Hall, the voting trust consented to sell, but only at a price — double per share the amount

Hall paid Apps — they believed Lincoln National could not meet.

Hall promptly went to the president of the National Bank of Commerce of Detroit and announced, "I want to borrow $100,000 next Thursday for thirty minutes." The bank president, who had come to know Hall, replied, "Very interesting, indeed, but why do you need to keep it for such a long time?"

Hall got the money at the appointed time and went immediately to the meeting of the voting trust. He paid them the amount they demanded and he insisted then that they sign over their shares immediately, giving Lincoln National full control of Michigan State Life. Hall thereupon declared a cash dividend of $100,000 out of the Michigan State Life surplus and returned the loan to the National Bank of Commerce, all within thirty minutes. Later in 1914 Lincoln National reinsured by assumption the entire Michigan State Life block of business and merged the company's assets into those of Lincoln National's. Overnight the size of Lincoln National had nearly doubled. By 1915 Lincoln National held more than $25 million in insurance in force, had in excess of $2.4 million in assets and realized a premium income of nearly $1 million.

Lincoln National again greatly increased its size and expanded its distribution with the acquisition in 1917 of Pioneer Life, of Fargo, North Dakota. At the time of the transaction Lincoln National carried $31 million insurance in force; the Pioneer Life acquisition added an additional $19

million. As with the Michigan State Life purchase, the acquisition of Pioneer Life required the special talents of Hall. Lincoln National had managed to acquire sixty-seven percent of the Pioneer Life stock, but again there emerged a powerful group that opposed the sale. This time it included the governor, the state attorney general and the insurance commissioner. A hearing in Fargo began at 10 a.m. with the governor and the attorney general declaring their opposition to the sale, but Hall would not give up. He proceeded to argue his case for the next seven hours without a break. In the end, the North Dakota authorities had changed their minds. The attorney general commented afterward that "Mr. Hall could make the people of Louisiana vote a bond issue for irrigation ditches."

The notable aspect of this acquisition, however, was the nature of the distribution system used by Pioneer Life. Rather than general agents, Pioneer Life used what was then called a "bank agency force." Business was written through the numerous small town banks scattered across the Dakotas, Montana and Minnesota. The bankers would identify potential customers and a field force of Pioneer Life's "special salesmen" actually sold the policies. A note was taken for the first premium, which the banker discounted and collected. Because this system worked quite well in the upper Midwest and was so vastly different from the Lincoln National's normal sales methods, Hall did not attempt to merge the Pioneer Life into Lincoln

The First Home Offices (1905-1912)

During the time when the company was being organized, between May and September 1905, meetings of the board were held in the Commercial Club rooms of the I.O.O.F. building on the corner of Wayne and Calhoun streets (where Lincoln National's offices would later be located) and in the German-American Bank. The earliest offices of the company were housed in a small rented space on the second floor above the Strauss Brothers Company Commercial Bank and the Western Union telegraph offices on Calhoun Street (this building still stands and is located next to the new Norwest Bank building erected in 1994-1995). The interior was notable for its cheap, second-hand furniture and lack of storage and working space.

Once the company was organized, the offices were moved to a building on Wayne and Clinton streets, but soon needed more space and remained there only from September 1905 through February 1906. The offices were moved to their third location when Lincoln National rented the entire second floor of the I.O.O.F. building, just below the Commercial Club where the original board meetings were held (the Commercial Club was the forerunner of the Fort Wayne Chamber of Commerce). By this time the furniture had been improved and the company had six employees, but fear of fire in the old I.O.O.F. building caused Lincoln National to establish its fourth office on the spacious seventh floor of the new Shoaff Building on the corner of Calhoun and Berry streets. This was a modern building, built in 1909 to resist fire; the building that preceded it was the Aveline Hotel, the scene of Fort Wayne's deadliest fire in which twelve people died when the hotel was destroyed the previous year. Lincoln National remained here for nearly three years, from late 1909 to November 1912.

Lincoln National's first office, on Calhoun Street in September 1905.

The second office (1905 - 1906) was on the corner of Clinton and Wayne Streets.

The company's third home (1906-1909) was in the IOOF building on the corner of Calhoun and Wayne Streets.

The fourth office (1909-1912) was located in the Shoaff Building on the corner of Calhoun and Berry Streets.

Lincoln National offices, ca. 1918.

National, letting it continue to function as it had always done. Lincoln National administered the agents from a Minneapolis office, which was called the Northwest Department. It operated in this manner until the early years of the Great Depression when scores of bank failures ended the system.

Lincoln National focused on internal developments and the construction of the new home office in the early and mid-1920s, but in 1928 the company was ready to make another major acquisition. The Merchants Life Insurance Company of Des Moines, Iowa, was owned almost entirely by its president, William A. Watts. In 1928 Watts, fearing another agricultural depression, such as he had experienced in 1893 and 1921, wanted to liquidate his holdings and move his family to California. Hall learned of the availability of Merchants Life from A. J. McAndless,who knew Watts' son-in-law, Russell Norton, a Merchants Life vice president. Watts initiated the transaction, which McAndless later recalled was notable for the rapidity

with which it was concluded. Unlike the struggles Hall experienced before, this purchase went smoothly. The process took only two days to seal the bargain. Lincoln National reinsured by assumption the policies of Merchants Life and moved the operation to Fort Wayne. As a result of this purchase, Lincoln National's insurance in force swelled to nearly $660 million.

The growth of the company since 1905 had been outstanding and attracted the attention of the industry and investors. Of the life insurance companies organized in 1905, eleven were still in business in 1929, including Lincoln National. Yet Lincoln National had $300 million more insurance in force than the total of all ten of the other companies combined and had income $2 million higher than the other ten added together. There were, in fact, only four life insurance companies west of Philadelphia with as much insurance in force as Lincoln National, and these were all older companies. The company advertising of the World War I era

and the 1920s delighted in comparing its accelerating growth pattern with the flat performances of older, more established companies. By 1920 the company could proclaim that it maintained agency offices from California to North Carolina and were licensed in eighteen states; by the end of the decade Lincoln National was doing business in thirty-three states. Further, after 1925 Lincoln National was also able to demonstrate a steadily declining expense ratio, thanks to attention to training and office efficiencies realized with the opening of the new home office building in 1923. Not surprisingly, Hall began to promise openly that the company would reach the magical $1 billion in force by 1930.

Although the Great Depression, which began late in 1929, delayed Hall from reaching his goal as soon as he hoped, Lincoln National was sufficiently strong to take over three insolvent companies in 1933: Northern States Life Insurance Company in Hammond, Indiana; the Old Line Life Insurance Company of Lincoln,

Nebraska; and the Royal Union Life Insurance Company of Des Moines, Iowa. Each company was reinsured by Lincoln National through management contracts that protected policyholders' interests until all liens were satisfied. Once the encumbrances were met, the policies were merged into the Lincoln book of business, adding more than $250 million insurance in force.

Reinsurance, although almost invisible to the public, grew dramatically during the late 1920s under Mead's direction and McAndless' sales efforts. At the end of 1929 Lincoln National had reinsurance contracts with more than three hundred other companies covering almost $400 million in term business. Ten years later, Lincoln National had contracts for more than $600 million. As Hall himself admitted in 1930, the company "had realized greater earnings from reinsurance in the five previous years than our other insurance," and McAndless told the agents in 1944 that "reinsurance has provided the profit margins out of which we develop our direct business." Nearly all the companies reinsured by Lincoln National were smaller life insurance companies, giving rise to the reputation, as Walter Menge later expressed it, that Lincoln National was something of a "mother hen," or guardian of the small life business. Reinsurance, the backbone of the company throughout the Depression years of the 1930s and the war years of the 1940s, was a key reason for the company's prosperity.

During the 1930s Lincoln National also entered the international marketplace for the first time. The company opened an office in the Canal Zone in 1934 and in 1936 began doing busi-

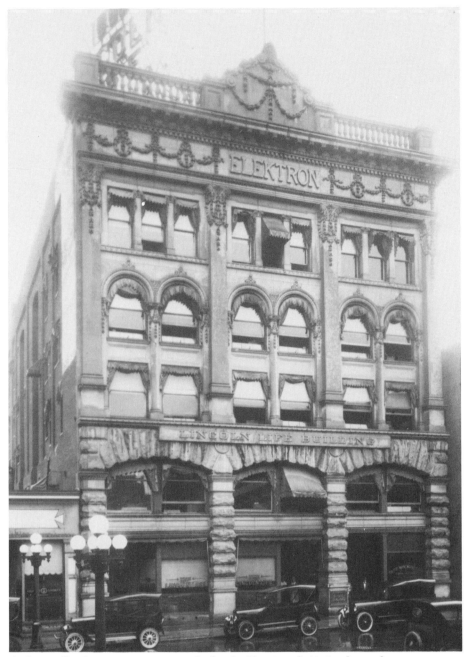

The home office from 1912 to 1923 was the first building Lincoln National owned.

"Lincoln Life, oh yes, the little company over the grocery store"

Reflecting its growing prosperity, Lincoln National purchased its fifth office in 1912 when it acquired the "the Elektron Building" in November one of the more notable buildings on Fort Wayne's east side. Designed by Fort Wayne architects John Wing and Marshall Mahurin, the building, also known as the Standard Building, was erected in 1895 by Ronald McDonald, a founder of the Jenney Electric Light Company and early electrical engineering entrepreneur (hence the word "Elektron" inscribed on the cornice of the building). For four years, from 1898 to 1902 the building served as the Allen County courthouse during construction of the present courthouse, and in 1904 it housed the Allen County Public Library while its first permanent facility was being built. Perhaps more important for Lincoln National executives, however, was that the building was also designed as a "fire-proof structure."

At the time the company took over the Elektron building, it was necessary for Lincoln National to occupy only the third floor. The first floor was rented to the International Business College and the White Fruit Company. The presence of this latter tenant gave rise to the jibe by the envious, "Lincoln Life, oh yes, the little company over the grocery store."

The Hoosier Youth

The dream of having a statue of Abraham Lincoln in front of the new home office on South Harrison Street had been part of Arthur Hall's vision for the building since its first plans were sketched. It was also part of the earliest concepts that this statue of the 16th president would be a significant work of art and not be the usual representation showing Lincoln bearded and mature in his well known double-breasted frock coat. Rather, it would illustrate the president in his youth, as a perpetual vision of emerging greatness of the spiritual figurehead of the nation and the personification of its ideals.

Upon the advice of the building architect, Benjamin Wistar Morris, the company was guided to Paul Manship, at the time one of the world's significant emerging sculptors. Born in St. Paul, Minnesota, in 1885, Manship won his first national prize for his work in 1909 when he was only twenty-three. By age twenty-six he was recognized internationally. Manship found his technical inspiration in the monumental sculptures of the ancient world and Renaissance Italy, but, as one British critic noted, "He has seen and studied with a passionate interest the work of sculptors of other ages and from it has formed a powerful and intensely personal style which never diverges one inch from the standards set up by his predecessors. ... Manship knows exactly where to stop; he never allows his inspiration to carry off his originality and, while his outlines, his decoration and his reliefs may be ... derivative from the early Greek in every detail, yet they do not create any illusion of Greek art." By the time he began the commission for Lincoln National, his works were in many major American art museums and in the plazas of Rome and Paris.

The challenge to create Lincoln as a youth was difficult, for no image exists of Lincoln before he was thirty-seven. To overcome this, Manship immersed himself in Carl Sandburg's books about Lincoln and in conversations with Abraham Lincoln scholar Ida Tarbell, "who vivified my impressions which led to

Paul Manship and his sculpture of "The Hoosier Youth."

the desire to represent the youth as a dreamer and a poet." He also travelled the countryside that Lincoln knew in his youth with the director of the Lincoln National Life Foundation, Dr. Louis A. Warren. Here he learned about the wilderness life of Lincoln, his devotion to his dog, his hard work, his determination to learn and his will to persevere in the face of hardship. He told Dr. Warren at the end of the trip, "I hope that you will feel with me that in the fact that I found a four-leaf clover on the site of the Lincoln cabin there is a symbol of good luck for this enterprise upon which I have set my heart."

After a year of study he submitted his design to Lincoln National's executive committee in 1929 and it was accepted. He completed his plaster model by 1931 (he even used as a model a dog from across the Ohio, like Lincoln's), and the bronze castings done in Belgium were shipped to Fort Wayne in early 1932. Four medallions representing the themes of patriotism, fortitude, justice and charity, which have been cited by many critics to be as important as the statue itself, were also completed for the base. The architect of the building, Benjamin W. Morris, and the sculptor closely collaborated on the construction of the statue base and pedestal to insure that all would be in harmony with the building. The statue itself was the bluish-green of aged bronze to blend with the Indiana limestone of the building.

In ceremonies held on September 16, 1932, the statue was unveiled before the employees and hundreds of invited guests. An opening speech was made by Dan Beard, the founder of the Boy Scouts of America, and at the appointed moment Arthur F. Hall III, the company president's grandson, pulled the cord that released the veil on the statue. Ida Tarbell was the special guest and Secretary of Agriculture Arthur M. Hyde gave the principal address. The proudest person on the plaza that day, however, was the founder of the company and the visionary who had first pursued the relationship between the company and the most renowned of the American presidents.

ness in the Hawaiian Islands through the British brokerage and general sales firm of Theodore H. Davies & Company, Ltd.. The Hawaiian entry was not as simple as might be thought. In Hawaii the Davies firm was known as one of the "big five corporations," selling everything from groceries to insurance and automobiles. Theo. H. Davies & Company also had significant operations in the Philippines. The firm approached McAndless in 1936 with the idea of placing a Lincoln National agency in the Philippines. McAndless responded that the Philippines were not in the company's strategic plans, but would be interested if Theo. H. Davies would support a Lincoln National agency in Hawaii also. Davies agreed and the deal was made. The volume of business in these agencies grew steadily until World War II. The war ended all business in the Philippines, but when Japanese forces were defeated in the islands, the agency was restored. Nearly all the old Lincoln National accounts were settled and three hundred of the original 1,500 policyholders were reinstated. The war with Germany also isolated many South American insurance companies from their traditional reinsurer, giving Lincoln National its first opportunity to enter the South American markets where the company has continued to maintain a significant presence.

After World War II the company was ready to expand again. This time Lincoln National concluded what was then the largest transaction of its kind in the history of the industry: the purchase of the Reliance Life Insurance Company of Pittsburgh. The transaction, which made Lincoln National a nationally prominent company, began in June 1950. Henry Rood, then a vice president, was the man who got the Reliance deal started when he had an unexpected visit from Henry Curry, a customer relations vice president of the Mellon Bank of Pittsburgh. Curry dropped in to the home office in Fort Wayne ostensibly for a casual visit with President McAndless. As it happened, McAndless and the senior vice presidents were out of town and so Curry met with Rood. In the course of their generally light conversation, Curry mentioned the need for the Mellon to divest itself of the Reliance.

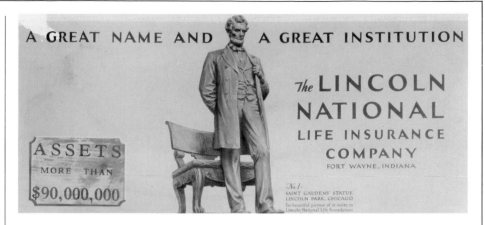

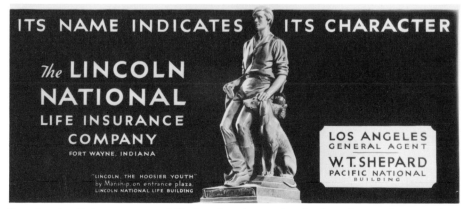

Several nationally known statues of Abraham Lincoln served as the theme for Lincoln National advertising in the 1930s.

Henry Rood and representatives of the Lincoln Philippine Life Company in 1965.

The Mellon Bank, he explained, had been directed by the U.S. Comptroller of the Currency to divest its interests in the insurer by 1951 or be in violation of the National Banking Act of 1930. Rood brought the matter to McAndless's attention the following day and negotiations were soon opened. For weeks after the deal was initiated, Henry Rood and Lincoln National attorney Clyde Cover held preliminary meetings with officers of the Reliance and Mellon Bank at the Duquesne Club in Pittsburgh. These were exciting days for the negotiators, though even decades later Rood recalled vividly the tiring nature of the seemingly endless train trips between Pittsburgh and Fort Wayne. The process reached a standstill when Lincoln National offered $27 million but Mellon held out for $28 million. Back in Fort Wayne, McAndless met with Menge whose solution was simple: split the difference and offer $27.5 million. At the negotiation table, though, even the Lincoln National officers did not know how McAndless would proceed. Then in the middle of a discussion he blurted out the figure Menge had suggested, taking everyone by surprise. As it turned out, the wily McAndless had offered what Mellon

The Lincoln in the Philippines during World War II

The nearly 10,000 air miles and two-week postal time that separated Fort Wayne from Manila always created a unique situation for the agency of Lincoln National Life in the Philippines. It had special underwriting rules, for instance, that allowed the agents to issue policies that were bound by the company before they were actually received and approved in the home office. Records-keeping also became a special responsibility of the agency office, again because of the great distance between it and the home office. As war seemed imminent in the Far East in 1941, the home office issued instructions to Manila to be sure to add war clauses to any new policies. The Philippine office never got the instructions, but had already taken it upon themselves to do just that. When hostilities broke out in December 1941, all communications with the home office were broken for the duration of the war. The agency continued to issue policies until the end of December and then it ceased to exist. Nevertheless, during the course of the war about twenty percent of the pre-war policies were kept in force by policyholders or their relatives continuing to send payments to Fort Wayne.

When the offices in Manila were closed after the Japanese captured the city, the agency sought a safe place to store the records. One fear an agency officer expressed was that the Japanese might seize the records and make fraudulent claims against Lincoln National — a truly unique way for the Empire of Japan to fund its war effort. The records were all baled and turned over to a Swiss national named Gus Laurent who took them to San Pablo, a provincial capital about sixty-five miles southeast of Manila. There he stored them in a building owned by another Swiss national who operated a copra plantation and oil mill, and the records stayed safe throughout the Japanese occupation. When the U.S. Sixth Army came through, however, San Pablo became a battlefield and the Swiss nationals abandoned their homes and the Lincoln National records. The victorious Americans commandeered the house of one of the Swiss for a headquarters building. Seeking to use all the available space, the GIs burned the bales of what they considered rubbish — the Lincoln National records of the last policies issued, policies for which no other records existed. In a painstaking investigation of half-burned envelopes and index files, the company was able to communicate with nearly all the Lincoln Philippine Life policyholders and restore or settle their accounts.

The man who successfully reopened the Lincoln National agency in Manila was Robert Slane, who had been the manager before the war. After the Philippines fell, Slane joined the U.S. Navy but was captured by the Japanese and held as a prisoner of war for three years. Shortly after his liberation in 1945, Commander Slane visited the home office in Fort Wayne and agreed to return to Manila to reopen the Lincoln National operation.

considered a fine price, although he had been prepared to go as high as $28.5 million, he later recalled.

Lincoln National, however, also stipulated that the deal could not be completed until it held at least ninety percent of the stock. Mellon Bank only held fifty-one percent and was concerned that if enough stockholders balked at the deal, the resultant turmoil of a failed deal would irreparably damage the agency force of the Reliance and Mellon would be left with an insurer of greatly reduced value. Rood stepped forward with the solution, also simple: if there were difficulty in the stock sale, Lincoln National would agree to reinsure the life insurance business of Reliance, and the Reliance corporation could then be dissolved. That proposal cinched the deal and it was signed on October 16, 1951. A new board was chosen and Menge was elected president and Rood vice president.

The challenge then centered on managing the news about the sale and, more importantly, keeping the Reliance sales force intact. Rumors about a sale had already begun to appear in the Pittsburgh newspapers as the transaction was being finalized and there some who were able to take advantage of inside information (later, the Securities and Exchange Commission would force a reversal of those transactions). Lincoln National officers quickly decided to meet with all the leading agents and managers in Pittsburgh. Within days of the announcement of the sale, McAndless and his key officers explained that advanced notice of the sale was withheld from the field force in order to protect the stock purchase part of the deal.

Reliance's greatest assets was its field force in the East and South where Lincoln National did little business. McAndless, concerned that the Reliance sales force remain in place, took aggressive measures to assure the Reliance agents that they would prosper as part of Lincoln National's organization. He organized three teams to visit each agency and meet with all the agents in their own territories: each team was composed of two Lincoln National officers and one Reliance officer. McAndless led one team himself, Menge another and

Henry and Ruth Rood and Walter and Elsie Menge attend their first Reliance convention, held at Atlantic City, New Jersey, in 1952.

Cecil Cross, head of Lincoln National's Agency Department, took the third. Within two weeks every Reliance agency in the country was visited. The deal was made attractive, too, with Lincoln National guaranteeing Reliance agents that they could either keep their old Reliance contract or take the new Lincoln National one, whichever most benefitted them.

The impact of this personal attention was reflected in Menge's meeting with one of the older agents in Reliance's Atlanta office. "I'm so glad to meet with you," the elderly man said in a pleasant drawl. "I've been with the Reliance Life forty-nine years and I never met the president of the Reliance Life, nor have I ever seen him." Menge replied, "That's not the way we do business at Lincoln Life. We're more democratic." Only two or three agents left the company; the rest remained and formed the core of a new, expanded sales force. The Reliance continued to operate as a separate company for about sixteen months, and then was merged completely with Lincoln National Life. The policies were reinsured by Lincoln National, the records were merged and the Pittsburgh offices with more than three hundred employees finally moved to Fort Wayne in 1955. The Reliance had been a strong, proud company and careful attention was given to ensure that the strengths of Reliance continued, enabling a new loyalty to Lincoln National to evolve. A similar technique would be used nearly a decade later when Lincoln National acquired another strong, proud company — American States.

The Reliance transaction brought to Lincoln National Life $1 billion of insurance in force and $300 million in assets, with thirty-five branches and more than seven hundred agents working in twenty-five states. Lincoln National now held nearly $7 billion of insurance in force, with agencies in every state except New York. The company was now the ninth largest life insurance company in the United States in terms of insurance in force and the second largest life reinsurer in the world.

"Expanding horizons" was a phrase Menge liked to use when he became president of Lincoln National Life in 1954. It is a fitting theme to describe the growth of the next 15 years. Characteristic of the company's continued aggressive growth is expansion into new arenas, new lines of business and new products. These "expanding horizons" also required a dramatically new organization of the company.

After the Reliance deal and the 1955 celebrations, Lincoln National looked for a new field to expand life insurance sales. In 1957 an opportunity came when Menge learned from a brokerage firm in Cleveland that John Seagram, the principal owner of Dominion Life Assurance Company in Waterloo, Ontario, was interested in selling. The board was interested in the acquisition and Menge estimated that the shares might be valued as much as $200 each, but Canadian market restrictions made it difficult to get a strong estimate of real value. The board voted to give Menge full authority to negotiate as he saw fit, but Menge asked rather that the board limit his authority to $195 per share. In this way, he could use the board position as his negotiating leverage. When Menge and Ed Auer, the chief investment officer, and the principals of Dominion discussed the deal,

1955: The Golden Jubilee

In 1955 Lincoln National celebrated its golden anniversary proud of its accomplishments and eager for the future. Lincoln National began the year as the nation's ninth largest life insurance company with more than 1 million policyholders, 2,500 agents, 2,000 employees and $1 billion in assets. The company was rebounding from the unexpected loss of its president the year before, but now under the direction of Walter Menge it was humming with anticipation for new growth and vitality in the wake of completing the largest acquisition in life insurance history, the purchase of the Reliance. Lincoln National continued to be a close- knit company, but the old "Lincoln family" that depended so heavily on the paternal role of the president for unity, camaraderie and team spirit had been replaced by a new "Lincoln family" that depended on employee-driven organizations and activities, most notably department functions, LINCS and the Loyal Service Club.

The year was full of activity for the new "Lincoln family." The first months of the year were filled with card parties, travelogues, trips, contests, fashion shows, and special events. The February party held by LINCS featured an evening of bridge and in March the featured speaker gave a speech on touring Europe. In May LINCS held its annual "Mother-Daughter Party" to celebrate a new addition to the cafeteria, highlighted by a round of songs dedicated to moms.

In June the 1,800 agents holding their convention at the Palmer House in Chicago celebrated Lincoln National's fiftieth anniversary. More than seven hundred agents and their families were brought to Fort Wayne on chartered trains for a special reception and celebration at the home office.

The year's activities reached their peak with the great Fiftieth Jubilee celebrated on September 15. A day of celebrations planned by a committee headed by Vice President Allen Steere began early when all the Lincoln National home office employees assembled in the plaza on South Harrison Street. Noted historian and Fort Wayne native Holman Hamilton (his grandfather had been Allen County's first sheriff) gave the opening address on "Lincoln, the Hoosier Youth," comparing the rise to greatness of Abraham Lincoln from humble beginnings to the evolution of Lincoln National from its meager beginnings in 1905 to one of the nation's most important life insurance companies. Harry E. Wells, the insurance commissioner of Indiana, and Fort Wayne Mayor Robert Meyers added their best wishes to the event, and Menge proudly recounted the Lincoln National's history and boldly predicted its future. Menge then cut a red ribbon stretched across the great front doors of the home office, helped by Bertha Imbody, the oldest employee by service and Sue Plasket, the newest. Then, he and all the other employees entered the building for a symbolic rededication of the company at the moment of beginning its second half century. All departments had their own celebrations, and a grand luncheon, including a fiftieth birthday cake, was provided by the company. Then everyone had the afternoon off for special receptions in anticipation of the evening's gala affair at the Allen County Memorial Coliseum.

The Jubilee was climaxed by the appearance that evening of the popular Fred Waring and his Pennsylvanians for nearly 7,500 employees and their families and friends. Those who were single were invited to bring "that special friend," if they wished. Claris Adams, executive vice president of the American Life Convention, opened the evening event with a brief talk that proclaimed the unparalleled achievement of Lincoln National in the life insurance industry. It was, he said, "One of the great romances of American life insurance." Then Waring's company gave a special preview presentation of its show, "Hear, Hear," which was bound for Broadway. The two -and-one-half-hour show was a rousing musical review with hundreds of costumes, brilliant lighting and multi-colored revolving sets. The music crossed every interest from American folk songs like Across the Wide Missouri, spirituals such as Deep River and He's Got the Whole World in His Hands, patriotic songs, love songs, minstrel show tunes, classical pieces (Nutcracker Suite), "electronic ballet," sacred songs and songs of collegiate conviviality, which included the Whiffenpoof Song and, for all the actuaries at Lincoln National, the Toast to Michigan. The show concluded with a special tribute to Lincoln National as the cast sung The Battle Hymn of the Republic and Where in the World but in America. After the Fort Wayne performance, the show was taken to Pittsburgh for the employees of the Reliance, and then it went on to New York and an opening at the Ziegfield Theater.

SONGS SUNG AT THE COLISEUM BY LINCOLN PEOPLE

(to the melody of *The Happy Wanderer*)

We gather here ten thousand strong
  A happy, loyal band
To sing the praise of Lincoln Life
  The finest in the land

Chorus:

  Fal-de-ree ... fal-de-ra
    Fal-de-ree ... fal-de-ra-ha-ha-ha-ha-ha
  Fal-de-ree ... fal-de-ra ...
    The finest in the land.

Lincoln National settled back into its normal pace of employee social and athletic activities for the remainder of the year. LINCS organized a wiener roast at McMillen Park in October, complete with hot dogs, marshmallows, apple cider and potato chips and games. There were relay races in "bustin' balloons," contests to see who could hold a lighted match longest, bingo-like card games and challenges to take gum out of a purse while wearing large "working-man's gloves." Earlier in the month the LINCS fall trip took Lincoln National women on a two-day tour of southern Indiana to see Brown County in its fall glory, to tour the James Whitcomb Riley home in Greenfield, to visit art galleries in Nashville and to hob-nob with the students in Bloomington. A highlight of the trip was ending the day in the lobby of the new IU Hotel watching the recent novelty of television.

The Christmas season was full of parties. The Loyal Service Club held a banquet in which the members tried, amid peals of laughter, to emulate the Fred Waring show with their own singing efforts called "Here, Hear."

Fred Waring (right-center) and a few of his Pennsylvanians helped Lincoln National celebrate its fiftieth anniversary.

Menge was able to say at one point, "I am authorized to go to $195 and if I cannot buy the company for $195 then I would have to go back to the board for a new authorization." Upon that declaration, Menge and Auer got up from the table, got their coats and headed for the door, giving the impression that they believed the deal to have collapsed. Just as they stepped through the door, however, Seagram called to them, "Come back, come back. I want to talk to you some more." He agreed to take the $195 a share offering, or approximately $2.36 million. The acquisition of Dominion was an important milestone, providing access to what was hoped would be a good market. It also made Lincoln National feel as if it were functioning as a "corporate family," rather than as a single company.

Menge decided not to make any changes in Dominion, apart from the election of Auer as chairman of Dominion's board of directors. Auer became an important liaison between the corporate center in Fort Wayne and the Dominion operations in Ontario, a role that foreshadowed the one he would play with American States five years later. Unlike the Reliance acquisition, however, Lincoln National was never able to merge Dominion into the Fort Wayne company since Canadian law barred actual merger. In addition, Canadians were fiercely proud of their own institutions and businesses and resented American participation. Lincoln National management hoped that in time, these barriers would fall, but while a profitable association with Dominion was maintained for the next twenty-eight years, the cultures remained quite distant. In the end, the company could not benefit from the economies of unification of the two life insurance businesses.

Lincoln National's growth at the mid-century was not solely in individual life insurance. In 1944 the Group Life Insurance Department was created under the direction of then-Vice

President Menge. Lincoln National had sold its first group life policy in 1916, but the line of business did not develop until after the Depression. When business revived in the early 1940s, Menge noticed that insurance companies that sold group policies paid little attention to small businesses. The Group Department, consequently, focused on developing products for companies that had less than fifty employees. Characterized by efficient administration, strong training and support for agents, the Group Department mushroomed in eight years to become a significant line of business. In 1952 group life premium income had reached more than $11 million. Encouraged by this growth, Menge focused on the extensive market represented by even smaller companies employing between ten and twenty-five people. Four years later, Group Life was producing more than $30 million in annual premium income.

The strength of the Group business encouraged Menge to explore ways to enter the market in New York, the only state in which Lincoln National was not licensed to do business. It made sense to position Lincoln National to offer its small-group products in a market in which so many companies had their headquarters. However, New York insurance regulations were so different from other states that Menge decided to form a new, specifically organized company. He had hoped originally to find an established company to acquire, but no suitable opportunity presented itself. On May 2, 1960, the Lincoln National Life Insurance Company of New York was chartered. The effort to operate a subsidiary in New York was pursued for seventeen years, but the company never reached the necessary level of profitability and was sold in 1977.

Menge's last major acquisition was his most important. In a dramatic departure for a company that had heretofore focused on life insurance lines of business, Lincoln National purchased American States Insurance, a property and casualty insurer in Indianapolis — the largest non-life company in Indiana — with several affiliates of its own, including a life insurance company, in 1963. Menge was particularly interested in the "all-lines" nature of the American States system, in which the general agents sold both life insurance and property and casualty insurance coverage. Menge believed that the affiliation with American States would place Lincoln National in a favorable position if the sales trends showed "one-stop shopping" for insurance was gaining favor among consumers.

Recognizing that Lincoln National people in Fort Wayne had no expertise in the property- casualty business, the company chose to give American States considerable autonomy. Menge's trust in American States' President John Phelan and his team was an important factor in this decision. The critical difference that allowed the American States affiliation to work where the Dominion failed was that Lincoln National and American States, both Indiana companies, shared a great deal in their values and their approach to business. The new entry became one of the most successful mergers of a life insurance company with a property-casualty company.

American States' home office in about 1930.

American States Insurance

American States was created in Indianapolis in 1925 by two young brothers, Dudley R. and Edward F. Gallahue, both in their early twenties. The original company was called the American Automobile Indemnity Company, and in 1930 it was incorporated as the American States Insurance Company. The only product the company sold during its first years was automobile insurance, but in 1941 the American States Fire Insurance Company was formed to take advantage of a new Indiana law that allowed a company to write both fire and casualty insurance. Enabled by new state legislation in 1947 to operate as a multi-line company, American States expanded over the following decade through acquisition and the creation of new companies.

Some of these early acquisitions, such as the Dubuque Fire and Marine Insurance Company, were struggling companies and proved good acquisitions. John Phelan, who was later president of American States, remembered going into the Dubuque offices and being appalled by the conditions of the facilities. Dingy eight-foot-high Sandborn Map cases formed the partitions between office areas and one man with a small window air conditioner had covered his area with a plastic sheet so that he could keep the cool air in his space. Phelan was struck by the number of dead flies lying all over the plastic sheet and the light cord string that extended from the ceiling light through a hole in the sheet to the desk below. As Phelan noted, however, "no property- casualty company is so bad that it doesn't have some remnant of an agency force, and what we were looking for was presence in new markets. Then we would fix it." In the case of Dubuque, American States' target was to enter the Iowa market; however, it found that Iowa's insurance regulations would not allow an out-of-state business to own an Iowa company. Phelan and President Edward Gallahue then arranged with one of their Iowa reinsurers to reinsure Dubuque Fire and pass the liabilities on to American States. Gallahue, the story goes, kept the Iowa insurance commissioner in an elevator going

American States office personnel, ca. 1930.

between floors until the deal gained state approval.

In addition to acquisitions, American States also organized new companies, such as the American Economy Insurance Company, to be more competitive in the automobile insurance industry. One of the significant new companies was the American States Life Insurance Company, which was organized in 1957 with help from Lincoln National. In the course of the previous two decades American States had come to realize the potential advantage of "one-stop sales" — that is, customers being able to buy life insurance and property and casualty coverage from one agent. Also known as the "multiple line agency system," there were a number of reasons that made "one-stop sales" attractive. Property-casualty policyholders were a good market for the agent to sell other types of personal insurance coverage and customers often preferred one agent or one company to meet their needs. This was beneficial to the company because it improved persistency, that is, a customer might be willing to overlook an unattractive product since other coverage was with that company. In addition, the impact of proper- ty- casualty cycles was lessened because the life insurance business had more predictable earning patterns. Finally, the agents had an additional source of income.

Combining sales of life and proper- ty-casualty products in the single

agent was an unusual concept, although American States was explor- ing new ground. Lincoln National's role in the creation of American States Life was financial, as well as lending its expertise and its advice. John Phelan and several other senior execu- tives visited Ed Auer, the senior investment executive at Lincoln National and succeeded in convincing him to make a major investment in the new American States enterprise. This connection with Lincoln National and Auer marked the begin- ning of a five-year relationship that led to the acquisition of American States by Lincoln National and laid the foundations for a relationship between the two companies that has been one of the most successful affilia- tions in the insurance industry.

In the last years of the 1950s there were a lot of companies for sale, but most were not good investments, gen- erally because they had poor operating ratios. American States, however, was a very solid company (Lincoln National even considered purchasing Western Casualty and Surety in Fort Scott, Kansas, which ironically would be acquired by American States in 1985). The possibility of Lincoln National purchasing American States began about 1958 with conversations between Auer and Edward Gallahue, who were summer home neighbors at Lake Wawasee in northern Indiana. Lincoln National CEO Walter Menge was interested at first, but declined to

American States executives visit Lincoln National executives after the acquisition in 1963. Walter Menge and John Phelan walk in front.

negotiate because American States had two classes of stock of unequal value: Class A had three times the voting power of the other, Class B. Although the Gallahue brothers owned most of the Class A stock and were anxious to sell, Menge feared that Lincoln National would face negative reactions from the Class B because of the disparity in value of the two classes. Menge instructed Auer to tell Gallahue that Lincoln National would be very interested if there were only one class of stock for American States. Over the next three years the Gallahues succeeded in exchanging one share of the Class A stock for three of the others. In 1961 Menge told Auer to begin negotiations.

The sale was signed in 1963 while the ASI senior executives were in Nassau for an agents' convention when Ed Gallahue told them of the sale. The news was greeted by silence and then by a firm determination to convince Gallahue that he was making a big mistake. "We were independent as hell," Phelan recalls, "and we did not want to be sold." There was no turning back, although, as Menge recalls, "We were very fortunate in the fact that American States already had a senior officer who was quite capable and that was John Phelan." Lincoln National executives worked hard to make the new affiliate welcome. Recalling the carefully managed transition that had been crucial in the Reliance acquisition a decade earlier, Henry Rood invited the leading American States men and their wives

to Fort Wayne for a "blue-ribbon" visit. One American States officer clearly recalls the somber trip on the bus to Fort Wayne, but how impressed he and the others were when they pulled up to the home office and found Walter and Elsie Menge and Henry and Ruth Rood, with all the other leading Lincoln National executives and their spouses on the Harrison Street steps waving a greeting. That simple gesture of friendship erased many fears.

American States and Lincoln National management soon recognized the mutual benefits that arose from the affiliation: ASI, which had been in a period of expansion, gained access to much needed capital to continue to grow and Lincoln National Corporation gained a very successful new profit center in a line of business where it had little expertise. One key to the excellent working relationship that evolved was Lincoln National's willingness to allow American States to operate with a minimum of interference. Auer, who was elected chairman of the board of ASI, was instrumental in this, as was the existence of an outside board of directors for American States.

Phelan remembers that Auer was supportive of the American States business philosophy. "Nobody in Fort Wayne knew a thing about property and casualty," Phelan noted in a 1994 interview, "and that was just fine with us. As I told Rood, 'Leave us alone and we'll make a good profit for you'." Perhaps more important for the work-

ing relationship was the two companies' shared Midwestern culture. This was especially evident, people throughout both companies agree, in the fundamental values that each held high: integrity, competency and creativity, respect and community involvement.

A traditional strength of American States has been its sales and service to customers, reflecting the expertise of personnel both in the home office and in the field. Phelan, from the outset of his presidency, strove to make American States more professional. Don Conover followed in his footsteps with the same policy. Agents were exhorted to become better salespeople and employees were given incentives to complete the rigorous training for the chartered property and casualty underwriter (CPCU) designation.

American States continued throughout the 1960s and 1970s to acquire smaller insurers, and in the late 1970s created the multi-regional operating structure. The most significant acquisition by the company was the purchase of the Western Casualty and Surety Company of Fort Scott, Kansas, in 1985, during the tenure of Edwin Goss as CEO. This consolidation essentially doubled the American States operation and enabled it to realize the full power of its operating structure. The acquisition transformed American States from a regional enterprise into a nationally significant business through dramatic expansion throughout the West and Midwest. The merger was a good blend. As with the affiliation of Lincoln National and American States, both the Western and American States shared common Midwestern values and business philosophies that provided a firm foundation for combining activities.

The deal also reflected the style of leadership provided American States since 1981. No sooner was the sale completed than Goss took pains personally to assure the employees of Western Casualty and the people of Fort Scott that the merger would strengthen the newly acquired company and that the community would not lose its most important employer and corporate citizen. A Fort Scott newspaper editorial read, "Not every chairman, not every company president would make themselves available at a time when the easiest course is that of silence. This speaks well for Edwin Goss and for his company." Similarly, McCurley — then president of Western Casualty — rushed back to Kansas as soon as the sale was agreed upon to inform the employees before

American States sets up its disaster scene claims office in 1978.

ASI and Technology

One of the foundations of the American States' success since joining Lincoln National has been its innovation and use of technology. By the late 1970s the company had developed systems for handling its business that provided it an edge over its competitors — an edge that it still enjoys. Data processing did not always run smoothly, though. For example, John Phelan remembers that once in about 1965 he had a problem he wanted to resolve and asked for certain reports, only to be told that there were other requests ahead of his and that the president of the company would have to wait. "So, I told them to have on my desk the next day a simple list of the projects that made it impossible for the president of the company to get a report. After that, I formed a Data Processing Priorities Committee, and I was its chairman." Similar problems led Phelan to recruit Richard Linton to begin to change the way data was managed. Phelan had met Linton at an industry trade show and was impressed with his abilities to grasp the broader needs of the rapidly growing industry, especially in relationship to marketing issues. Beginning in 1969, the company started to make notable improvements in its fundamental data management skills under Linton's direction, and the stage was set for the great technological strides of the 1980s.

In 1978 American States made a major commitment to develop a fully integrated system for managing information and automating the production process. During the presidency of Edwin Goss, who had come to American States in 1951 and rose in the company on the sales side, this process came to fruition. The first system to be successfully developed was on the commercial side and it was called Comline. For the first time in the industry, both commercial and personal insurance lines were fully automated by 1981 at American States. Seeking to move toward greater efficiencies by putting automation in independent agencies in the early 1980s, the company developed a system which was called "Interaction" that was designed to integrate fully the central business systems with the agents' regional and personal offices. To match the advances in automation, American States also changed its work processes through the "Quality Commitment" program adopted by Lincoln National. This combination of new technologies and work management methods in the home and regional offices enabled American States to meet new competitive demands. In the 1990s American States continues to evolve its automated systems and their interactive capabilities.

This manner of placing advanced technological tools in the hands of agents was in keeping with American States' oldest traditions. In the days of Edward Gallahue, Phelan and Don Conover, great amounts of energy were spent tending to the agents' well being, to make sure they knew they were an important part of the business. During the tenures of Goss, Bob Anker and the current CEO, Cedric McCurley, the company has devoted substantial efforts to reduce the labor- and paper-intensive portions of meeting customers' insurance needs. In effect, the "Interaction" program, which provided both in-depth information and automated processing, made the field agent appear to be an underwriter and thus capable of better service at the point of sale. The automation of the field force gave ASI the capacity to write significant new business without hiring additional staff or impairing customer service. Under this system, policy can be initiated, underwritten and issued as a printed document within 24 hours, a distinctive sales advantage.

John Phelan (right) poses with Walter Menge shortly after Phelan became president of American States.

the news was given to the media. His comments were met by applause, not because Western Casualty had been sold, but because the president's sincere efforts were seen to be in the company's best interests.

The numbers also made clear that the merger was in the best interest of both property- casualty companies and Lincoln National. In 1985 Lincoln National and its affiliates ranked thirty-fifth nationally in the property-casualty arena. With the acquisition of the Western Casualty, LNC jumped to rank twenty-fifth in the country.

When he assumed leadership of the company, Goss brought an entirely new style of governance. He transformed American States and its affiliates with new strategies, new tools and greater participation in decision-making by employees. A native of New York who attended Fordham University, Goss began his insurance career with the Royal Liverpool Group Insurance Company after a tour of

duty in World War II. He came to American States in 1951 and worked mostly in sales, first as a branch manager in the field and later in the home office. When he became president, the organization of the company was flattened considerably, reflecting a more participative style of leadership.

Goss also was very conscious of the need for depth in management expertise, particularly in an organization whose structure was as flat as American States. Whereas the company had a history of strong functional managers, the new structure Goss implemented with its 22 divisions required a team of general managers who could exercise total accountability. Goss built a depth in management ranks to realize the potential in the new structure and keep American States growing.

If there were any lingering doubts about LNC's commitment to American States, they were dispelled in 1984. In the course of six months, American

JOHN PHELAN

John Phelan led American States for nearly two decades, marking a time when it became one of the best managed and most innovative property-casualty insurers in the nation. Born in 1914 in Kalamazoo, Michigan, Phelan attended Carleton College in Northfield, Minnesota, where he was Phi Beta Kappa in English and had ambitions of becoming a newspaper reporter. His first job after college was as a cub reporter for the *New Bedford* (Massachusetts) *Standard-Times* for $15 per week, he recalls, "I didn't eat lunch on Saturdays until 2:30 because we didn't get paid until 2 p.m.." Convinced by his father to explore a career in insurance, he landed a job with Hardware Mutual of Stevens Point, Wisconsin, in 1936. During the nine years he was at Hardware Mutual he did a little bit of everything and learned a great deal about insurance. He also became a firm believer in the virtues of "hands-on" learning and managing. A salty, down-to- earth man, he received his training on the job. Once, when assigned by a supervisor to write the new sales manual, he protested, "But I don't know a damned thing about the business," only to be answered by the supervisor, "You will when you get through." Frequently given tough assignments, he quickly developed a reputation for being able to solve problems and get things working, sometimes in a heavy-handed way.

In 1945 he was offered a job at American States by one of the owners of the company, Edward Gallahue, and, in keeping with his reputation as a trouble-shooter, Phelan was given the assignment of sorting out a branch office that needed help. He then was assigned the same task over American States Fire Insurance, and presided over this subsidiary's merger into the parent company when Indiana passed its "Multi-Lines Law" that allowed a single company to write both fire and casualty insurance. For the next decade Phelan again served in many different capacities at American States until he reached the rank of executive vice president in the early 1960s.

Following the acquisition of American States by Lincoln National, Phelan was made president of his company, a position he held until 1979. He governed American States with a firm hand and came to be known as a man of outspoken opinions and deep pride in his company. He eventually became an expert in property and casualty insurance, publishing several articles and one book on the subject and serving as national president of the Chartered Property and Casualty Underwriter Society. His "hands-on" style of management became a key to the success of American States, which earned a reputation for toughness in the marketplace under his leadership. When necessary, he did not hesitate to spend the time to examine the smallest details. "I remember one February, when the numbers were all going to hell, sitting in my basement office at home with several officers; we were going over the agency sheets, agent by agent by agent. Sure, we had guys who were running the regions, but we looked at every damned piece of the operation to see how we could improve." He believed that he should be able to do anything he asked his agents to do, so Phelan, already a CPCU, studied to become a chartered life underwriter as well. As he recalls it, he went through the CLU exams at the same time he was studying for his instrument rating as a pilot, "which was frustrating since I was not interested in becoming a CLU but I did want to qualify for instruments; but I studied it anyway. If you want to know pressure, just take the CLU exams; and it was doubly bad because I had to pass; the boss simply could not fail in front of the others."

He learned to fly so that he could go often to the agencies and their regional offices. "I used the airplane extensively so that I could boost morale by meeting everybody. It was good for them to see the boss come to town, have lunch with him, get a picture taken, buddy-up and make it personal."

States management secured nearly $400 million from the corporation to grow its business. The first event was the acquisition of Western Casualty, which totalled $270 million. The acquisition was the largest in LNC history until the corporation bought Delaware Management Holdings in 1995. The second event was tied to the so-called property-casualty cycle — the pattern of profitability the industry seemed to follow. American States believed the part of the cycle bringing low profits was about to end and it was a good opportunity to get a jump on the industry. In a phone call to Ian Rolland in August, Goss asked the Lincoln National chairman for

$100 million to finance internal growth. "I have one question," Rolland said. "Are you sure that's enough?" "Clearly this was an enormous bet on the property-casualty business and American States' skills," Anker said many years later. "It paid off."

Anker, then executive vice president, was a key associate in bringing about the transformation of American States into a powerful national organization. Anker had been a math major at Lawrence University in Appleton, Wisconsin, who — in his words — "sort of stumbled into actuarial sciences" and ended up working for the Wausau Company for ten years. A col-

league had gone to American States in the late 1960s and recruited Anker in 1974 to come to Indianapolis as a second vice president and actuary. Anker said the president of the company, Phelan, especially fascinated him as brilliant, someone from whom he could learn. His job description was to create a professional actuarial department, "so that," Anker recalls tongue-in-cheek, "Phelan could tell the folks in Fort Wayne, 'See, I have an actuary, too. True, he is just a property-casualty actuary, but he is a real actuary.' " Anker was, in fact, the first Fellow of the Casualty Actuarial Society employed by American States.

Anker was instrumental in expand-

The "Electronic Brain" Comes to Lincoln

"Lincoln Life's Four Marsmen" was the way the 1956 Lincoln Log described the team that began to put Lincoln National into the computer age.

In early 1955 Walter Menge asked Vice President Henry Rood to organize a special committee to investigate whether it would be wise for Lincoln National to invest in one of the new "Giant Brains," or, as it was more commonly called, the "Electronic Brain." To scientists it was the Electronic Digital Computer. To users of personal computers in 1995, which includes nearly all Lincoln National employees (and their children), there is little notable about this. In the mid-1950s, however, the television and tape recorder were still relatively new and there was no such thing as a hand-held calculator. Most people were aware of the marvels of the Remington-Rand UNIVAC, which was first used in national elections in 1952 and 1954 and appeared on the Saturday night television quiz programs, but its use in business was rare.

Lincoln National, like all insurance companies, wrestled constantly with the issue of accurate computations and data management. In the 1930s the company was especially proud of its accomplishments in "scientific filing" and other office efficiencies. Lincoln National was hailed by *Forbes Magazine* in 1935 as a leader in the industry for the way it managed its data. Still, the processes were entirely manual with some help from machines such as the "Addressograph." Under A.J. McAndless, Lincoln National acquired sophisticated card-punch tabulators and electric calculating machines in 1946. By 1955 Lincoln National was using the IBM 604 computer, which still maintained data on punch-cards. The technology of the future promised to put the data of stacks of punch-cards on mere inches of magnetic tape at lightning speed.

The "Electronic Brain" committee of 1955-56 became immersed in the new technology of electronic data processing. Fellow workers overhearing their conversations were puzzled by references to "bits," "input," "buffers," "sequential programming," "binary coding" and "debugging," all terminology new to the 1950s. In 1956 the Lincoln Log assured employees that "as yet no decisions have been made as to which, if any, of the electronic machines the company might install." While the editors were enthusiastic about the possibility of new technology, they also were careful to explain that new machinery did not mean lost jobs.

In 1958 Lincoln National decided to invest in the IBM 705; the new data processing system — a "Giant Brain" — was installed in early 1959, marking the beginning of an important new phase in the race to manage and use information.

Leadership of Lincoln National's operations in 1970: (left to right) E.G. Shafer of Dominion Life Assurance Co., John Phelan of American States, T.B. Flemin of Dominion- Lincoln, Ltd., F.W. Goodrich of Chicago Title and Trust, Mikael Hagopian of CORENA and Henry Rood.

on preferred personal lines of business. "But, as an underwriting theme, we came to the realization that if we couldn't automate it, we were not going to write it," Anker said. "That may be an over-simplification, but its essence was true — we had to have cooperation between underwriting managers and technology staff in order to be a leader."

After the acquisition of The Western, Anker was elected president of American States, and the company expanded further in 1988 with the acquisition of Covenant Corporation of Hartford, Connecticut, expanding its market from thirty-eight to forty-six states. In February 1991 Goss retired, leaving behind a record of remarkable growth Anker was elected chairman of the board and McCurley became president of American States. In January 1992 Anker was named president and chief operating officer of Lincoln National Corporation and McCurley became chairman of American States.

The American States story, to some extent, has always been one of its continuing ability to adapt to different operating environments. It has remained successful from a period when the independent agent controlled the marketplace to one in which direct-writers have become a dominant factor. It has adapted in the personal lines market where lower

ing the use of technology throughout American States. A knowledgeable, self-taught user of computers, he helped break down barriers in the company, helping the data processing personnel communicate more effectively with the underwriters and others who would use the new automated systems. Anker realized that automation was the key to controlling

expenses. Traditionally, the insurer provided the agent with facilities to write almost every kind of coverage. That changed as American States began to focus on its areas of expertise and stopped writing lines of business where it suffered losses — crop-hail insurance, for example. Thus, in the early 1980s, it formed American States Preferred Insurance Company to focus

Lincoln Defends "Tokyo Rose"

Lincoln National had the curious distinction of defending "Tokyo Rose," the woman who for many Americans was the voice of treason during World War II. Her real name was Iva Ikiko Toguri D'Aquino, a Japanese-American who, like so many others, was caught up in the shattering events of the beginning of the war.

Actually, several women were named "Tokyo Rose." The name was the invention of American GIs to identify an attractive, English-speaking female voice on the propaganda programs beamed at them by Radio Tokyo. After VJ Day, the myth of a single, beautiful "Tokyo Rose" with an alluring, sexy voice, trying to make U.S. soldiers unhappy and homesick was very much alive and caught the popular imagination. Correspondents set out to try to find this person. In their searches one woman, Iva Toguri D'Aquino, stepped forward to reveal that she was the voice for the propaganda program "Zero Hour." The reporters were happy to name her "Tokyo Rose," and she submitted to an interview and a press conference. Because she was an American citizen, she was arrested for treason. Despite her protests that she had been trapped in Japan at the outbreak of the war and was forced as a matter of survival to participate in the broadcasts (she called herself "Orphan Ann" in the shows), she was convicted in 1949 in what became the longest treason trial in U.S. history. She was sentenced to ten years in prison and fined $10,000.

After serving six years and managing to pay nearly $5,000 of the fine, she was released in 1956 and returned to Chicago where she lived on a pittance working in a Japanese food store. The government, however, wanted the rest of the fine, and after a delay of several years federal prosecutors turned to her Lincoln National insurance policies, which had cash values amounting to nearly $5,000. In the ensuing court actions in 1968, the government sought to garnish the funds directly from Lincoln National, but Carl Baker, a young attorney who had just joined the company's legal department, successfully defended the integrity of the policies on the basis that only the policy holder herself could be garnished and the company would not surrender the cash value except to her. As it turned out, Ms. D'Aquino took her cash value and settled with the government by 1971, ending Lincoln National's role in the affair.

prices were not enough; companies now have to have improved procedures and lower costs of operations. And it has adapted from an era when companies sought to be general writers of all lines a time in which companies have to be more focused.

EXPLORING GLOBAL VENTURES

Shortly before he became chairman of the board, Menge sought to extend Lincoln National's direct sales presence in Europe and create yet another leg in the "corporate family." The company's reinsurance department had been active in Europe for many years, but had never been satisfied with the volume or type of business, much of which was the second layer of a large European reinsurer. Many Europeans in the generation of World War II had lost faith in life insurance, but studies showed that among the rising younger generation, especially of the middle class, there was potentially a strong market for life insurance. Consequently, on September 26, 1963, Lincoln National opened an all-lines reinsurance company in Paris called the Compagnie de Reinsurance Nord-Atlantique, or CORENA. For chairman of the board, Lincoln National selected Jacques Rueff, the internationally known financial advisor to Charles DeGaulle, and elected as the general manager, Mikael Hagopian a highly respected professional with thirty years experience. A native of Istanbul, Turkey, Hagopian moved with his family to France when he was seven years old and developed fluency in English while serving as a French liaison officer with the British military command in North Africa in World War II. After the war, he earned a law degree from the University of Paris. The company prospered moderately well in western Europe and was able to expand into African and Asian markets by the mid-1960s.

When Rood became president in 1964, he explored further expansion into international markets with the creation in 1965 of the Lincoln Philippine Life Insurance Company whose purpose was to create a native company capable of surviving the impending nationalization of foreign companies. Policyholders were given

Lincoln National goes on the Tokyo Stock Exchange. Left to right are Richard Robertson, Robert Crispin, Ian Rolland and Max Roesler.

the choice of continuing their policies with Lincoln National, which most Americans did, or becoming a part of the new Philippine company, which could write more, smaller policies. Most Filipinos did this, but nationalization went forward. By 1973 the Lincoln Philippine Life Insurance Company was no longer permitted to write business in the Philippines and Lincoln National sold the company to the original British factors, Theo H. Davies Co.

In Rood's first years Lincoln National also expanded its business into the British Isles with the creation of the Dominion-Lincoln Assurance Company, Ltd.. This company, like CORENA in France, focused on the emerging middle class market through the typical American agency system, rather than the brokerage techniques used by British companies. Rood also was drawn to the idea of creating a new line of business for Lincoln National Life. In 1966 he directed Rolland, then a young associate actuary, to develop the product from scratch. A year later, the Annuity Department was in full operation and had written its first cases, establishing an important new product line for Lincoln National as a financial services business.

In 1967, on the eve of entering a new phase of its corporate life,

Lincoln National was the tenth largest life insurance company in the United States in terms of insurance in force and the largest life reinsurer in the world. The company had $16.5 billion of life insurance in force (in addition to $2 billion in life policies issued by affiliates) and $2 billion in assets. The Group included six major components: Lincoln National Life, Dominion Life Assurance in Canada, American States, CORENA, Dominion-Lincoln Assurance in Great Britain and Lincoln Philippine Life in Manila. As Menge had noted as early as 1964, however, the nature of Lincoln National had changed and, being more complex, required new techniques for holding all the parts together and achieving common goals. Menge's solution was to create a holding company.

LINCOLN NATIONAL CORPORATION

On January 17, 1968, Menge's vision was realized with the formation of the Lincoln National Corporation (LNC), one of the first holding companies in the insurance industry. Menge had first spoken about the need for a holding company in the late 1950s when he talked about the "family of Lincoln companies" in his

Allen Steere directed much of Lincoln National's governmental relations for decades, until his retirement in 1973.

speeches describing the life insurance company which owned other companies that were not to be merged into Lincoln National Life, as had been the practice in the past. The difficulties associated with a life insurance company's acquiring a new line of business, such as the property-casualty company of American States, however, led Menge to consider more effective and efficient techniques of organization. He also recognized the need to have legislation passed in order to make it possible to form a holding company in Indiana. Accordingly, he directed the company's chief governmental relations officer, Allen Steere, to oversee the two-year process of guiding the necessary measure through the Indiana General Assembly. It turned out, as Steere remembers, to have been "one of the toughest legislative fights in his career, primarily because holding companies had earned such poor reputations during the 1930s and a number of senators were determined to block the holding company bill." After various amendments to the bill were developed by the Lincoln National legal team, however, Steere was able to assuage the senators' fears and see the enabling legislation promptly passed. The process was quickly set in motion to create a parent organization and in June 1967 shares of the new stock were exchanged for shares of the old Lincoln Life stock on a one-for-one basis. Through a grandfather clause, the directors of the life insurance company were made the directors of the new corporation. As Menge recalled, "We had a brand new company with enlarged powers that took us out of the jurisdiction of the state insurance department. We could now do anything any other corporation could do."

The objectives of the new holding company set the stage for the events of the next two and a half decades: The corporation would (1) improve the efficiency and performance of the affiliates; (2) broaden the product lines and improve marketing; and (3) expand investments of policyholder and shareholder funds. This new structure for the corporation gave Lincoln National the flexibility it needed for yet further expansion. There was celebration in Fort Wayne when Lincoln National Corporation offered its stock on the New York Stock Exchange and Midwest Stock Exchange in August 1969.

The first manifestation of the flexibility of the new corporation was to organize the Lincoln National Development Corporation. The purpose of the first wholly owned subsidiary of LNC to be formed was to enter the real estate market to obtain quality real estate and develop skills not currently a part of Lincoln National Life's regular investment program.

The same year Lincoln National Corporation appeared on the stock exchanges, it acquired Chicago Title and Trust Co., another very different line of business for Lincoln National. A company that traced its beginnings to 1846, Chicago Title and Trust played a historic role in the great Chicago fire of 1871. While most of the property records of the central Chicago districts were destroyed when the fire swept the Cook County deeds office, copies of the records were preserved by Chicago Title's predecessor.

The holding company's first years yielded no grand design for molding each of the parts of the corporation under one strategic plan. The leadership simply sought to exploit the new flexibility and pursue good opportunities for growth. The organizational chart depicted three legs of the corporation: Lincoln National Life, American States and Chicago Title and Trust, each with its subsidiaries. Functionally, however, only the Fort Wayne based operations of Lincoln National Life were closely tied to the corporate structure. Indeed, there was little effort to set the corporate entity apart from the life insurance company. In the minds of Lincoln National employees in Fort Wayne there was no real change: the fact that the life insurance company now had a parent had little impact. It was the same for American States and Chicago Title and Trust, which continued to function independently as they had done when they were affiliates of the life company.

As Thomas Watson became CEO of the corporation in 1971 the company continued to show a steady pattern of growth in terms of net income and accumulation of assets. The corporation in this year had $65.7 million in operating income (over the $52.4 million in 1970) and assets of $3.3 billion (over the $3 billion of 1970). The earnings per share had increased to $5.80 over the 1970 earnings of $4.60. Despite these measurements of growth, Watson was troubled by the lackluster performances of the foreign companies and the expenses of segments of the domestic operations. He determined to eliminate these problems and focus on the area he believed had the greatest opportunity for growth and profitability, life insurance. Consequently, Watson divested the company of Dominion-Lincoln in Great Britain (1973), Halsey, Stuart & Co., a brokerage firm and subsidiary of Chicago Title & Trust (1973), Lincoln Philippine Life in Manila (1975) and CORENA in Paris (1976).

Watson's principal concern was to bolster direct sales of life and health insurance, the traditional strengths of Lincoln National. The solution was the formation of the Lincoln National Sales Corporation (LNSC) as a marketing arm for a novel concept of the agency system. The original impetus for LNSC stemmed from the difficulty faced throughout the industry in recruiting quality agents in the 1970s. Selling life insurance was seen by some as a job of last resort, one into which a person simply drifted for want of a better opportunity. This was especially true when one considered bright college graduates who were increasingly attracted to the glamor of the investment firms and brokerage houses. In the minds of many young professionals, selling life insurance and related products had become trivial. A model for a different approach existed in one of Lincoln National's own general agents, John Marsh of Washington, D.C.. Marsh, who in the mid-1960s had developed the Variable Annuity Life Insurance Company (VALIC), pointed the way to the future and, for a while, alarmed the traditional insurance industry with his bold concept of life agents selling products other than life insurance. His agent, Mitchell Curtis, eventually had financial clients all over the world. These men lived like princes. Marsh had a private dining room in his office suite, staffed by his private chefs, and he hosted only the most important Capitol City figures. Clearly, selling insurance could be very respectable. The problem lay in translating the Marsh and Curtis experience into something all agents might enjoy in some degree. As early as 1968, when Watson was president of Lincoln National Life, the company experimented with the corporate agency system using selected regional offices, such as Baltimore and Chicago, as pilots. Encouraged by the results, Watson determined to develop the system fully after he became CEO.

The vision of LNSC was to create a single general agency that would unify the marketing operation for all product lines. In essence, each agency would become a little corporation, complete with corporate titles and a corporate image that would be an added incentive to bright young sales professionals. Henceforth, the general agent in Atlanta, Baltimore or Cleveland would be the chairman, president and CEO of XYZ Corporation, an affiliate of Lincoln National Sales Corporation. His agents might have titles such as vice president, secretary or executive vice president. This brought a new measure of dignity and acceptability to the business of selling life insurance.

The second principal feature of the LNSC concept was extensive financial support for the corporate agencies. More funds would be made available for recruitment and training of agents as well as for the expansion of facilities, equipment and expertise to sell and service the new products that appeared in the late 1960s and early 1970s, such as variable annuities, pension funds and financial planning. Management of the system would be decentralized and carried out through regional offices.

LNSC was formed in September 1973, with Jack Rawles as its first president. He was soon followed by Howard Steele, who had been in the Chicago office with Watson. A recruitment program was launched and thousands of potential agents were brought to the home office for training each year. Increasingly attractive incentives were offered for sales performances. In the first few years of the LNSC operation before Watson's retirement, sales figures shot up and the overall operation drew the serious attention of the industry. By the end of his tenure as CEO in 1977, there were seventy-eight subsidiaries of LNSC serving as agencies for the selling and servicing of Lincoln National Life products.

Watson's organization of the Lincoln National Investment Management Company (LNIMC) was a relatively minor event in December 1973, but in little more than a decade it would prove to be one of the most important platforms upon which Lincoln National Corporation would position its growth for the twenty-first century. LNIMC traced its origins to the creation of the LNC Investment Management Corporation in 1969, which was formed by Rood from the life company's investment committee to provide advice and management services to all the affiliates of the corporation. In 1970 its name was changed to LNC Investment Advisory Corporation. The origins of LNIMC can also be traced to the origins of a mutual fund, Security Supervisors, Inc. in 1971. Watson consolidated this mutual fund with the LNC Investment Advisory Corporation into one entity called LNIMC in 1973. The new organization then administered five mutu-

Walter Menge, joined (left to right) by John Phelps, Henry Rood and Gordon Reeves, signs the documents that create CORENA.

al funds and served as investment advisor to the Lincoln National affiliates under the direction of Senior Vice President Walter Gadient, the corporation's chief investment officer.

When Watson stepped down as CEO in 1977, Lincoln National had income of nearly $131 million and total assets of $6 billion. The corporation had recovered from a mid-1970s slump in earnings, but for the incoming CEO, Ian Rolland, it was clear that a new corporate organization had to be developed if the company were to compete effectively in the coming decade. Among the many systemic

changes of Rolland's tenure was the introduction of orderly strategic business planning. What made Lincoln National's planning distinctive in the industry was its decentralized process. Responsibility for strategic planning was placed with the operating managers of the business units — those most familiar with the line of business — with technical support provided by a small corporate staff. Each business unit was required to undertake a formal planning process, creating their own five-year (later three-year) plans for reaching corporate goals, before assembling for a corporation planning

session with the CEO and the board of directors. The first planning conference was held in 1980 in Florida. Soon, a corporate office for strategic planning was created to augment the process, and strategic planning became an institutionalized function of the culture of Lincoln National.

The planning process showed that LNSC had proven to be far too expensive, an issue that would have to be addressed over the next several years. Gradually, the number of agency corporations was reduced from a high of seventy-eight to the thirty-six regional agencies that are the core of the field

Lincoln and the Restoration of Ford's Theatre

In January 1967 Lincoln National gained national attention for its role in inaugurating the restoration of Ford's Theatre in Washington, D.C., the site of the assassination of President Abraham Lincoln. The most famous theater in American history had been closed as a stage since April 14, 1865, when the actor and southern radical, John Wilkes Booth, shot Lincoln in the head during the performance of *Our American Cousin*. An outraged nation took its revenge on the theater as well as the assassins and refused to allow Ford's to reopen. Draped in black, the building stood empty for many years until the government purchased it and turned it into a storage facility.

The restoration of the theater as a monument to the fallen president was started by North Dakota Senator Milton Young who introduced a bill in 1946 that would give the National Park Service authorization and funding to initiate the project. Following numerous studies, Congress gave full funding to the restoration in 1964, including the installation of a museum in the basement. At a cost of $2.7 million, the theater was fully restored, including furnishings, by the end of 1967. Recognizing that attending the theater was one of Abraham Lincoln's favorite ways to relax, the plan also called for the revival of theatrical productions, and this became the chief purpose of the Ford's Theatre Society.

Secretary of the Interior Stewart L. Udall, with Lincoln National President Henry Rood, announced on October 4, 1967, that Lincoln National Life was the first corporate underwriter of the project with a major challenge grant of $250,000. In addition, Lincoln National announced that it would sponsor a nationwide telecast of the inaugural program on January 30, 1968. Rood noted that Lincoln National's role was in keeping with other major efforts the company had made to commemorate the great president and his ideals, from the Lincoln Library and Museum and the monthly publication of Lincoln Lore to the Paul Manship statue of "Abraham Lincoln: The Hoosier Youth." Even Arthur Godfrey on his popular morning radio program praised the company by noting "that many companies are named after Lincoln, but Lincoln Life is one that does something about it." The grant succeeded in attracting the remaining necessary funds for the Ford's Theatre Society to be able to create a professional resident repertory company that would produce plays typical of the Lincoln era.

The grand hour-long "Inaugural Evening at Ford's Theatre," which aired on CBS, was staged as a documentary interpreting the life and ideals of the president when the nation was deeply divided in Civil War. Notably, in 1968 the nation was again deeply divided and theater-goers had to pass through crowds of protesters of the Vietnam War. Directed by the distinguished screen producer-director John Houseman, the show was a collage of Lincoln-era speeches, poems and songs, which opened with an appearance by Helen Hayes. "The first lady of the American stage," was the first actor to perform in the old theater since the assassination. Other performances were given by Henry Fonda, Harry Belafonte, Robert Ryan, Julie Harris, Andy Williams, Richard Crenna, Odetta, Fredric March, Jean Thielemans, Herb Shriner and Carmen de Lavallade.

The responses to the production were overwhelmingly favorable, with major reviewers across the nation praising both the show and Lincoln National. Special praise, however, was reserved for the moving performance by Belafonte of the authentic rendition of the "Battle Hymn of the Republic," which black soldiers modified to tell their own story of the struggle to end slavery. Following the inaugural event, the National Repertory Theater began its first regular season of period productions, initiated by the Lincoln National's challenge grant, that continue to the present.

Lincoln National continued to support the Ford's Theatre. In January 1978 the company sponsored the commemoration of the tenth anniversary of the reopening of the theater. Entitled "A Celebration of Theater," the Ford's Theatre Society presented a variety show of songs, dances and dramatic pieces featuring such performers as Henry Fonda, Billy Dee Williams and Jane Alexander that was aired on NBC television. The guest of honor was President Jimmy Carter.

Three years later, in November 1981, Lincoln National's own Choraliers appeared on stage with Richard Blake, who portrayed Abraham Lincoln in a production of "An Evening with President Lincoln." Lincoln National CEO Ian Rolland was the guest of honor. Lincoln National had also come to Washington to inaugurate the Lincoln Lecture Series on Liberty and Equality. Sharing a heritage that the ideals of the sixteenth president, the lectures were held at Gallaudet College, the national college for deaf students chartered by Abraham Lincoln.

force in the mid-1990s. This process of reducing the numbers of corporate agencies was done gradually in order to preserve the best elements of the system. In 1990, however, some of the agencies were still so individual that they suppressed their relationship with Lincoln National Life Insurance Company. In Rolland's view, it was critical for both Lincoln National Life and the agency corporation that there be an obvious and well advertised connection between the two. Accordingly, in 1994 the name of the agency organization was changed to Lincoln National Financial Group in order to give a consistent identity. Henceforth, each agent and each agency would be readily identified with Lincoln National without giving up any real benefits of a strong agency corporation.

In the late 1970s and early 1980s Rolland took advantage of the research skills of the respected consulting firm of McKinsey & Co. to achieve an effective overall operating reorganization for Lincoln National. Again, the strategic planning process clarified the corporation's goals and directions by involving all levels of executives in the process for determining future direction. It was agreed that the overall goal was to provide

superior service to customers, and it was thought that this could be achieved by putting all aspects of a line of business together under one head, a strategic business unit, or SBU. It made sense to place all the facets of a particular line of business, such as Group Life and Health or Pensions, under the umbrella of its special area of expertise. All the advertising, market research, infrastructure, training, internal and external promotions, and so forth would be arranged under the head of the line of business. In this way, there was clear accountability as well as clarity of focus for those working in the unit.

Simultaneously with the reorganization of the corporate structure, Lincoln National launched an aggressive acquisition program which aimed at increasing diversity of products and their distribution. In 1979 the company acquired Security Connecticut Life Insurance Company, of Avon, Connecticut, a company that had been organized in 1955 as a subsidiary of Security Insurance Company of New Haven, Connecticut. In the years after 1970, under the direction of then CEO John A. Solomon, Security Connecticut had become a dynamic company maintaining a growth factor of twenty-five years. Security

Connecticut was attractive to LNC because of its strong distribution system of life and annuity products through independent agents and brokers.

Two years later Lincoln National entered the new field of universal life insurance with the purchase of First Penn-Pacific Life Insurance of Oakbrook Terrace, Illinois. This company was known for its administration of universal life, a product that filled the increasing desire of customers to have an insurance policy with current interest crediting rates and flexibility. Of special importance at First Penn-Pacific was a sophisticated data processing system which enabled the company to compete in the rapidly intensifying universal life market of the mid-1980s. With this acquisition Lincoln National became one of the first major insurance companies to sell universal life.

There were further strategic acquisitions in 1984 and 1985, several of which were made by Lincoln National to give greater depth to the insurance capabilities of the corporation. The specialty company, K & K Insurance of Fort Wayne, focusing on insurance for sports and recreational activities, was acquired in 1984. National Reinsurance Corporation of Stamford, Connecticut,

Harry Belafonte sings the black soldiers' rendition of the *Battle Hymn of the Republic* during the gala inauguration of Ford's Theatre in Washington, D.C..

A standing ovation greets the performers at the curtain call of the Ford's Theatre inauguration.

The Lincoln Museum

Once Lincoln National had become firmly established and was beginning to enjoy prosperity in the early 1920s, Arthur Hall decided to expand the association of the company with the legacy of Abraham Lincoln. Hall's personal attachment to the historical figure of the sixteenth president was a legacy from his mother who adored Lincoln and cherished a dried rose she collected from the president's coffin as the funeral train crossed the Midwest in 1865. Harriet Hall had been on the Indiana committee to replenish the flowers on the president's casket as he lay in state in Indianapolis; when the flowers were removed, Mrs. Hall was given one as a memento, a cherished gift she gave to her son. Hall established the Lincoln Historical Research Foundation in 1928 and recruited Dr. Louis A. Warren to come to Fort Wayne to bring the foundation to life.

Warren was ideal for the job. Born in 1885 in Holden, Massachusetts, Warren came from humble beginnings and worked his way through school. He earned a degree in theology from Transylvania University in Lexington, Kentucky. And perhaps prophetically, his first pulpit for the Disciples of Christ was in Hodgenville, Kentucky, Abraham Lincoln's birthplace. Rumors and unsubstantiated stories about Lincoln's youth led Warren to spend his spare time scouring local records for solid information about the president's earliest years. In the process this vocation became a new career with the publication of his first book, *Lincoln's Parentage and Childhood*, in 1926. As a Lincoln scholar Dr. Warren was well received and it was one of his lectures in behalf of a Lincoln memorial that brought him to Hall's attention.

The blend of Hall's desire to create a special memorial to the namesake of the company and Warren's knowledge of Lincoln were perfect. The goal for the foundation was quickly set after Warren arrived in Fort Wayne: The company should develop and house the country's most significant research collection of Lincolniana. Warren promptly began to lay the foundations for the Lincoln Library and established its scholarly reputation in 1929 with publication of the first issue of *Lincoln Lore*, a one-page bulletin on Lincoln and his times that has been produced continuously for sixty-six years.

The beginnings of the collection began with the acquisition of the library of Judge Daniel Fish of Minneapolis. This was one of the largest collections of books about Lincoln and documents in the nation. Warren quickly added two additional significant collections through astute trading and sale of duplicates. Despite early misgivings on the part of some company leaders about the wisdom of an insurance company's operating a scholarly library, the connection between scholarship and business made a happy union. The first permanent displays on the fourth floor of the home office were artifacts and documents assembled to show something of the life of Abraham Lincoln to the employees and other visitors. But it was left to Warren's successor to develop this into a more significant museum.

With the foundations of the Lincoln Library well established, the amiable Dr. Warren retired at age seventy-one in 1956 and turned the operation over to R. Gerald McMurtry, a young Lincoln scholar who had established a reputation for collecting Lincolniana as the archivist for Lincoln Memorial University in Harrogate, Tennessee. A native of Elizabethtown, Kentucky, another boyhood home of Abraham Lincoln, McMurtry graduated from Centre College in Danville, Kentucky, and worked for a time during the Depression in the Lincoln Museum under Dr. Warren. Under McMurtry, an accomplished writer and public speaker, the collection was greatly enhanced by the acquisition of numerous objects touching Abraham Lincoln's life and era -- from personal items in his office to a portion of the flag that draped the presidential seats at Ford's Theater the night of the assassination. Perhaps the finest acquisition made by McMurtry was the inspiring life mask of Lincoln's face and hands made by the noted sculptor Leonard Wells Volk in 1860, just before Lincoln became president.

McMurtry's tenure witnessed important changes for the foundation and its holdings. He directed the complicated move from the fourth to the first floor of the Harrison Street building and an extensive increase in the number of exhibits open to the public. As a member of the national Lincoln Sesquicentennial Commission in 1959, he made appearances throughout the world giving presentations on Lincoln and represented the company during the Civil War centennial celebrations (1961-1965) at a host of related commemorative events. All the while, the research and publications reputation of the Lincoln Library and Museum continued to grow. "His life was a ceaseless round of discoveries; sometimes he marvelled quietly that he got paid to do exactly what he wanted to do." In many ways, the job was a scholar's dream.

In 1972 McMurtry retired and Mark E. Neely Jr was recruited by Vice President Allen Steere to take his place. Neely, a graduate of Yale University, had very large shoes to fill and he did so with great professionalism. He quickly developed a wide reputation as a scholar and a witty and provocative public speaker who was always in great demand. He oversaw the important move of the facilities to the first floor of the new Clinton Street addition and the expanded exhibition area of the sixty new displays of the career, times and significance of the president. The foundation honored its first director by renaming the institution the Louis A. Warren Lincoln Library and Museum and in 1978 the second director was honored with the establishment of the widely respected annual R. Gerald McMurtry Lecture, which brings an outstanding lecturer on Lincoln and his age to Fort Wayne each May.

Neely, like his predecessors, made key additions to the collection and enhanced the scholarly reputation of the institution. During his stewardship, the museum added one of the most important collections when he successfully negotiated the acquisition of the Lloyd Ostendorf Collection of Lincoln photographs. Perhaps the most precious item added to the collection, however, was the last portrait painted of Lincoln from life, executed by Matthew Wilson about one month before the assassination in April 1865.

In addition, travelling exhibits were created and the first conservation and preservation efforts were initiated, elevating the curatorial functions of the museum to the professional standards demanded by the importance of the collections. Important objects were collected, such as Lincoln's White House chair and his personal cordial wine set, and the Mary and Robert Todd Lincoln "Insanity File" was acquired only when her descendant, Robert Todd Lincoln Beckwith decided that only the Lincoln museum would treat the sensitive materials with the care and sympathy they deserved. As the author of the *Lincoln*

was purchased in 1984 to increase Lincoln National's presence as a direct writer in the property-casualty reinsurance market. Western Casualty and Surety Company of Fort Scott, Kansas, was acquired in 1985 by American States Insurance, propelling the corporation's property-casualty operations into national significance. The Western, like American States, sold its products through a system of independent agents and the acquisition increased American States' market share in many states, particularly in the Midwest. Thus expanded, the property-casualty operations wrote approximately $1.5 billion in annual premiums in 1985, or nearly 1 percent of the total national market.

Lincoln National also re-entered the British life insurance market in 1984 with the acquisition of Cannon Assurance Ltd. of Wembley, England. This gave Lincoln National a new direct presence in the United Kingdom, which would become an important platform for dynamic growth in the 1990s. The next year Lincoln National strengthened its position for investment management with the purchase of Modern Portfolio Theory Associates (MPT) of New York City, an investment management firm with strong quantitative skills. Lincoln National also acquired Lynch & Mayer Inc. of New York City for its growth investing techniques.

The strategic plan also called for the divestiture of operations that no longer fit the company's business mix for the late 1980s. Accordingly, it was decided that Chicago Title and Trust had little synergy with Lincoln National's other insurance lines and was sold in 1985. Meanwhile, the foreign ownership of Canadian-based Dominion Life Assurance had proven to be too great a burden and it was sold to a Canadian firm. Finally, the strategic plan determined that there was an opportunity to reduce profitably the corporation's exposure to real estate and thus Lincoln National Development Corporation, which had been formed in June 1968, was sold in 1984.

As a result of these changes, Lincoln National Corporation in 1985, at the time the nation's fifteenth largest diversified financial services company, had attained a new business mix that gave increased depth to the three central businesses: individual life insurance, employee benefits and property-casualty insurance. In 1985 the corporation had $13.5 billion in assets, total revenues of nearly $5 billion and operating income of $185.5 million, a twenty-eight percent increase over 1984. Of significance, though, was the fact that the group health business was evolving into a new line of business, managed health care.

GROUP LIFE AND HEALTH / EMPLOYEE BENEFITS

For nearly half a century the group department was a major part of

Gerald McMurtry, director of the Lincoln Library and Museum (right), interviews Abraham Lincoln scholar Carl Sandburg on the occasion of his appearance at Lincoln National.

Lincoln National Life. In 1980, at the time it was transformed into the Employee Benefits Division (EBD), it had become one of the largest parts of the corporation in terms of revenue, but dramatic changes in the health care industry placed enormous pressure on the company, leading to its divestiture in 1992. This was the first line of business created by Lincoln National which the company aban-

The Lincoln Museum (continued)

Encyclopedia, which was nominated for the Pulitzer Prize in history, and co-author of *The Lincoln Image* and *The Confederate Image* and other works on the Civil War era, Neely was a guest at the White House to inaugurate a presidential lecture series. The pinnacle of Neely's career at the Lincoln Museum and a highpoint for the foundation came in 1993 when he was awarded the Pulitzer Prize in history for *The Fate of Liberty*, Neely's study of President Lincoln and civil liberties during the Civil War. Ruth Cook, Neely's long-time assistant in the museum, recalls that the announcement of the Pulitzer came as a complete surprise to him — he did not know the book had been nominated. That same year Dr. Neely decided to return to teaching and accepted the prestigious John Francis Bannon chair in history at St. Louis University.

In 1993 CEO Ian Rolland decided that the national treasure the museum collection represented needed to be shared with a greater audience. As a result, plans were developed to greatly expand and enhance the museum operation. The goal was to increase the visibility and excitement about the museum theme without sacrificing the great scholarly reputation achieved over six decades. To do so, Joan Flinspach, the director of the Boys Town Hall of History in Lincoln, Nebraska, and a woman highly respected in museum circles, was recruited to lead a team in the development of a new Lincoln Museum. To continue the scholarly function of the institution, Dr. Gerald Prokopowicz, a Harvard graduate in American history, joined the team.

This new museum opens to the public in 1995. More than merely moving the existing museum to a new location in the corporate headquarters of Renaissance Square, relocation allows the facility to house nearly 30,000 square feet, three times the size of its site at Clinton Street. The museum will include eleven state-of-the-art galleries with eighteen computerized or hands-on exhibitions and four theaters. The project represents a $6 million investment to make the legacy of Abraham Lincoln accessible into the twenty-first century.

The directors of the Lincoln Museum

Louis A. Warren, director 1928-1956

R. Gerald McMurtry, director 1956-1972

Mark E. Neely, Jr., director 1972-1993

Joan Flinspach, director 1993-

doned and, as such, the divestiture was the most wrenching in the company's history.

Lincoln National had sold a small amount of group life insurance as early as 1916, but there was no effort to organize a department for the development, sales and administration of a group product until 1943. The effort to create a group department began when President A. J. McAndless was approached by his long-time friend, Tom Robson, president of the Fort Wayne Knitting Mills, a large hosiery manufacturing company on the city's near north side which was a part of the Munsingwear Corporation. At a luncheon meeting with McAndless and Senior Vice President Walter Menge, Robson related how he was unhappy with his current group coverage, which also provided accident and health benefits. He asked whether Lincoln National would be interested in entering that line of business, adding that he would be able to attract several other employers in the same business to come to Lincoln National if the company was interested. Menge recognized the opportunity to get into the accident and health insurance business and by 1944 the Group Department was in full swing under Menge's direction. A home office staff of fifty was organized in the northwest corner of the second floor of the Harrison Street building, while group field offices were established for a specialized sales force of Employee Benefits Mangers (EBMs) who would singly and with the regular Lincoln National agents sell the group products. At the end of the department's first year it proudly tallied just under $45 million of insurance in force and annual premiums of about $700,000.

The group operation grew rapidly. Under the direction of Thomas Watson, who had started with Lincoln National in the group office in Chicago, the department more than doubled in size by 1953 and took over the second floor of the Wayne Pump Building on Coombs Street. In 1956, just over ten years after its organization, the department celebrated having $1 billion in group life insurance in force with over $30 million in premiums. Five years later Group reached the $2 billion mark and by 1967 held

Ian Rolland (center) and Howard Steele (to Rolland's left) lead in the kick-off for the fall sales campaign in 1978. Drawings for prizes were pulled from the bear's "honey pots."

over $5 billion in force. By this time there were more than three hundred employees in the department, which then occupied the entire fourth floor of the main home office building.

Among the major clients of Group Life and Health by the 1970s were Magnavox, Simonize, Sherwin-Williams, Eli Lilly, State Farm Insurance, Peter Eckrich Foods, Central Soya, Hart, Schaffner & Marx, Michigan State University, Southern California Gas, the National Football League and Safeway. But one of the chief reasons for the success of Group was its ability to develop packages for small businesses, which it began doing in 1956 when the first products for groups of ten to twenty-five lives were made available. The department also developed in the early 1950s a number of retirement programs, such as pensions and group annuities, which grew rapidly and, in the case of pensions, became a major business unit in itself at the end of the 1970s. In 1965 the department even expanded into the field of credit insurance.

The struggles began for Group in 1970 when health costs began to rise sharply. In addition to the pressures of rapidly increasing inflation, the industry had to cope with wage and price controls set by the federal government. These controls limited the ability of insurance companies to respond to the unusual conditions in the health care industry. A comment in the Lincoln National annual report for 1971 foreshadowed the dramatic decisions of the mid-1980s when it stated

that, in order to meet the new pressures of inflation and the health care marketplace, the company affirmed its "willingness to innovate and successfully adapt to changing circumstances while maintaining profit objectives [to] help us expand our role as major insurers of group life and group health insurance risks." Adaptation and innovation characterize the history of Group in the 1980s and 1990s.

Group also was affected by internal pressures. In 1973 when Watson launched Lincoln National Sales Corporation (LNSC), Group was required to help finance the development of the greatly expanded agency force. In addition, Group also had to shift its old sales force of EBMs to LNSC, increasing their number to match the creation of new agencies and thereby losing the direct relationship with the sales force that had been a defining characteristic since its beginnings. Former members of Group agree that this development bore a direct relationship to underwriting losses in the mid-1970s and the eventual loss of several large clients.

The first response by Group to rising health costs and inflation was traditional: Adjust pricing and tighten underwriting. The severe inflationary pressures of 1974 and 1975, combined with a normal cyclical downturn and the demands of developing LNSC, however, outstripped the department's ability to keep pace and resulted in the largest losses ever suffered by group health. Group maintained profitability through its investments, pension and group life sales, a pattern that would continue into the late 1980s. Although a recovery in group health occurred in 1977-1978 during Ian Rolland's first years as CEO, low profit margins were foreseen for years to come. This was also the first time the company announced that it would begin to focus on ways to control the costs of providing health care as a part of its strategy for continuing in the health insurance business.

Under the direction of Executive Vice President Howard Steele, the Group Department was reorganized in 1980 as the Employee Benefits Division (EBD). Group Life and Health became a department of the division under Senior Vice President Don Fackler. The division took over the entire former Magnavox office complex on the outskirts of Fort Wayne that became known as "Lincoln West." EBD at its beginning employed more than five hundred in Fort Wayne and six hundred field benefit employees in twenty-seven

offices. In order to enhance service to clients, the Group Life and Health Department began to implement a sophisticated automated claim system in 1980 and streamlined the regional claims offices. Two years later the operation sought to expand its business quickly by acquiring blocks of business and to reach a goal of $2 billion in premiums, beginning with the purchase of the group business of Inagon Life in Winston-Salem, North Carolina, and Southwestern Life of Dallas, Texas, which resulted in an immediate twenty percent growth in the group area. The central difficulty, however, remained the rising cost of health care, which now was increasing out of proportion to other areas of the national economy. Consequently, in 1984 Lincoln National embarked on an important new direction for group health when it entered the managed health care field. In part as a result of a study undertaken by the consulting firm of McKinsey & Co., Lincoln National determined to develop alternative techniques of dealing with

health care. In the past, traditional indemnity coverage simply provided that the insurer pay the medical bills as submitted. The new managed care approach, however, envisioned a system that provided the same quality of health care to clients but allowed for the insurer to manage certain aspects of the care. For example, in addition to more efficient administrative procedures, the concept encouraged such techniques as preventative care and multiple medical opinions, discouraging repetitive and unnecessary testing or procedures and covering generic rather than brand-name medications whenever possible.

In order to enter the managed health care business, Lincoln National formed a group called ACT, or Alternative Care Technologies under the direction of Steve Berkey. Housed in an office near Lincoln West, it was a small, enthusiastic operation that moved into the uncharted waters of the new concept. ACT's primary function was to acquire health maintenance organizations (HMOs), preferred provider organizations (PPOs) or to enter into joint ventures with health care providers in order to begin to control health care costs. Lincoln National also sought to compete with third-party administrators (TPAs) — that is, providing a number of health cost containment programs in addition to claims processing and payments for employers who assume all or part of the risk — with the formation of Lincoln National Administrative Services Company (LNASC). At the same time, Steele, the division executive, entered into negotiations with U.S. Healthcare, Inc. of Blue Bell, Pennsylvania, a company that owned HMOs and PPOs in the eastern half of the country, principally in Florida, Chicago, New York and Pennsylvania. The arrangement that resulted was a merger of Lincoln National's group indemnity strength in Florida and Chicago with the HMO and PPO strengths of U.S. Healthcare to form a company called Healthwin. What made this novel was the opportunity for Lincoln National to offer employers an attractive triple option — HMO, PPO or traditional indemnity coverage.

From 1984 through 1988 Lincoln National's managed health care efforts

Thomas Watson in the Group Department, ca. 1960.

centered on the activities of ACT, Healthwin and LNASC, but it was clear by 1988 that the company needed additional specialized expertise. Complicating matters was the fact that there were serious management problems in the Healthwin operation. Consequently, upon the retirement of Howard Steele, the company recruited as his successor a managed health care expert, John Cole, who had been with Blue Cross and Blue Shield of California. Healthwin was divested in 1988 and ACT was dissolved. EBD, now under the direction of Cole, was reorganized into three major business groups: Employers Health Insurance (EHI) — a company acquired in 1986 and known today as EMPHESYS Financial Group, Inc.; Administrators Network (ADN); and Managed Health Care Group (MHCG).

The Managed Health Care Group was the center of change and marketing energy in EBD between 1988 and 1992. Cole, whom some described as a dynamic visionary, was deeply devoted to his concept. To some who experienced those years, Cole's aggressive enthusiasm for managed health care, while infectious and stimulating to the marketing side, masked financial perils. Growth was the objective and marketing was the tool. The organization was divided into a western market group and an eastern market group and were encouraged to be highly competitive with each other in order to provide the strongest possible performance overall. Staffing grew as did administration costs. In this atmosphere, overhead rose at an alarming pace.

A critical component to the success of managed health care was also the need to develop a technological advantage through the implementation of a superior, comprehensive data process-

"The Sony of American Life Insurance"

In June 1990 Lincoln National Corporation formed a strategic alliance with Dai-ichi Mutual Life Insurance Company, Japan's second-largest life insurance company and the world's third largest life insurer. This agreement marked the largest investment in a U.S. insurer by a Japanese insurer. Under the terms of the agreement, Dai-ichi purchased a significant block (9.6 percent) of Lincoln National's stock for $312 million and entered into a reciprocal business relationship in the areas of investment management, reinsurance, pension products and group health products. The agreement also featured an exchange of trainees to strengthen each company's understanding of the other's markets. For Lincoln National, the alliance not only brought capital to the corporation, but also offered opportunities for the corporation to gain greater visibility in the international equity markets.

One of the important factors that made the alliance of the two companies possible was that they had known one another for nearly three decades. In March 1956 a group of Japanese insurance leaders visited the United States to learn from 13 selected companies about American insurance practices. One of the companies the group visited was Lincoln National and among those in the group were Tsunehisa Yada, the managing director of Dai-ichi Mutual, and the group leader, Shin-Ichiro Kiga. Henry Rood, then senior vice president of Lincoln National, was the host for the group as they attended presentations by all the major divisions of the company. Rood also had Kiga and his son Yasuo as guests in his home in Fort Wayne. The younger Mr. Kiga was deeply impressed by the Rood family hospitality and by the way Lincoln National was managed.

In the course of the decades that followed, Lincoln National entered into reinsurance agreements with Dai-ichi and in December 1987, the company celebrated its listing on the Tokyo Stock Exchange. It was during a visit by Lincoln National officers in 1988, however, that the idea of an association was first broached. This time Yasuo Kiga, the young man who had visited Henry Rood in the 1950s and who now was a senior officer at Dai-ichi Mutual, returned the earlier kindness and hosted a luncheon for Lincoln National executives Richard Robertson, Robert Crispin and Lincoln National Reinsurance's Steve Clinton. During the course of the luncheon, Kiga asked the Lincoln National men what the reaction would be if Dai-ichi were to suggest that it make an investment in Lincoln National.

Dai-ichi's international research department had made a thorough study of the U.S. company. The report, which was written by Taira Suekane, recommended consideration of Lincoln as an investment, noting Kiga's familiarity with the company and the strengths of Lincoln National especially in the areas of reinsurance, pensions and investment management. The report at one point glowingly characterized the corporation as "the Sony of American life insurance."

When negotiations eventually began in 1989 the talks were held principally in New York in the law offices of Sullivan, Cromwell, Dai-ichi's legal advisors. The Lincoln National team was led by Jeff Nick, who was senior vice president for corporate planning and development. The talks were drawn out and sometimes difficult; everything had to be defined and worked out line by line. The negotiations were never acrimonious, however, as it became clear why the Dai-ichi executives were called in Japan "the gentlemen of the life insurance industry." For Lincoln National, however, the deal had to be large enough to be significant and yet with sufficient safeguards to prevent a takeover. In the process, a "marketing agreement" was drawn up that defined the relationship of the two companies in terms of mutual respect and reciprocity in order to lay the foundations for a stable association.

The process reached a climax after a day-long session when talks came to a standstill over a number of outstanding issues. Nick determined that although the deal so far was a good one, it was not a compelling one. When the Japanese would not move from their position, the Lincoln National team left the table and returned to their hotel. The Japanese team was surprised that Lincoln National would apparently call off the deal at that point and called Nick to return for further talks, but still no agreement could be reached. The Dai-ichi team returned to Japan empty-handed, but in the ensuing months compromises on both sides were made and an agreement was reached in the spring.

The signing ceremony took place in the office of General Douglas MacArthur, which had been preserved since the post-World War II years in the headquarters of Dai-ichi. For both parties the setting was impressive and full of meaning. MacArthur, an American hero as commander in the Second World War, was also held in high esteem in Japan for bringing democracy and economic stability to the country after the war. Moreover, Japanese insurance companies had played a particularly important role in the MacArthur Plan for post-war Japan, providing the financial backbone for economic recovery.

THE FUTURE IS HERE.

An EBD advertisement of 1989.

ing system. Called System for Managed Care, or SMC, the technology was expensive and untried. Yet, it promised to give MHCG the competitive edge it required, and indeed, in many ways the system presaged later technological developments. Yet, after four years of effort, its completion was still but a promise and long-term prospects proved to be far more expensive than the company was willing to underwrite. The capital required and the risks involved with SMC, the skyrocketing overhead of the Managed Health Care Group and the changing political environment all led to the decision to sell EBD.

Still, the excitement of these years is evident in the recollections of those who worked there. "Every day was

Fort Wayne employees of EBD at Lincoln West in 1989.

The executive foyer of the Lincoln National corporate headquarters. The design by Schenkel Shultz is inspired by Ford's Theatre in Washington, D.C. centering on the replica of the theatre's domed ceiling. In the center of the foyer is a reproduction of the painting executed by Matthew Wilson in March-May, 1865, the last portrait of Abraham Lincoln done from life, the original of which is in the Lincoln Museum's permanent collection.

The award-winning American States Insurance offices of its Pittsburgh Division. Design by Schenkel Shultz.

Ken Dunsire, chief administrative officer of LNC, in 1994 stands at the rail of the newly renovated fourth floor of Renaissance Square, Lincoln National's corporate headquarters.

The "Vision Room" is the central conference room of Lincoln National Reinsurance Companies. Design by Schenkel Shultz.

The Quays, the striking headquarters of the Lincoln National (UK) in Uxbridge, United Kingdom.

Renaissance Square was renovated to become the corporate center and home of the Lincoln Museum.

new," one employee remembers, echoing the comments of many others, "We were excited to come to work, join teams to solve problems and be a part of something big and important." For others, the developments during these years held anxiety. "We worked very hard to dismantle all that we had done in the old Group in order to build something entirely new. In the end, we lost the old business we had and we were left with something that was too expensive to keep." As another employee recalled, "We built an organization that was entirely new to handle the complexities of the triple option approach to managed health care, but that operation became too expensive to justify in view of the disappointingly low volume of business being generated." In 1992 Rolland made the painful decision to sell EBD. It was the appropriate business decision, but it was also a move that had profound impact on every part of the corporation, not least of all on the more than three thousand employees of Group.

INVESTMENT MANAGEMENT

Investment management has become one of the principal pillars of Lincoln National Corporation, but in the company's earliest years, it was a simple matter. State regulations for permissible investments were strict. In accordance with the Indiana Insurance Act of 1899 under which Lincoln National was organized, the company's investments were limited to U.S., state and municipal bonds, real estate mortgages, policy loans and a few bank instruments. The allowable list of investments for insurance companies expanded slowly over the next three decades. Beginning in the mid-1920s, however, the laws governing insurance company investments changed. In 1929 the company hired Frank Travers to form the Investment Research Department, and soon thereafter Lincoln National's investments began to diversify through investment in common stocks and bonds. Still, in keeping with the imperative to meet long-term liabilities such as ordinary life insurance, most investments before the 1970s were still made in real estate, residential and commercial

Takahide Sakurai (left), president of Dai-ichi Mutual Life Insurance Co., presents Lincoln National CEO Ian Rolland with a multi-volume history of Dai-ichi During his visit to Fort Wayne in 1991.

Mark Neely, director of the Lincoln Museum, shows Takahide Sakurai, Ken Dunsire, of Lincoln National's Corporate Operations, and interpreter Kazuko Sherman artifacts from the collection of Lincolniana.

mortgage loans and other long-term vehicles, such as thirty- year utilities bonds and forty-year railroad trust certificates. This style of investment worked well at a time when interest rates remained stable and there was little competition among the different types of financial institutions. Banks, savings and loans and insurance companies each had their clients for different types of financial needs and seldom competed with each other.

Before 1970, the corporation's investment program was very largely the responsibility of Lincoln National

Life's investment department, and the skills required in the traditional insurance investment program were easily within the expertise of the home office personnel. With the acquisition in the late 1960s and early 1970s of new lines of business and the development of new products, however, investment challenges became more demanding. Watson's solution was to consolidate the management of the Lincoln National's investments in a new organization, Lincoln National Investment Management Company (LNIMC), which he created in 1973. He placed

Matsumi Ono (left) and Shingo Fujii (center), two employees of Dai-ichi in training at Lincoln National, talk with Sara Powers, an LNC intern, during the local Three Rivers Festival in 1991.

ly advanced, the most sophisticated money management decisions were still being made as a result of personal contacts and those with the greatest skills to do so were centered in cities like Chicago, New York, London and Tokyo. The operation launched by Watson and Gadient began the evolution of a strong, individual corporate investment division that would be critical to meet the challenges of the decades of the 1980s and 1990s.

The year 1979 marked a dramatic change in the manner in which all insurance companies managed their investments. In order to curb inflation, which had reached dangerous proportions, Federal Reserve Chairman Paul Volker decided to curtail the money supply rather than interest rates. With less money in the market, inflation was slowed, but interest rates rose sharply. Coincidentally, the government sought to increase competition by deregulating portions of the financial services industry. As a result, insurance companies found they had to compete not only with other insurance companies, but also against other financial institutions. Everyday consumers entered the investment marketplace in large numbers and began to make decisions for themselves as to where their investments would be placed. For insurance

Walter Gadient in charge of LNIMC and made him the corporation's chief investment officer. Gadient, an outstanding investment analyst whom Watson had recruited from the Dean Witter Company in 1971 as a part of his strategy for strengthening investments, preferred to remain in Chicago in part to be in the environment of a major financial city and near the important investment operations of the Lincoln National affiliate, Chicago Title and Trust. For Gadient this made sense because in the 1970s, a time when telecommunications and computer technology were as yet not high-

"Making a Mint"

Before 1928 there was little diversity in Lincoln National's investment portfolio. Most of its funds were placed in real estate, much of which were agricultural lands. In its earliest years these farm properties were located near Fort Wayne and never beyond the boundaries of Indiana and Ohio. With the acquisition of Michigan State Life in 1914, real estate investment was extended into Michigan; and when Lincoln purchased Pioneer Life in 1917, the company entered the extensive agricultural market of the Dakotas and Montana. These long-term, conservative investments served the company well until the agricultural depression of the 1920s.

While Wall Street boomed during the "Roaring Twenties," the post-war years brought recession to rural America and a precipitous rise in foreclosures on farm properties. Lincoln National, like many other insurance companies, was deeply affected. Lincoln National's experience was severe: in the period between 1905 and 1919 Lincoln National had no mortgage foreclosures; but beginning in 1920 foreclosures rose at an alarming rate. In 1928 alone, Lincoln National had in excess of $2.3 million in farm foreclosures. Lincoln National found itself the holder of millions of dollars in farm real estate and little hope of selling it anytime soon.

In order to protect the real estate values of so many farm properties, the Finance Committee decided that Lincoln National ought to operate the foreclosed farms. Accordingly, the home office established an ad hoc farm department, with executives visiting the rural properties, hiring crews for painting, fencing, carpenter and drainage projects to keep up the properties. Lincoln National began purchasing railroad car loads of drainage tiles, fertilizer, live stock and feed. Cowhands were hired to tend the livestock.

Intent upon exploring every avenue for generating income from the rural properties, several farms were devoted to growing and distilling mint. It was believed that the essence of mint, which sold in 1925 at the substantial price of $30 per pound, would turn the farm losses into profit. The company vault was used to hold vials of the precious stuff. But within two years the price of essence of mint fell to a mere $3 per pound and the scheme was abandoned.

Lincoln National's farm operations were ended in 1927 and in 1928 the company began to resolve its investment issues by developing a diversified portfolio.

companies, the early 1980s became a very difficult time as owners of low-earning whole life policies borrowed against their cash value and invested in money market funds and certificates of deposit at higher yields. The impact on Lincoln National, like other insurance companies, was to shorten significantly its traditional long- term liabilities. Insurance companies, which usually met their long-term liabilities with long-term assets with little liquidity, now had a badly mismatched situation: short-term liabilities and long- term assets. Insurance investment personnel began talking about "asset-liability management" in order to manage better the risks of interest rates. Many insurance companies experienced severe liquidity crises by the mid-1980s and some other financial institutions, notably the savings and loans, had difficulty even surviving.

In the difficult conditions of the early 1980s, however, Lincoln National had to abandon its traditional methods of handling investments and adopt new processes. The company was one of the first in the industry to create a number of individual portfolios of invested assets and selected product liabilities in order to manage more effectively the interest rate risks. Many of these portfolios started to invest a significant amount of new cash into public bonds that offered attractive returns and could be easily sold. In addition, Lincoln National started using some of the newer investment vehicles in the early 1980s. The company, for example, was one of the pioneers in the industry in the use of interest rate futures contracts, for example. These contracts were an efficient way of securing the high yields common in the early 1980s by agreeing to purchase bonds in the future at current prices. Further, in order to achieve specialized expertise in equity investments, Lincoln National also acquired two investment management firms in 1985, Lynch & Mayer Inc. and Modern Portfolio Theory Associates Inc. (MPT), which changed its name to Vantage Global Advisors in 1992.

To meet the new investment challenges, CEO Rolland recruited Robert Crispin from Capital Holdings Corporation in the fall of 1986 to be the chief investment officer and a cat-alyst for change because of his skills as an investment strategist and his extensive contacts in the investment world. In accordance with the strategic plan developed in 1986, the decision was made to restructure the investment operation, create the necessary infrastructure and switch to a process of managing the company's funds with a focus on "total return investment." This was a new concept in the industry. It centered on a disciplined approach to investments by focusing on categories that are determined to produce the highest future value based on both price-change characteristics and current income, rather than just the industry practice of focusing on current income. The "total return" philosophy evolved from the belief that the corporation's primary responsibility was to its shareholders and its clients and that Lincoln National ought to manage investments in the corporation in such a way as to give them the greatest risk-adjusted returns. On January 1, 1988, Lincoln National became one of the first insurance companies to manage its assets on the "total return" basis and LNIMC's position in the corporation was enhanced to be the primary investment advisor of all Lincoln National companies.

The internal process began with personnel. LNIMC sought to work primarily with existing employees who were retrained and put in different places with new functions. They were given the responsibility — and accountability — for their new areas, but a clear system of rewards was also put into place. According to Jon Boscia, who succeeded Crispin in 1990 as chief investment officer, "their contributions were sought and valued; people were made to feel good about the process and they responded enormously well. The same group of people who were here in the early 1980s are the same people who have helped produce one of the best investment operations in the industry." New talents, however, were also recruited in order to quickly enter market areas in which Lincoln National had not yet developed the internal expertise, such as high- yield bonds and real estate acquisitions. According to Thomas McMeekin, the current president of

Edward Auer, chief investment officer, during the 1950s and 1960s.

Lincoln National investment strategies are discussed by President Gathings Stewart (left), CEO Thomas Watson (center), and Walter Gadient, chief investment officer in 1974.

LNIMC, the present and future strength of the investment operations depends on the diversity of its personnel, who combine the best of the existing personnel with that of new expertise drawn from every facet of the investment world. In this way, McMeekin notes, LNIMC was able to organize itself efficiently in the late 1980s and early 1990s to meet the demands of rapid change in market opportunities that lie at the heart of the "total return investment" concept.

It also enabled Lincoln National to avoid the investment problems affecting some other major insurers. A handful of companies became insolvent because they went outside the mainstream of investment practice, placing too much emphasis on one asset class — like high-yield, or "junk," bonds — or one region, such as commercial mortgage lending in the oil-producing states hard-hit in the late 1980s. McMeekin said in a 1995 interview that total return moti-

vates investment managers to do "some contrarian things," like avoiding high-yield bonds when underwriting is loose and yields overly competitive. "We do not chase 'hot markets' because of the way we measure ourselves," McMeekin explained.

Lincoln National was among the first insurance companies to use external money management firms to expand its investment capabilities. Believing that in the increasingly complicated and volatile marketplace

The American Legacy

In 1994 the variable annuity business of Lincoln National had a record year of earnings and marked its fourth consecutive year as the nation's largest seller of individual annuities. Income from operations just since 1990 rose from nearly $40 million to $120 million in 1994. This phenomenal record of growth is due primarily to a dynamic approach to distribution that began in 1987 with the appearance of the American Legacy Fund.

In 1982 Lincoln National created its first expanded fund with the Lincoln Multi-Fund, which originally included four variable fund options in addition to various fixed accounts. Although the new products were sound, the distribution structure was too limited. The decision was made in 1983 to develop what were called alternative distribution systems, and this marked the beginnings of growth on a rapid scale for the annuities business at Lincoln National. The first line of distribution continued to be the field force of Lincoln National, which numbered more than 1,300 career agents at the time. Contracts were made with scores of firms that specialized in selling annuities in certain markets, such as hospitals and schools, which created numerous new large cases.

The unique breakthrough that put Lincoln National in the forefront of annuity sales, however, came in 1986 when Lincoln National held discussions with Capital Research and Management, one of the nation's largest and oldest investment management organizations, regarding its family of mutual funds known as American Funds, a California firm highly regarded for its high-quality customer service. The deal began when executives of Capital Research and American Funds contacted Ken Dunsire, then in charge of Lincoln National's Individual Products Division in the life insurance company. For American Funds, which was unhappy with its relationship with another life insurance company, the original idea was to see if Lincoln National, would be interested in creating a variable life insurance policy. American Funds was attracted to Lincoln National because it was a high quality insurance company known, like itself, for its superior customer service. American Funds, however, was interested in Lincoln National for other reasons also. The Tax Reform Act of 1986 had made variable annuities more attractive and Lincoln National was well known in the industry for its abilities in this line of business, particularly for its long experience, administrative expertise and strong client relationships.

Discussions soon led to variable annuities and Dunsire brought into the conversation Robert Nikels, the head of what was then called the Savings Products Department, which included Lincoln National's annuities. In March 1987 an agreement was reached and Lincoln National created the American Legacy Variable Annuity. By this transaction, Capital Research would manage the various segments of the American Legacy Fund, American Funds would contract with fund planners and broker-dealers to sell American Legacy and Lincoln National would provide product development and such insurance functions as contracts and administration. In addition to the expertise of each of the partners, the great strength of the deal was that the annuity was distributed by the huge nation-wide American Funds network of more than 45,000 stockbrokers and 400 broker-dealer firms, in addition to Lincoln National's usual sales outlets.

Growth was modest in its first years, primarily because of the crash of the stock market in the fall of 1987. Operations in Fort Wayne were managed by only a handful of personnel. But investor confidence rebounded quickly, particularly among older Americans who took pride in providing for their own retirement plans, and caused sales of American Legacy Variable Annuities to grow steadily from 1989 to 1990. No one expected, however, that sales would explode in 1991. Executives in 1990 anticipated sales for 1991 to be around $900 million, but that mark was passed by mid-year. Eight hundred calls a day on toll-free lines were handled and the pace of sales by July was $32 million per week. Finding staff and space and providing training became urgent issues. Overworked personnel were jammed two or three into cubicles and equipment was shared until support could catch up with the sales demands. Even chairs were hard to find. By the end of 1991, American Legacy had become the largest selling individual annuity in the United States and it continues to be so to the present. American Legacy deposits in 1994 exceeded those of all the other Lincoln National annuity plans together and continues to be one of the company's most significant driving forces.

highly specialized skills and technologies were necessary to give shareholders and customers the strongest level of service possible, Lincoln National began to augment its capabilities by contracting with various "sub-advisor" asset managers, such as Provident Investment Counsel, Capital Technology and Putnam.

Investment issues in the 1990s had become global in scope. As with other financial organizations, economic activity around the world affected Lincoln National operations and the complexity of financial instruments greatly increased, creating new demands for additional expertise not only in the area of "exotic" financial instruments, but also in traditional ones as well. Most importantly, stronger ties were developed internally between areas of investment and those of the business units whose products the investments supported. Thus, such activities as product development, asset-liability management and potential investment returns emerged as additional factors as significant in the company's profitability as underwriting returns, the traditional source of profitability.

LNIMC by the mid-1990s was evolving into a major new profit center for the corporation. The most dramatic event in the process of augmenting Lincoln National's investment capabilities occurred in April 1995 with the acquisition of Delaware Management Holdings, Inc. of Philadelphia, one of the nation's oldest and most respected firms in the investment management industry. Founded in 1929, Delaware Management is known in the industry as a "value" investor, that is, an investment style that focuses on stocks with low price-earnings ratios and above- average dividend yields. This investment style has made Delaware one of the leading pension and mutual fund managers. At the time Lincoln National announced the agreement, Delaware Management had about $25 billion under management and net assets of $9.2 billion. Rolland said, "the acquisition, when completed, would create a company with more than $60 billion of assets under management, a wide array of investment products and styles as well as a diverse distribution network." This acquisition was also an important part

A tax-favored investment for financial independence

The first American Legacy prospectus, 1987.

of Lincoln National's recent efforts to achieve the vision identified in its latest strategic plan: "To become a high performing financial services company with benchmark service, growth and profit." As a new Lincoln National line of business known as Investment Management, which includes LNIMC, Delaware Management Holdings, Lynch & Mayer, Inc. and

Emerging Markets: Lincoln National in China

John Cantrell, senior vice president for international strategies, 1994.

On April 28, 1994, Lincoln National opened its office in Beijing, China, with a banquet for nearly two hundred government and business representatives. This marked the beginning of a significant effort by the company to extend its expertise into the single largest national market in the world. The People's Republic of China, with 1.2 billion people who are accustomed to saving, an economy growing by thirteen percent a year and a rapidly growing middle class, offered high potential for sales of insurance products in the future. In 1994 Lincoln National was one of only four insurance companies allowed liaison offices in China hoping to be licensed to sell insurance. A second office located in Shanghai was scheduled to be opened in mid-1995. Before licensing, however, Lincoln National has begun to establish a serious presence in the country by investing in China and creating partnerships within the Chinese business community.

Although Lincoln National had long maintained reinsurance relationships in the Far East, the effort to secure a position in China evolved from events that began in 1991. Officers of Lincoln National Investment Management Corporation (LNIMC) were attracted to the possibility of investment opportunities in China and sent then-Senior Vice President Thomas McMeekin to investigate. At the same time, Eldon Mayer of Lincoln National's affiliate, Lynch & Mayer, had undertaken his own research and encouraged CEO Ian Rolland to pursue establishing contacts with China.

The old advertising slogan for Lincoln National, "Its Name Indicates Its Character," acquired special meaning in the initial efforts to establish the company in China. Of all the U.S. presidents, only four are readily recognizable to the Chinese: George Washington, Abraham Lincoln, Franklin D. Roosevelt and Richard M. Nixon. Of these, Lincoln is the most respected and often quoted. In one meeting Rolland attended, the vice premier of the People's Republic indicated that as a young boy he had memorized the Gettysburg Address, acknowledging Lincoln National's unique connection to the sixteenth president. Indeed, Lincoln's name is one of only a handful of American words that has its own character in the Chinese language — a notable benefit in the difficult process of establishing recognition in a foreign culture.

The EMANCIPATOR

NO. 533   PUBLISHED WEEKLY FOR THE FIELD REPRESENTATIVES OF THE LINCOLN NATIONAL LIFE INSURANCE COMPANY, FORT WAYNE, INDIANA   DECEMBER 7, 1964

It's A New All-Time Record

$118,695,671

Lincoln National Life celebrates a successful "Persons Month" sales campaign in 1964 (front row from left to right: Cliff Gamble, Henry Rood, Henry Persons and Jack Rawles).

Vantage Global Advisors, Inc., the company's investment operations had evolved into one of the most sophisticated and effective in the insurance industry.

THE FIELD FORCE

At the spiritual core of Lincoln National is the original function of the company — sales of life insurance. Carried out only by individual career agents at first, the rapid growth of the business soon led to the development of agencies and a home office management system under a director or supervisor of agencies. As with other companies which sold their direct business through agents, this system worked well until the late 1960s, when new products and new market conditions required different approaches to the field operation. In addition, the field force itself was changing as agents began to assume more sophisticated — and demanding — roles with their clients. This is a process of change that continues to this day. Still, at the core of the new field force is the old drive and excitement for sales and the thrill of success as an independent entrepreneur.

The head of the first field force for Lincoln National was Arthur F. Hall, the company secretary and general manager in 1905. Hall's only training and experience was a few months

part-time selling for the Equitable Life Insurance Company in Indianapolis. Hall recruited two independent Fort Wayne agents, Max Blitz and William Bishop, to join him as the first field force. These three were later joined by William Ingham and by early September had secured the necessary 250 applications for Lincoln National to begin business as a life insurance company.

Blitz was a tough salesman who was known in Fort Wayne for his persistence. Not a few of his contemporaries remember throwing him out of their places of business because he would not take "no" for an answer. Bishop, a portly, more affable man, was not as successful initially. A former housepainter from Bluffton, Indiana, Bishop decided he ought to go back to his old profession where he could earn $15 a week and better support his family. Blitz convinced him to stay and gave him a couple of good leads. Through his own brand of persistence and the liberal use of gifts, such as little statues of Abraham Lincoln or cats and dogs, Bishop gradually improved his sales. By 1909 he was the top salesman of the company, an honor he earned for three more years.

Developing field agents continued to be a problem in Lincoln National's first years because the company could not afford experienced agents who, in the absence of general agents, demanded advancements directly from the company. Consequently, Hall began to recruit part-time agents, especially school teachers who could sell aggressively during the summer months. The teaching skills were valued as well. Those who succeeded and wanted to stay with the work were given full-time contracts. As part of the development effort, the company held its first sales convention at Lake Wawasee in northern Indiana in August 1906. Hall told them, "This little crowd of successful producers forms the nucleus around which The Lincoln National Life Insurance Company will in a few years build a great agency force, and I hope to see these same men at our annual meetings for years to come." He noted further that thanks to the agents the company had 702 policies, representing $1.6 million of insurance in force with more than $60,000 in premiums.

The average policy was $2,400 and the average premium was $37.

In 1907 the company needed to expand its business beyond Fort Wayne and the surrounding small agricultural communities. Hall decided to extend the field of operation with experimental large city agencies, previously thought to be too expensive because of more intense competition. To do this, Hall recruited the company's first agency executive, Walter T. Shepard, in 1909. Thanks to Hall's powers of persuasion, Shepard was induced to leave his comfortable job as field superintendent of Security Mutual Life to join Hall in Fort Wayne. The two made a good team. Soon Hall and Shepard had secured agency contracts in several large cities, including Dayton, Cincinnati and Columbus. Although the operations in Pittsburgh and Cleveland did indeed prove to be too expensive and were closed in 1910, others prospered. The gamble on the large cities succeeded. By 1931 the agency committee decided that henceforth Lincoln National would no longer operate agencies in communities with populations under one hundred thousand.

Without general agents to recruit and manage the agents, the company had to bear all the costs for establishing agents, charging advances against commissions and renewals. In order to contain the agents' expenses as much as possible, Hall created the Agency Committee in 1910. Every Saturday the committee would meet and go over each agent's expense claims with a fine- toothed comb, finally placing the field force on a commission basis only. It was Shepard's job to manage the change, and the result was that the company surplus doubled in 1911 and sales increased.

To encourage the agents, Hall and Shepard initiated the first sales contest, called Hall Month, to mark the company president's birthday in May 1911. Later known as President's Month, the contest was also the beginning of the Hall Rose tradition. During this Month each application for insurance was accompanied by a greeting card on which was printed a large rose. The rose had special significance for Hall whose mother had retrieved a rose from the casket of Abraham Lincoln when his funeral

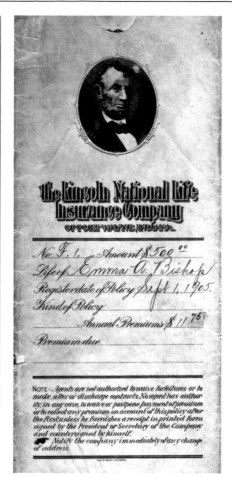

The first life insurance policy issued by Lincoln National.

Max Blitz, one of Lincoln National's first salesmen.

The first Lincoln National sales convention was held at Put-In Bay, Ohio, August 5-7, 1909. Arthur Hall is in the front row, third from the left; on his right is Walter Shepard.

train passed through Indianapolis.

The promotional activity of the home office under Shepard grew quickly. Starting a long tradition, the first sales club to be formed for high production was The Lincoln National Life Club in 1916. Special benefits and bonuses were won by those who made quotas that earned them such titles as "Lincoln Knights," "Emancipators" and "Railsplitters." Monthly contests were held to challenge the agents: February was Lincoln Month, March was Lions and Lambs Month, April was Agents' Month, and so on. At the 1917 agency convention banquet Hall

closed his remarks with a challenge characteristic of his zeal for the company:

"We look to you Emancipators and Railsplitters — to you leaders — to light the pathway of the company's future progress, and I ask you to please rise and drink a toast that I have to offer

'With good hard work
We will write a plenty,
To make a 100 million
By 1920'

Hall's toast worked. The goal of $100 million in annual sales was reached one year ahead of schedule, in 1919. In

1920 sales reached $159 million.

Communication with the agents has always been a priority effort. The sales conventions served the purpose on a personal basis, but as the company grew, more frequent and more encompassing techniques were adopted. The home office began publishing a newsletter for the field force in 1916 called the *Lincoln Life Salesmanship Bulletin*. It was a mimeographed sheet that gave advice on sales to agents, typically stressing melodramatic stories about the "man who procrastinates" to convince reluctant prospects to take out a policy before it was too

"Do It For Shep"

It could be said that Walter I. Shepard, Lincoln National's first agency executive, pulled success out of the jaws of failure. Born in 1873 in Newark, New Jersey, Shepard began his professional career as a dentist, but he suffered serious problems with his eyesight and, as one friend later expressed it, "Shep had to go blind in order to see the light of life insurance." A friend helped Shepard get a position as a special and later general agent for the Provident Savings Life of New York. Soon thereafter his father-in-law, Charles M. Turner, who was president of Security Mutual of New York, recruited Shepard to help him transform Security Mutual from an assessment company to a legal reserve organization. By 1908 he had become the superintendent for all the Security Mutual agencies in the Midwest and he had offices in Chicago and Minneapolis.

When Arthur Hall looked for an agency executive for Lincoln National he was guided to Shepard by Jack Oliver, the editor of the Insurance Indicator, a trade journal published in Detroit. Oliver said of Shepard, "He's the best man in the whole darned business," and Hall wrote to invite Shepard to Fort Wayne to discuss a position developing Lincoln National's agency force. Shepard, upon learning about the small size of Lincoln National, politely declined, telling Hall that it simply was not worth his while to come all the way to Fort Wayne. Characteristically, Hall wired Shepard, who was in New York at the time, suggesting that "if it is too expensive to come to Fort Wayne, then why don't we meet in Pittsburgh?" Shepard, bowing to persistence and a sense of courtesy, went to Pittsburgh. Once in Shepard's presence, Hall turned on his powers of persuasion with his vision of the challenge of developing the agency force. Shepard, much to his own surprise, gave up his comfortable job at Security Mutual and joined Hall in Fort Wayne in June 1909 for half his former salary.

In the two decades that followed, Shepard created the Lincoln National field force and he became an industry model of the agency executive as the volume of sales exploded from $1.2 million in 1910 to nearly $239 million in 1930. "Walter Shepard had that rare quality of leadership," it was said of him later, "coupled with a delightful and inspiring personality that stimulates men to greater efforts and thus to larger success. Pep and enthusiasm ooze from his

Walter Shepard

every pore, but with no ill effects insofar as go his fashion-plate clothes and gray spats. As his friends often said, 'A few minutes with Shep leaves you walking on air with your head in the clouds.' It was his compelling personality in those early days that won for The Lincoln sales men and women of exceptional ability to its agency force."

Shepard himself attributed his success always to the agents. As he told an associate in 1928, "I am certain the agency workers in the field are the most loyal, most faithful and most efficient bunch of men and women any company has every had. In almost twenty years of close association with them I have never asked them to do a thing — whether it meant added money or mere unrequited toil — but that they have come through one hundred percent."

In 1933, when he turned sixty, Shepard left the home office and became the general agent for the company in Los Angeles. In 1945, he retired from Lincoln National and in 1952 died in Los Angeles at age 79.

LIFE INSURANCE PREMIUMS HELP FINANCE THE WAR EFFORT

Hall Month campaign poster used during World War II.

The cover of the first issue of the The Emancipator, April, 1918, the company's publication for the field force.

late. In 1918 *The Emancipator* was first published as a more sophisticated tool for communicating with the sales force. It continues today as the longest continuous publication in the company. The home office experimented with the telephone in 1934 both to communicate news and to kick off a sales campaign. On May 11, a one-day sales effort was promoted in honor of President Hall. Arrangements were made for the field agents to gather in the larger agency offices across the nation. At appointed times early in the day, Hall and agency superintendent Al Dern called each office in a sort of one-way conference call. In the field office the speeches made over the telephone by Hall and Dern were broadcast into the room filled with agents. The technique worked. In that one day Lincoln National agents wrote $2.75 million in new insurance.

Dern had joined Lincoln National after the acquisition of Pioneer Life in 1917. Another talented agency builder, Dern succeeded Shepard in 1933 and emphasized careful recruitment of new agents and continuous training. He brought industry attention to Lincoln National with his chairmanship of the agency section of the American Life Convention and his directorship of the Life Insurance Sales Research Bureau.

When Dern died unexpectedly in 1947, he was succeeded by Cecil F. Cross, one of the most important agency executives in Lincoln National's first half-century. Trained as an actuary at the University of Michigan, he served as an artilleryman in France during World War I. After the war, he worked in two insurance companies before being recruited by A. J. McAndless in 1920. Much admired for the courage with which he endured his failing vision, Cross became manager of agencies at a time when Lincoln National needed to expand its sales force beyond areas traditionally served by the company. This was one of the principal reasons Lincoln National acquired the Reliance Life in 1951. The Reliance agency system extended into regions such as the South where Lincoln National had little exposure. The challenge was to bring the Reliance sales force to the Lincoln National agency system as intact as possible. Along with McAndless and then-Senior Vice President Walter Menge, Cross nurtured the blending of the sales operations.

After the first half-century, the Lincoln National field force numbered more than 2,000 agents and 125 general agents doing business in forty-six states, the District of Columbia, Hawaii, Puerto Rico, the Canal Zone and the Philippines. In 1963 a Management Development Program was established to provide incremental training to those in the field sales force interested in pursuing management roles, and in 1968 the agency organization was restructured. Under the new organization, the country was divided into four territories, each placed under the management of a vice president who maintained an office in the region. This structure continued until 1980 when the four vice presidents were returned to the home office in order to centralize overall direction of the field force and give greater uniformity to management.

Women in the field force played an important role in the growth of sales from the early 1920s when Zura Ziegler Brown burst into the male domain and quickly carved a place for herself as a specialist in sales to women. After the 1940s women entered sales in increasing numbers. They found the flexible hours attractive: They could be home if they need-

"The Lincoln Life Man"

(Song sung by agents to the 1920s, to the tune of "Peggy O'Neill")
If he's boosting for the right, he's a Lincoln Life man;
On the job with all his might, he's a Lincoln Life man;
If he's rendering service always,
If he knows that a smile always pays,
And if he snappily does his best happily,
He's a Lincoln Life man.

ed to watch over school-age children or could sell through community friendship and club networks common in the 1950s and 1960s.

In 1973 a major change occurred for the field force with the formation of Lincoln National Sales Corporation (LNSC). This was an innovative concept originally developed for CEO Thomas Watson by one of his senior vice presidents, John Mascotte. It was believed that careers in insurance sales would be more attractive by changing the structure of the agencies to corporations affiliated with Lincoln National Life and by linking the

agents to the regional offices. In addition, the concept envisioned extensive financing of agency development and marketing efforts. Many of the general agents who had developed their regional agency offices now became CEOs of incorporated Regional Marketing Offices (RMOs) and some members of the agency became officers of the RMO. Agents increasingly were referred to as producers, emphasizing the essential part they played in the company. The role of the agent, however, was itself rapidly changing in the 1970s and 1980s. Formerly, agents had a relatively narrow line of

Manager of Agencies Al Dern makes a telephone broadcast to the Lincoln National agencies on Hall's birthday, May 11, 1934.

"The Devil's Work:" The Extraordinary Sales Career of Os Gilliom

"Never take 'No'" is a well known adage in life insurance sales, and such persistence pays off. Few life agents, however, have experienced the extraordinary challenges and success that Oswin "Os" Gilliom experienced as a salesman for Lincoln National from 1911 to 1952. Gilliom's particular burden was not only to sell as high a volume as possible, but to do so in a community that considered life insurance sinful and the salesman an agent of the devil.

Born in 1886 on a farm in Adams County, Indiana, near the town of Berne, Gilliom learned the virtues of hard work. Young Gilliom attended the local one-room school, but largely was self taught. Determined to be a teacher, Gilliom qualified to teach three terms of grammar school while still a teenager (as a minor, he turned over all his earnings to his father) and then finished a degree program at Tri State College in northern Indiana. By 1910, at age twenty-five, he was a respected teacher and principal of his own one-room school. That same year Walter T. Shepard stopped his horse-drawn buggy at the school and began to talk to Gilliom about being an insurance agent for Lincoln National. Gilliom would have none of it, but after Shepard made his sixth stop at the little school during the year, Gilliom relented and signed a contract.

Although enthused about the idea of selling life insurance, Gilliom well knew the great obstacle he faced in Adams County. The community — as was Gilliom — was Mennonite and these deeply religious folks viewed life insurance as tantamount to gambling on God's creation. One minister taught from the pulpit that "Any man who offers us life insurance is in the same league as the man who leads youth to destruction with strong drink." The life insurance agent in Adams County was, in short, an "agent of the devil." As Gilliom began to make his calls, he shocked the community. It was discussed in school, on the streets and in the Sunday schools. His family members counselled him to stop. His minister counselled him to go back to teaching. His friends begged him to stop. He was told, "Why, we'll kick you out of the church! Go into something that is honorable and respectable. The insurance agent is in the same class with the saloon-keeper, the gambler and the scoffer." He was offered a job at the bank, if he would stop. His wife feared to visit her own mother because of the disapproval she knew she would meet. Still, he peddled his bicycle for miles over the countryside and heard hundreds of "No's." At one point a public debate was held in town hall on the topic, "Is Life Insurance Right or Wrong?" Farmers from miles around came to town to participate, and the verdict at the end was that "life insurance was positively immoral, irreligious and wrong." Gilliom saw all this as so much good advertising and was yet more determined to make his case.

He first managed to sell some policies to his former students who believed in him — and were not Mennonites. His breakthrough came when he began to focus on converting first the hardest prospects by comparing the usefulness and appropriateness of fire insurance, which most farmers carried, to that of a term life policy. Another approach was to sell the hard cases on the sensibility of buying health and accident insurance and from that inroad make the case for a life policy. Either way, once the toughest opponents were won over, the rest soon fell in line. As for the religious scruples against life insurance, Gilliom used the local newspapers to report on policies that have matured or claims paid and as a subtle educational campaign he had published (without his name attached) various selections from sermons or other writings that spoke favorably about life insurance. In time, as Gilliom recalled, "these positive notions were digested and into their system completely."

The results were astonishing. There was a revolution in thinking about life insurance, and by 1920 Gilliom had sold policies to ministers, deacons and professors in the denominational schools. Once the wall was breached the flood of applications soon thrust Gilliom into the number one spot among Lincoln National agents six times. By the early 1920s he maintained the astonishing pace of one application per day for every working day of the year and sold one policy a week for 1,307 consecutive weeks — or just over twenty-five years — until he was stopped by illness, a record still unbroken in life insurance sales in the industry.

As for his place in the community, Gilliom was taken back into his church and soon operated one of the largest Sunday schools in the Mennonite church. He became a national trustee and four-time president of the Christian Endeavor Society. Toward the end of his career, he viewed his success very simply: "Accept the challenge of hard work which life insurance salesmanship offers. Be determined to do that hard job well." Having done so, Gilliom retired from active sales in 1952 because of failing health and died two years later, a loved member of his community.

Cecil Cross

products to offer clients and their services were generally limited to insurance-related advice and maintenance of policies in force. After 1979, however, and the beginning of deregulation of the insurance industry, new products like universal life and new services, such as comprehensive financial planning and employee benefit planning, became a part of the agents' sales portfolio. The enhanced RMO, combined with the expanded home office services, financing and training, resulted in much higher levels of sophistication and responsibility for the agent and the agency.

LNSC and the number of corporate agencies grew dramatically in the late 1970s, but so did the expenses, reducing the profitability of the sales effort. Gradually, the number of corporate agencies was reduced to as few as thirty-six RMOs (two new RMOs were added in 1994), and the entire system was renamed in 1994 as the Lincoln National Financial Group in order to represent more clearly the diversified products and services of the regional sales operations. The RMO in the Fort Wayne region, Lincoln Financial Group of Northern Indiana, illustrates the complexity that has evolved in the field force. Focusing on customer service, the Lincoln Financial Group of Northern Indiana offers the full line of company products and services. It also has evolved a specialty in business and financial planning for which it maintains thirty associates with professional designations and operates satellite offices in four regional communities.

In 1994 the Lincoln National field force is a complex organization. There are about two thousand career agents associated with thirty-eight Regional

Z. Z. Brown: Lincoln's First C.L.U. and The Mistress of Sales

Zura Ziegler Brown, a Fort Wayne woman, became in 1929 the first member of Lincoln National Life's agency force to win the designation of chartered life underwriter (CLU) and for a time was the only female CLU west of Ohio. Born Zura Shumaker in Butler, Indiana, in 1892, she was a voracious reader and expert tennis player. Caught up in the heady days of the years before World War I, it was her firm belief that every young woman intellectually ought to have a career, earn an independent income and see the world. She went to Normal School, earned her teaching certificate and then met and married Charles Brown. Choosing a path natural at the time, she immersed herself in motherhood and abandoned her career. Her husband, a Montana rancher, died five years later, however, and Zura returned to Fort Wayne with her two boys and took a job in the steno pool at the S. F. Bowser Pump Company. She had a deep interest in people and soon took a job at the Wayne Knitting Mill in what was then known as "the welfare department."

She met an old friend from Butler named Roy Oberlin who had become an agent for the Lincoln National and he tried to sell Ms. Brown on the idea of selling insurance. She hesitated at first, but when a report from the local Irene Byron Sanitarium revealed that she had the early stages of tuberculosis she determined to take the Lincoln National job so that she could spend more time out of doors. In February 1924 she became a full-time Lincoln National agent. Typically, she read everything about insurance she could and joined the Fort Wayne Underwriters' Association — insurance became her life apart from her two sons. She quickly became one of the most successful sales persons at the company. She consistently led the female agents and usually was listed among the top ten male agents and exceeded the sales of many of them. Within five years, she became especially well known as an expert on annuities and retirement packages.

Zura Ziegler Brown

Her most notable specialization came to be the unique field of insurance for self-supporting women. Her success in selling policies to women was renowned in the company. In 1928 she sold over $300,000 mostly to women and had two straight years without a single lapsed policy. She attributed her success to knowing the Lincoln National products well and tailoring her presentation of the products to meet the needs of women, whether business women or housewives. "Do you know what I don't do?" she said to a reporter in 1928, "I don't argue. I try to be tactful. I never say, 'Here, you need this insurance and I'm going to see that you take it.' Dominance and domineering will not sell women. Women, contrary to the old adage, know their own minds nowadays."

Long associated with the Fort Wayne agency, she died in 1978 as one of Lincoln National's most successful and revered sales agents.

Wilson Slick, successful LNL agent of the late 1920s.

Thomas Watson (center) and Jack Rawles (right) pose for the opening of the annual sales campaign in 1976.

Marketing Offices. In addition, there are more than twenty thousand brokers who regularly handle sales of Lincoln National products.

LINCOLN NATIONAL REINSURANCE

A core business of Lincoln National Corporation that has its origins in the early years of the company and has been a mainstay of its growth throughout its history is life-health reinsurance. Today, Lincoln National Reinsurance Cos. (LNRC) is one of the world's largest life- health reinsurers and the premier life-health reinsurer in the United States. Its lines of business are individual life, disability income, financial reinsurance and various group markets, such as health maintenance organizations. It is also one of the nation's leading life-health underwriting authorities, a hallmark of the operation that distinguished Lincoln National for the past seven decades.

Lincoln National made its first reinsurance contract in November 1912, and before the year ended fourteen life insurance companies were using Lincoln National's new service. The beginning of Lincoln National reinsurance coincides with the arrival of Franklin B. Mead at the company a year earlier. Mead, who came from Michigan State Life Insurance

Esther D. Pincus and the President's Club

During the middle decades of the century Esther Pincus of the Ben Simon agency in Norfolk, Virginia, was the top saleswoman of Lincoln National Life and before the 1960s the only woman to have qualified for the President's Club.

Born in 1901, her first experience in sales was when she joined the company in 1937. During World War II she sold war bonds as well as insurance and in 1944 she became the first woman ever to qualify for the President's Club. She won the club distinction seven more times, the last when she was 80 years old. During her long career of fifty-five years she was a model for young women seeking a career in sales with her advice to be persistent: "Just call, call, call; somebody is out there who will buy."

Esther's Insurance Motto:
Now I lay me down to snore,
Insured for several thousand more.
If I should die before I wake,
My wife would get her first real break.
But, should I live for twenty years,
My wife and I shed no tears.
We can retire and fish and rest,
Back comes my money with interest.
In our old age we can keep our house
And not live with our daughter's spouse.
So thank God for the great endurance
of the person who sold me life insurance.

Company, had been keenly interested in reinsurance, that is, the mechanism of one insurer's passing on part of the risk of a life insurance policy to another insurance company in exchange for part of the policy's premium. Mead also had an abiding interest in substandard life insurance and clearly saw the connection between the special risks of impaired lives and indemnity reinsurance. When he came to Lincoln National he put the two together as a means of developing a new and aggressive line of business for the company — one that would set it apart from the rest. The reinsurance business was an immediate success and it is safe to say that had it not been for Mead's promotion of reinsurance, Lincoln National might well have disappeared, as did all the other insurance companies that existed in Indiana when Lincoln National was founded.

Although Lincoln National was successful in its early experiences with reinsurance, the dramatic boost to this line of business was a result of good fortune and World War I. The only significant reinsurer in the United States in 1917, the year the nation entered "the Great War," was the Pittsburgh Life and Trust Company. For reasons other than reinsurance, however, Pittsburgh Life and Trust failed in 1917 and its business was assumed by the Metropolitan Life Insurance Company, which was interested primarily in the Pittsburgh real estate portfolio. Simultaneously, the war brought about the isolation of the world's largest reinsurers, Munich Life and Colgone Life. At the end of the war, the two German companies were taken over by the U.S. Property Custodian as part of the war reparations provisions. The net effect of these events was to create a vacuum in the normal course of reinsurance service, and Mead was quick to see the opportunity for Lincoln National.

Anticipating the fate of the German reinsurers, Mead addressed the meeting of the Medical Section of the American Life Convention in 1917 and astonished the participants when he announced that Lincoln National was going to take the place of Pittsburgh Life and the German companies in the reinsurance market. Lincoln National, on the other hand,

had already begun to develop the skills required for evaluating and pricing substandard cases. It also possessed some of the most advanced reinsurance skills and knowledge. When Lincoln National stepped forward to offer to accept from small insurers more applications for standard and impaired risks, the response was positive. Smaller insurers began to turn to Lincoln National for assistance and guidance and the company came to call itself the "life insurance company's life insurance company."

In 1919 A.J. McAndless was recruited by Mead to join Lincoln National and take over the reinsurance operations. It was McAndless who made Mead's vision for Lincoln National reinsurance a reality. Throughout the 1920s McAndless travelled tirelessly from one life insurance company to the next to develop reinsurance contracts. By its nature a business built on personal relationships founded very largely on trust between the ceding company and the reinsurer, the reinsurance services offered by Lincoln National owed their spectacular growth to the personality, energy and skill of "Mac." He was deeply trusted to give the best advice, offer a reasonable price and keep the confidence of his clients. This became the hallmark for how Lincoln National did business, which McAndless passed on to his successor, Leland "Pete" Kalmbach, who handled reinsurance in much the same way throughout the 1930s and into the 1940s.

One important innovation developed by Lincoln National during the 1930s was modified co-insurance. Developed under the direction of Pete Kalmbach, the concept allowed the ceding company to keep all of its assets while a portion of the risk was still transferred to the reinsurer. This was a provision especially attractive to the larger life insurance companies, and in 1937, thanks to Kalmbach, Lincoln National landed its first reinsurance contract with one of the large eastern mutuals. This facet of the business grew rapidly, and by 1940 Lincoln National had its own underwriters working in the home offices of several of the largest companies.

As the business expanded, Lincoln National's skills in underwriting grew also. In 1923 Lincoln National was far

Leland "Pete" Kalmbach

ahead of the industry in its ability to accept applications; while the industry norm was to reject one of every nine applications, Lincoln National rejected only one out of every forty-seven applications. Further, Best's noted the high quality of Lincoln National's underwriting in 1923 when it commented on the company's exceptional mortality experience as being "remarkably low." Lincoln National also continued to develop its reputation for service to other life insurers, and by the mid-1920s there were an additional sixty-six companies writing substandard business as a result of visiting and studying the practices of Lincoln National.

Lincoln National entered the international markets in reinsurance in 1936 when a New York insurance broker named Robert Ahrens assisted the company in creating a reinsurance treaty with a Mexican life insurance company. Soon, nine small Central and South American life insurance companies were under Lincoln National reinsurance contracts. The Hispanic connections were continued in the late 1940s by Victor d'Unger, an employee of Lincoln National's home office. By 1955 the reinsurance contracts in Central and South America had grown to thirty-two and had extended its international services to individual lives in thirty-five countries.

Most notably, however, in 1955,

Second Vice President Melvin McFall greets visitors to Lincoln National Reinsurance Cos., 1994.

when Lincoln National celebrated its fiftieth anniversary, Mead's vision was realized as the company became the largest life reinsurer in the United States. At the same time, Lincoln National reinsurance served more than 450 American companies and maintained regional reinsurance offices in Dallas, San Francisco and Atlanta. In 1958, *The Reinsurance Reporter* made its debut. It quickly established itself as a premier reinsurance journal focusing on topics of concern to its clients. Of the magazine, then-President Walter Menge wrote in the initial issue, "... we hope to affirm the ideal that has always animated our reinsurance activities — service above and beyond the normal requirements of our business." Today, *The Reinsurance Reporter* continues to offer commentary and insight into insurance and actuarial issues. This theme of service through information and knowledge has been carried to other new publications aimed at Reinsurance clients: *Medical Resource* (since 1989), *Group Resource* (since 1987) and *LNRM Network* (since 1991).

The traditional principal reinsurance business in Lincoln National was individual life and health insurance, although at the end of the 1970s such products as disability income, group life and health and financial reinsurance also were sold. In 1978, however, the concept of modified co-insurance grew out of financial reinsurance as a means of gaining federal income tax advantage for mutual life insurance

companies. Nationally, insurance companies enjoyed considerable tax advantages using the loopholes provided by Modified Co-Insurance, but in 1980 the Reagan administration directed the closure of the tax advantages and this form of transaction disappeared. In its wake, however, an entirely new world of non-conventional reinsurance transactions began.

The 1980s proved to be a decade that marked the beginning of dramatic changes for reinsurance in the industry and particularly for Lincoln National. Thus, the company began to pursue lasting growth through new opportunities in non-traditional lines of business, such as "financial reinsurance," which focused on innovative capital solutions for clients. The company also pioneered in the area of annuity reinsurance, reflecting the dramatic growth of annuities beginning at the end of the decade. The greatest breakthrough in reinsurance marketing, however, began in the mid-1980s with the extension of reinsurance services to non-traditional risk-takers, such as employers who self insure, health maintenance organizations, preferred provider organizations, third party administrators and physician-hospital organizations. As in the era when Lincoln National entered the reinsurance field by specializing in helping small companies, which could not afford expensive actuarial and underwriting departments, Group Markets Reinsurance in the 1980s extended its reinsurance service to the non-traditional risk-takers and

assumed the role of actuarial, underwriting, research and medical analysis departments for many different clients.

The experience of the early 1990s was not entirely one of growth and innovation. During these years the industry also witnessed serious difficulties in the area of disability income and Lincoln National Reinsurance was one of the market leaders in this line of business. The difficulties stemmed from the business written during the 1980s when competition for upper economic customers was intense. During these years many insurers misjudged the risks and developed products fraught with underwriting dangers. For example, insurers allowed more liberal definitions of disability and broader definitions of income. They sold policies with cost-of-living adjustments benefits and higher maximums, and, most dangerous of all, lengthened the exposure periods first to age sixty-five, then to seventy and, finally, to the lifetime of the assured. To make matters worse, many policies were made non-cancelable, making price corrections impossible.

Lincoln Life's disability income experience deteriorated early in the 1990s, as it did for other life insurance companies. In 1991 it lost $1.6 million, then $19.6 million in 1992, showed a profit of $3.5 million in 1993, but lost $14.9 million in 1994. The experience in reinsurance mirrored that of LNL and was compounded by the industry-wide nature of the problem. Thus, in 1993 Lincoln National Reinsurance took a loss of $54 million. In both the life insurance company and Lincoln National Reinsurance strict measures were undertaken to reduce the impact of the problem and prevent future losses, such as more restrictive underwriting, tightening definitions and curtailing benefit periods. Still, the difficulties sown in this line of business in the 1980s will haunt the company for many years to come.

While Lincoln National was one of the first to diversify its reinsurance business, the company faced greatly intensified competition in all lines of business. Conditions associated with the stiff pricing competition by both direct companies and other reinsurers by the mid-1980s led Lincoln National

Lincoln National reinsurance operations, ca. 1930.

to realize it had placed too much reliance on its traditional individual life and health reinsurance products. As explained by Gabriel Shaheen, president of Lincoln National Reinsurance who succeeded Tom West in 1994, it was no longer necessary to struggle to hold the largest market share. Lincoln National Reinsurance concentrated, instead, on its emerging diversified markets and the technologies which gave the company the competitive edge. To large extent, however, relative ratings often devolved into a war of semantics of little significance to clients. Rather, those seeking the services of a reinsurer looked for service, price and confidence. To maintain a leading position in the field by these standards, Lincoln National focused on developing its skills in underwriting, which had been the traditional strengths of the company since the days of Mead.

The foundation of underwriting has been quality research and development operations under the office of the chief medical director, who since 1995 has been Dr. Donald Chambers. Concentrating its research strength on exceptionally broad-based, long-term studies of a wide variety of experiences, Lincoln National researchers have established a nationally significant record of developing data on most serious diseases and disabilities, particularly cardiovascular ailments, dia-

Paul Turner and Margarita Davis, specialists in international reinsurance, 1990s.

betes, blindness, AIDS and cancer. The dramatic breakthrough in underwriting services that gave Lincoln National technological leadership in expert systems, however, was made in 1984 by Dr. Art DeTore, a vice president in risk management, Russ Suever, director of technological services, and their staff with the creation of an automated life underwriting system known as LUS. More than a system, LUS is also a knowledge process that managed to go beyond mere calculations to capture the art of underwriting. So unique was this process that it was patented in December 1990, marking the first time in the insurance industry that underwriting software was patented rather than simply copyrighted. By thus enabling a higher number of cases to be underwritten electronically through the expert systems, LUS is a direct descendant of Mead's first efforts to accomplish the same results with "lay underwriters" in 1917. In order to concentrate more effectively on the technological opportunities of what has come to be called "knowledge-based systems," the Lincoln National Risk Management Company was formed in 1988. Constantly evolving and still in keeping with Mead's seminal ideas on efficient processing, LUS was joined in 1993 by an automated administrative system called Datalliance. This unique electronic data exchange system gathers and processes the various requirements identified by LUS, such as attending physician statements and medical information bureau reports, thereby dramatically speeding up the process from application to issuance of a policy.

FRAMEWORK FOR THE FUTURE

In the early 1990s Lincoln National embarked on a major process of transformation of the corporation. It had become clear by the late-1980s that the approach to the way the corporation functioned, which had been based on the SBU concept initiated a decade earlier, had to be re-evaluated. This was especially true for some of the SBUs that were part of Lincoln National Life, which had become too insular in the way they functioned. Businesses such as annuities, individ-

ual life and pensions operated independently, often causing confusion in the minds of customers about the identity and strength of the company. Effective marketing, too, was increasingly difficult for these product lines. Lastly, the economic and regulatory environment changed for each area, increasing the risks to which the businesses were exposed. In addition, the role of the holding company was obscure, since it was difficult to discern distinctions between it and the life insurance company. The early 1990s also witnessed major changes in the financial services industry that offered new opportunities for the corporation.

Rolland and the strategic planning committees developed Project Compass as the foundation for the strategies that would carry the company into the twenty-first century. In the broadest sense, Project Compass identified that LNC must first of all be of value to its shareholders and in order to do this, it must be transformed through a process that narrowed the focus of the corporation to those areas in which it excelled. The goal was to become a "benchmark" company in each of its lines of business; if it could not, the company should not be in that line of business.

To address issues in detail, Rolland formed a "Compass Task Force" in the summer of 1991. It was led by Senior Vice President Jeff Nick and, reminiscent of Rolland's own strategic planning committee of the mid-1970s, it was composed of seven other senior officers who largely represented the next generation of leadership. This group was charged to flesh out the new directions, particularly with respect to clarifying the relationship between the parent company and the subsidiaries. Special attention was given to eliminating the "fuzziness" between LNC, the holding company, and LNL, the insurance company, which had become, in Rolland's words, "a source of confusion to our customers, our producers, our investors, the media and even our own employees."

Among the findings that arose from Project Compass studies was the determination that each line of business would have to perform in keeping with three basic imperatives that were defined for the entire corporation: The businesses would have to be top-tier performers, create substantial value and control risk. Further, in order to give greater clarity to corporate structure, the holding company for the first time was clearly separated from the Fort Wayne-based companies and given a corporation-wide identity, ending the perception that the corporate officers, in reality, were simply the executives of Lincoln Life. In 1994 the renovation of a major Fort Wayne building was completed and the corporate headquarters were relocated to Renaissance Square, which occupied the entire block opposite the first Lincoln National-owned office, the Elektron Building, leaving the life insurance company as the sole occupant of the Harrison Street building complex. By the same reasoning, reinsurance was consolidated in its own separate facility, which had been known as Lincoln West and now was known as One Reinsurance Place.

The corporation opened the 1990s with the process of paring down its lines of business to those which met the strategic vision. It divested its stake in Western Security Life in 1991. The decision to exit the managed care and large— case group business was made in 1991 and was completed in 1992. In 1993 K & K Insurance, which specialized in sports and entertainment coverage, was sold. Additional divestitures occurred in 1993 when LNC completed the sale of Security Connecticut and partially sold Employers Health (now known as Emphesys Financial Group, Inc.). An additional 9.2 million shares of common stock were issued in 1994. These actions gave Lincoln National its strongest capital position ever and allowed the company to finance internal growth. In addition, the stage was set to improve customer service and to augment core areas of business through acquisitions, especially in the United Kingdom and in investment management. Thus, in mid-1993 Lincoln National made its first strategic acquisition in six years with the purchase of Citibank Life in Great Britain to be consolidated with Cannon to form Lincoln National (UK). Also, in late 1994, the company made a major strategic move when it announced the agreement to purchase Delaware Management Holdings, Inc.

of Philadelphia, as a means of dramatically strengthening the investment management sector of the corporation. The largest acquisition in the company's history, the purchase of Delaware Management was completed in April 1995 and established a new core business for Lincoln National: Investment management, to add to those of life insurance and annuities, property-casualty insurance and life- health reinsurance. This new core business, which in 1995 was called the Lincoln National Investments Cos., included Lincoln Investment Management (formerly LNIMC), Delaware Management Holdings and the investment management firms of Lynch &

Mayer and Vantage Global Advisors.

As for Lincoln Life, the original company founded in 1905 and the spiritual heart of the corporation, Project Compass pointed toward a process of transformation. Jon Boscia, formerly head of LNIMC, was elected president of the life insurance company in mid-1994. It was his charge to strengthen the life company through a thorough overhaul, beginning with a new marketing and design system and a national advertising program. The formula seemed simple: re-create the enthusiasm for the business and its potential for growth shown nine decades ago by its first chief executive officer, Arthur Hall.

Jon Boscia, right, president of Lincoln Life, poses with Brian Lamb, CEO of C-Span, in Washington February 1995 after Lamb was presented the Spirit of Lincoln Award by Lincoln Life and The Lincoln Museum for his television network's reporting of governmental affairs.

COMMUTATION COLUMNS 2 1/2%
Commissioners 1958 Standard Ordinary Mortality Table

Age	D_x	N_x	C_x	M_x
0	10,000,000.0000	324,850,104.9680	69,073.1710	2,076,826.7172
1	9,687,024.4290	314,850,104.9680	16,632.9566	2,007,753.5462
2	9,434,122.5838	305,163,080.5390	13,990.2787	1,991,120.5896
3	9,190,031.7084	295,728,957.9552	13,090.0808	1,977,130.3109
4	8,952,794.4741	286,538,926.2468	12,228.1241	1,964,040.2301
5	8,722,205.5791	277,586,131.7727	11,487.5189	1,951,812.1060
6	8,497,981.3556	268,863,926.1936	10,778.2903	1,940,324.5871
7	8,279,935.2370	260,365,944.8380	10,178.0782	1,929,546.2968
8	8,067,807.4636	252,086,009.6010	9,681.6066	1,919,368.2186
9	7,861,350.0557	244,018,202.1374	9,279.8558	1,909,686.612
10	7,660,329.9546	236,156,852.0817	9,042.8478	1,900,406.756
11	7,464,449.7860	228,496,522.1271	8,957.6178	1,891,363.908
12	7,273,432.4866	221,032,072.3411	8,940.8062	1,882,406.29
13	7,087,090.8833	213,758,639.8545	9,126.8500	1,873,465.48
14	6,905,108.1581	206,671,548.9712	9,364.0939	1,864,338.63
15	6,727,326.7826	199,766,440.8131	9,582.3146	1,854,974.5
16	6,553,663.2627	193,039,114.0305	9,846.7536	1,845,392.2
17	6,383,971.1254	186,485,450.7678	10,090.0279	1,835,545.4
18	6,218,174.4633	180,101,479.6424	10,252.3993	1,825,455.4
19	6,056,259.3006	173,883,305.1791	10,280.6243	1,815,203.0
20	5,898,264.9735	167,827,045.8785	10,300.1828	1,804,922.
21	5,744,104.7377	161,928,780.9050	10,255.1657	1,794,622.
22	5,593,749.4258	156,184,676.1673	10,150.6810	1,784,367.
23	5,447,165.8414	150,590,926.7415	10,044.0865	1,774,216.
24	5,304,263.9929	145,143,760.9001	9,883.7932	1,764,172.
25	5,165,007.9517	139,839,496.9072	9,725.3439	1,754,288.
26	5,029,306.7854	134,674,488.9555	9,617.0037	1,744,56?
27	4,897,023.7928	129,645,182.1701	9,507.1611	1,734,94
28	4,768,076.9758	124,748,158.3773	9,442.8900	1,725,43
29	4,642,339.5370	119,980,081.4015	9,420.4356	1,715,99
30	4,519,691.3751	115,337,741.8645	9,392.0634	1,706,5
31	4,400,062.8465	110,818,050.4894	9,401.2183	1,697,1
32	4,283,343.0569	106,417,987.6429	9,402.5686	1,687,7
33	4,169,468.7479	102,134,644.5860	9,437.1317	1,678,3
34	4,058,337.1968	97,965,175.8381	9,502.3390	1,668,9
		93,906,838.6413	9,672.2130	1,659,
		...5557	9,900.3401	1,649,
				1,639

CHAPTER III
LINCOLN NATIONAL AND THE INSURANCE INDUSTRY

Lincoln National has been a pioneer since its earliest years in many areas of the insurance industry and frequently has been a leader in resolving some of its thorniest problems. Early in the company's life, Lincoln National was fortunate in attracting one of the most creative insurance professionals of the early twentieth century, Franklin B. Mead, who, it appears, had been seeking a place where he could put into practice a number of ideas about insurance products and practices. His fit with Lincoln National and its chief executive officer, Arthur Hall, was a good one. The company soon came to be known for its reinsurance services — especially to smaller companies — and its ability to write profitably substandard policies, disability benefits and juvenile insurance. The company also pioneered lay underwriting and office management techniques, creating the Life Office Management Association (LOMA) which has served the industry since 1924.

Chief among the issues facing the insurance industry since the 1940s have been those that have centered on taxation, and Lincoln National has developed a reputation since the days of the "McAndless Rule" and the "Menge Formula" for taking a leadership role in resolving tax related issues. So, too, has Lincoln National exercised leadership when the industry has had to resolve internal difficulties, as in the disputes between stock and mutual companies over taxation concerns, matters of integrity or the solvency crisis of the late 1980s.

Lincoln National has also been in the forefront of a number of medical issues that have a serious impact on the industry and on public health, from coronary disease and diabetes to blindness and AIDS. The management through unique information management programs of knowledge derived from underwriting research has not only served Lincoln National well, it has allowed Lincoln to serve others in the industry also, particularly through the reinsurance business.

SUBSTANDARD RISKS

Lincoln National was not the first U.S. life insurance company to write substandard, or impaired, risk policies. It was, however, the company which showed the industry how to do the business successfully. Very early in its life Lincoln National demonstrated what became one of its principal strengths — the ability to identify and manage insurable risks.

It was common for life insurance

Franklin B. Mead.

companies at the turn-of-the-century to refuse to issue policies to a person who was rated less than 100 percent physically fit. Even the slightest impairment, including those associated with many types of occupations, were sufficient to deny a policy to an applicant. The earliest insurance company to issue policies on a person's life that did not meet the criteria for standard rates, that is a substandard risk, was the Travelers Insurance Company, which wrote a few impaired risk policies on a lien plan before 1900. Three other eastern companies had also written substandard policies on a limited basis before 1910. Indeed, Lincoln National's first medical director, Dr. Calvin H. English, who did all the underwriting at the time, issued a policy in 1909 on a railroad engineer, a member of what was then considered to be a hazardous profession. This was an unusual case, however, and based entirely on the subjective judgment of Dr. English.

When Mead joined Lincoln National as actuary in 1911, the issue of substandard risks was addressed quickly and placed on a statistical basis. Mead had had a long-standing

The actuarial department, 1920s.

interest in this line of business. To him it seemed logical to develop special rates for impaired risks in the same way fire insurance companies had special rates for different classes of buildings. Lincoln National, he reasoned, could do the same in the life insurance business. Mead had spent a number of years before coming to Lincoln National developing mortality tables from the records of his employer, the Maccabees, a fraternal association in Detroit that issued policies without concern for occupation or health. Consequently, Mead had records that showed a variety of mortality experiences and allowed him to develop a rate structure for the substandard cases based on real data. At Lincoln National he was able to put his tables to work since Lincoln National's chief executive officer, Arthur Hall, was unfettered by the common wisdom about the undesirability of substandard risks held among most insurance professionals.

Under Mead's program, Lincoln

Franklin B. Mead, the Other Founder of Lincoln National

Iriscrest was the name Mead gave his home in honor of his prized gardens.

The insurance professional who was most important in the survival of Lincoln National in its first decades, the man who led it into a leadership position in the industry, was Franklin B. Mead. Arthur Hall, who had the wisdom to hire Mead, described him in 1921 as "The Lincoln Life's 'Production Engineer.' He deserves that title," Hall continued, "because actuarial work with him begins where the figures leave off, which is the point at which actuarial work should begin in Mr. Mead's opinion."

Born in Greenfield, Ohio, in 1875, Mead entered the University of Cincinnati at age nineteen and studied English, classical literature and mathematics, but he was not an outstanding student. In 1897 he took a job as a brokerage salesman with the Security Trust and Life Insurance Company of Philadelphia, which wrote primarily substandard life insurance. Intrigued with insurance, he entered the University of Michigan to study more math in 1904 and was graduated with a bachelor of arts degree in 1906. Two years later, he went to work in Detroit for the Michigan State Life Insurance Company.

During his years at Michigan State Life, Mead became increasingly involved in industry conferences and presented a number of papers which drew the attention of his peers. One, "The Measure of Risk and Liability under the Total and Permanent Disability Benefits of Life Insurance Policies," was especially well received at the 1909 meeting of the American Life Convention because there was so little available information on the subject. It was probably at this or a similar meeting that Hall first met Mead. What is certain is that whenever the two met, Hall was deeply impressed and in 1911 offered him a place at Lincoln National.

If Hall was the patriarch and architect of the company, Mead was its intellect. While Hall gave the company its spirit, Mead brought to the Lincoln National the expertise and creativity of an insurance professional. Mead's personality was something of a paradox. He was precise and exacting and he was devoted to efficiency, yet he was also a daring thinker willing to take chances. He viewed statistics as a vehicle by which creative new approaches to fundamental insurance issues could be made. Like Hall, the natural leader who needed the right circumstances to demonstrate his abilities, Mead was a "natural actuary" who also needed the right atmosphere to allow him to flourish.

As Hall later explained, Mead's fertile mind went beyond statistics to imagine how insurance might work better and more profitably. Mead laid the foundations for Lincoln National's spectacular success, and probably its very survival, with an aggressive entry into the reinsurance market. His work on substandard risks became the benchmark for the industry and at Lincoln National set a standard for underwriting skills that continue to define the company. Mead was devoted to efficiency and constantly sought ways to manage work better. In order to cope with the overall dramatic increase in business in the 1910s and early 1920s Mead hired Frank L. Rowland, an efficiency expert to examine and overhaul office procedures to make the most of staff, space and equipment. The Life Office Management Association, or LOMA, originated with these efficiency activities.

Mead was also a connoisseur. He had broad interests that included collecting Chinese ceramics, etchings and rare books. He was an amateur photographer and enjoyed helping to mount exhibits at the Fort Wayne Art School. He held memberships in the Indiana Federation of the Arts, the Hoosier Art Salon, the Indiana Historical Society and the Royal Horticultural Society of England. This last reflects his deepest interest beyond work: his iris gardens. Mead's home on the corner of Parnell and State streets in Fort Wayne was called "Iriscrest," in honor of the flower he cherished most. Eventually the place had four acres of flowers and other landscaping. His iris collections were nationally recognized for their excellence and his articles on irises and gardening in general regularly appeared in *House and Garden* and *Country Life*. When he died the flowers were bequeathed to the City of Fort Wayne and became the foundation for the elaborate gardens of Foster Park on the city's south side.

For all his refined tastes, Mead was also remembered as a man who greatly enjoyed parties, good shows, good jokes and good food. He was a vigorous dancer, but an appallingly poor driver. Sitting perfectly erect on the front part of the driver's seat, Mead would barrel into the basement parking area of the Harrison Street building and invariably could not bring his car to a stop without hitting a wall.

When he died on November 29, 1933, at age fifty-eight, he was serving as president of the American Institute of Actuaries. The American Life Convention took special note of his passing, recognizing the many contributions he had made to the profession.

National issued its first properly rated substandard policy on April 6, 1912, to Daniel Thompson, who was a railroad and sawmill worker. According to Mead's tables, Thompson was rated to age forty-nine, though his insurable age was thirty-nine. It was a good risk. Thompson, as it turned out, lived to the policy's maturity and in 1932 used the proceeds to purchase a single premium life annuity from Lincoln National. Thereafter, he purchased two more Lincoln National policies before he died in his early nineties.

But in 1912 the company — and Mead personally — were hit almost immediately with a torrent of criticism from the industry. The objection was raised that such a small company should not assume such risks, especially since, they believed, it was impossible to estimate accurately the life expectancies of substandard cases. Even the American Life Convention levelled official criticism at the company in 1913 and one acquaintance of an agent expressed his "sorrow for the management of the little Fort Wayne organization." The agents felt otherwise, however, and increasingly brought their impaired business to Lincoln National. The mortality experience remained low and Lincoln National profited. Characteristically, Hall found a sales motto that fit perfectly: "Protection for the Greatest Possible Number at the Lowest Possible Cost."

In the early 1920s A. J. McAndless, who was working for Mead selling reinsurance services for Lincoln National, was able to use the company's rapidly growing expertise in the field to gain access to the reinsurance business of numerous companies. Many of the large insurance companies reinsured with European firms for their excess business. When McAndless was rebuffed in his bid for their business, his sales approach then turned to substandard reinsurance.

"Why not," he asked, "go ahead and keep your present reinsurance arrangements for your large cases, but let us provide you with substandard insurance service?" The idea made sense, and Lincoln National began to develop its role as a primary indemnity reinsurer.

LAY UNDERWRITING

Lincoln National was a pioneer in the area of lay underwriting, that is underwriting by individuals not trained as physicians. The growth in Lincoln National's business between 1912, when the company started writing substandard life policies, and 1920 was impressive. Between 1912 and 1920 business in force rose from $2.1 million to $50 million. Business doubled in 1915, 1916 and 1919. Gratifying as the degree of growth was, it also put a terrific burden on the simple underwriting process then used by the company. Before 1912 all the underwriting decisions were made by Lincoln National's medical director, Dr. English, with oversight after 1912 by a special underwriting committee. Even the help of a second physician, Dr. Bryan Barlow, and Mead, the company's actuary, did not alleviate the situation.

Matters reached a crisis in 1917 when volume doubled for the second straight year and the office manpower was reduced by enlistments in the military. Mead decided to cull all the applications that clearly were unimpaired and give them to Jean Pyle, one of the senior clerks, for her review. If she found nothing unusual, the applications could be forwarded to the Issue Department, which would prepare the policies. She was soon joined in these underwriting activities by Florence Warner and Clare McDarby, who worked under the supervision of Pyle. Henceforth, only those applications which were questionable in

Clyde Cover, a prominent attorney for the company during the 1950s.

some way were handled by the company medical staff or Mead himself. After the war, additional men and women joined the ranks of the underwriting staff, creating by 1919 an Underwriting Department that came under the direction of A.J. McAndless.

For nearly a decade thereafter, Mead held seminars at Lincoln National in lay underwriting for personnel in other companies, particularly for smaller Midwestern companies, and McAndless integrated these services with his sales efforts in behalf of Lincoln National's reinsurance business.

LIFE OFFICE MANAGEMENT ASSOCIATION (LOMA)

The problem of managing life insurance offices more efficiently had been a topic of discussion in the industry

The Chief Medical Directors of Lincoln National

Dr. Calvin A. English
Dr. Walter E. Thornton
Dr. William "Bud" H. Scoins
Dr. Harry A. Cochran Jr.
Dr. John W. Barch
Dr. Donald C. Chambers

The underwriting department, 1920s.

since at least 1921. In that year, Charles G. Taylor, the president of the American Life Convention, recommended that a section be formed in the organization to address office management issues. His successor, H.R. Cunningham, agreed with the idea and named Taylor to be the chairman of a committee to explore establishing an office management section. Arthur Hall, who had been a part of the original discussions, was not invited to join. After the committee had been formed for about a year and no report had been made, Hall asked the ALC to call for a report. Another year went by and Hall again called for a report, but there was none.

In the absence of any movement at the ALC for creating a section on office management, Hall and Mead took matters into their own hands. In the summer of 1924 the two men sent letters to all the ALC members inviting them to come to Fort Wayne to form an association of office management. The secretary and counsel of the ALC, Thomas W. Blackburn, was angered and sent a letter to the members saying that there were enough life insurance associations in existence already and that "the effort to organize another general life insurance association should be nipped in the bud and absolutely discredited." He believed that the ALC and the Association of Life Insurance Presidents were sufficient. Blackburn was supported in this by several of the large eastern companies, and the chairman of the Association of Life Insurance Presidents asked Hall and Mead to call

off their planned September meeting. Hall was incensed and sent another letter to the ALC members explaining his view of the situation and again inviting the companies to send representatives to Fort Wayne.

Hall and Mead were gratified on September 25 when 140 representatives from eighty-eight companies came to Lincoln National and organized the Life Office Management Association. Mead was chosen to be president and Lincoln National's efficiency expert, Frank L. Rowland, was elected secretary. On the closing day of the meeting Hall hosted a banquet for all the guests at the Fort Wayne Country Club. When he heard the news, the ALC's Blackburn resigned himself to the accomplished fact and wished the organization well. Mead remained a director for several years afterward and Rowland became the organization's first executive director and later its president. The first examination was given in Fort Wayne in 1932 and LOMA created the Life Management Institute the next year, establishing a new professional designation as Fellow, the Life Management Institute, or FLMI. From 1924 to 1934 LOMA operated in Fort Wayne, but in 1934 the organization was moved to New York City. By 1993, more than 43,000 insurance workers had achieved the FLMI designation.

JUVENILE INSURANCE

Lincoln National was a pioneer in issuing large amounts of life insurance

on the lives of children aged one day to fourteen years. The first juvenile life policies were apparently issued early in the century by the Old Colony Life of Chicago and the Public Savings Life of Indianapolis. According to A.J. McAndless, Lincoln National became active in the relatively rare business of juvenile insurance in 1924 when Dr. Charles Peters, formerly the medical director of the Public Savings Life, came to work at Lincoln National. The company hired Dr. Peters specifically to attend a ALC sectional meeting to discuss this line of business and he remained with Lincoln National to develop the product.

MEDICAL ISSUES

Lincoln National has long been respected as a leader in a variety of medical issues that affect the life and health insurance industry. This reputation is due in large part to the company's outstanding medical directors who began their work in the 1920s and the professional staff that has augmented their work since the 1940s. The company's reputation, however, also owes a great deal to the reinsurance business. Because reinsurance operations put Lincoln National medical researchers in contact with an immensely broad spectrum of morbidity and mortality experiences over long periods of time — generally far in excess of the studies conducted outside the industry — the medical department has been able to create highly refined risk classifications based on actual insured lives, allowing stronger underwriting and competitive product development. On the strength of these skills, Lincoln National has often emerged as the industry leader in confronting controversial public health and civil rights issues.

Lincoln National began to make its mark on medical issues before it was twenty years old. Dr. Calvin English, the company's first medical director, became intrigued with the accumulation of data connected to mortality. What made Dr. English's interests different in the insurance industry was his departure from the usual medical underwriting concerns that centered on infectious diseases, such as tuberculosis and pneumonia. Rather, Dr.

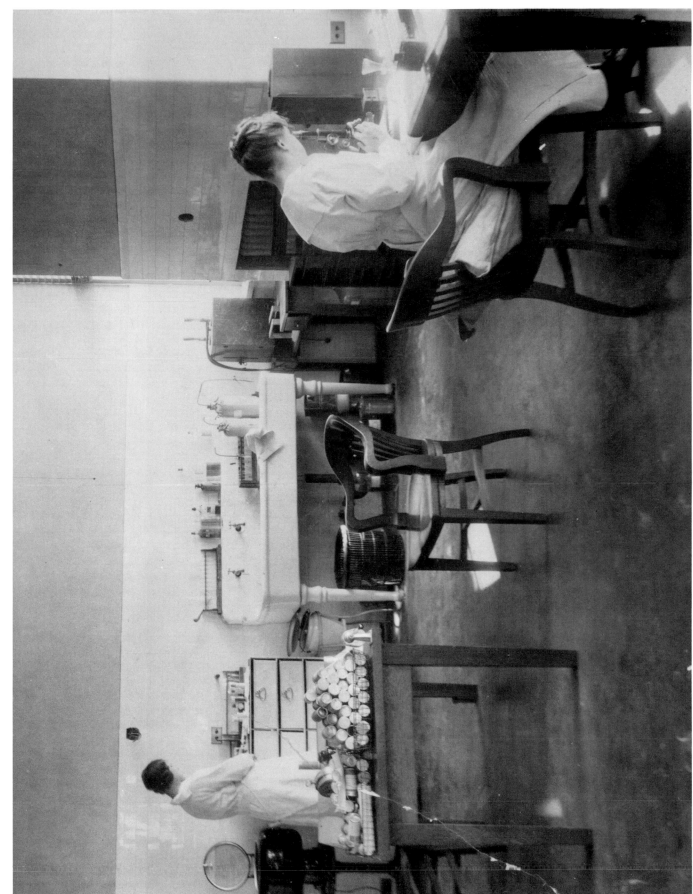

Lincoln National's medical laboratory, ca. 1925.

Dr. Calvin English.

English focused on chronic illnesses, such as heart disease and cancer. In a home-grown way in about 1915 he began to collect information from different sources and saw patterns emerge about the occurrence of cancer. Then, at the Medical Section meeting of the American Life Convention in 1922, Dr. English became the first person in the insurance industry to draw attention to cancer as a disease that was rapidly on the increase.

Three years later, Dr. English was again the first in the industry to make a similar observation about coronary disease. More than two decades later, Lincoln National's medical department launched a long-term study on heart disease — the Chest Pain Mortality Study — that continues today. In this study, which began in 1947, researchers track the mortality experiences of policyholders from data not only of Lincoln National Life, but also of the extensive reinsurance connections maintained by the company. Consequently, the company has been a leader for nearly five decades in its ability to underwrite lives with cardiac problems. Lincoln National developed the industry's first system of coronary risk analysis. The risk profiles were so well developed that underwriters not only could extend competitive coverage to a wider range of substandard risks, but also could move some of the old standard lives to superstandard categories called Preferred Plus.

In a similar project, Lincoln National's Dr. Harry Cochran began a study of diabetes in 1946, again using extensive insurance records in addition to the data produced by the medical profession. On the basis of the diabetes studies, Lincoln National was the first insurance company to offer coverage to individuals with the disease and still leads the industry in its ability to underwrite diabetic lives. In addition, later research based on a large number of policyholders' experiences over a long period of time revealed some unique aspects of tolbutamide, one of the oral drugs commonly used to treat diabetes, which contradicted clinical studies that suggested the drug was toxic. Based on the clinical studies, physicians stopped using the effective drug, but the information shared by the insurance researchers eventually were used to alter the physicians' protocol for the drug, thereby returning to use by diabetic patients a safe and beneficial treatment.

Similarly, an important study of cholesterol mortality was undertaken between 1959 and 1966 in collaboration with the University of Minnesota. Working with Professor Henry Blackburn, a noted specialist in cardio-vascular medicine, and Ancel Keys, a dietary specialist who had invented the famous "K-rations," Lincoln National researchers, led by the director of underwriting research, Jess Mast, and medical director Dr. Jack Barch, not only confirmed that individuals with high cholesterol experienced high mortality due to cardio-vascular disease, but also were surprised to learn that people with low cholesterol experienced high mortality due to an increase in cancer. Although the company was able to use the low-cholesterol information in its underwriting as a new indicator of cancer risk, the evidence from the studies was not accepted by the medical profession for many years and then only after numerous additional clinical studies were carried out.

Some medical issues have been highly politicized and charged with emotion. In the early 1970s, for example, growing concern for the welfare of physically handicapped individuals led to measures being enacted in some states prohibiting, among other things, insurance companies from requiring information about blindness on life policy applications. At times during the mid-1970s this became a heated issue between the industry and the National Institute for the Blind, which feared discrimination against its constituents. Lincoln National was able, however, to play a leading role in bringing about changes in state legislation and regulations by convincing legislators and insurance commissioners that considerations about blindness were legitimate underwriting concerns and that the industry could develop risk classification practices that favored the blind.

The most highly charged issue for life and health insurance companies, however, has been the AIDS epidemic. Again, Lincoln National has been the industry leader in the issue. Acquired Immunity Deficiency Syndrome (AIDS) was first recognized in the United States in June 1981, but public awareness of the crisis was slow to develop. The first conversations about AIDS at Lincoln National began in 1983, well before most people had heard of the disease. In early 1985 Dr. Donald Chambers, Lincoln National's chief medical director, took the issue to the American Council of Life Insurance (ACLI) and became the first person to warn the industry of the enormity of the emerging epidemic. Dr. Chambers continued to play a leading role in speaking to the insurance industry's concerns about AIDS late in 1985 when he testified before several state legislatures and the House subcommittee on Health and the Environment chaired by Congressman Henry Waxman of California. In the course of the next several years, Lincoln National's medical staff led scores of industry seminars, made numerous speeches, wrote many articles in professional and trade publications and became extensively involved in the media's coverage of the disease.

AIDS quickly became a intensely politicized issue because its initial developments were so closely related to the homosexual population. Gay and civil rights groups in some states vigorously resisted efforts by health agencies and insurance companies to use highly accurate antibody tests to determine whether a person had been infected by the human immuno-deficiency virus (HIV) that leads to AIDS. Fearing that such tests might be used to discriminate against homosexuals, the District of Columbia and several states, including California, New York, Wisconsin and Massachusetts, enacted measures limiting the use of HIV testing in underwriting insurance policies. For Lincoln National's medical department, the challenge centered on changing the AIDS issue from a political one to a medical one. After vigorous industry efforts, in which Lincoln National played a leading role, the most onerous of the restrictions were lifted and reasonable guidelines which allowed testing and also protected individuals' civil rights were worked out.

Because of his role in identifying AIDS as a serious issue for the insurance industry, Dr. Chambers wrote the ACLI "white paper" on AIDS in 1985 and was chosen in 1986 to be the first chairman of the AIDS committee of the ACLI Medical Section. At the same time, Lincoln National CEO Rolland became a charter member of the joint

ACLI-Health Insurance Association of America's (HIAA) CEO-level Task Force on AIDS. Driven by the seriousness of the AIDS epidemic, its complexities and the challenges it presented to the industry, Lincoln National was the first insurer to form a multi-disciplinary Corporate AIDS/HIV Task Force. The task force was organized in October 1985 to direct the overall management of the company's approach to AIDS, with an emphasis on technical medical research, the formation of policy and the exchange of information. Taking advantage of its early studies of the issues surrounding AIDS, Lincoln National personnel researched and formed opinions on AIDS questions that other companies had not begun to address. By 1987 Lincoln National was widely recognized as the industry leader in the development of AIDS management strategies.

GOVERNMENT RELATIONS

Since its earliest years, Lincoln National has been active in government relations. In the last half-centu-

ry, the company has been an industry leader in its efforts to represent and influence legislation and regulatory actions which affect insurance companies. Although Lincoln National has a long tradition of working closely with governing and regulatory bodies in the states in which it does business, the company has had its most dramatic impact on government relations at the national level.

The first lobbying effort undertaken by Lincoln National came in 1907, less than two years after the company started doing business. Caught up in the reforming zeal that marked the first decade of the century, Republican Governor James Frank Hanley sought to correct what he believed were abuses in the way Indiana's insurance companies used the first year's premium to cover sales and processing expenses, rather than putting the majority of the premium into the reserve fund. The accounting method for this activity is called "full preliminary term valuation," and it was the governor's intention to outlaw it. Because such a measure would be especially harmful to young companies with small reserves, the company's president, Samuel

Chief Medical Director Dr. Donald C. Chambers testifying before the Health Subcommittee of the U.S. House Committee on Energy and Commerce. Lincoln National's government relations officer, Michael Marchese (center), looks on.

Richard Baird, chief counsel for Lincoln National during the 1930s and 1940s.

Foster, and its secretary, Arthur Hall, personally assumed the task of convincing the governor and the legislature that prohibition of full preliminary term valuation would drive all the small companies from the state.

In the 1920s, when the company experienced rapid growth and prosperity, Lincoln National for the first time sought to have a state law changed. In this case, the state investment laws governing insurance companies were, in Franklin Mead's words, "the most archaic and strict of all forty-eight states." The company needed to reduce premiums and increase capital; the only way it could do this was to increase its presence in the investment world, but Indiana laws required that no more than ten percent of an insurance company's funds could be invested in equities, with the majority being placed in mortgage loans. Mead, and later Austin Stultz, led the lobbying effort in the Indiana General Assembly and the investment law was changed to a more liberal version in 1929, but the changes were so slight that the company pursued intensive lobbying efforts throughout the 1930s.

More significant in the 1930s was the drafting of a new Indiana Insurance Code, which substantially is the same state code under which life insurance is regulated today. Again, Stultz and his assistant, attorney Clyde Cover, were active with legislators and, in the end, made substantial

contributions to the formation of the new code. Lincoln National lobbyists also made a major impact on the first Indiana unemployment compensation laws that were passed in 1937 and, in 1945, loaned one of its actuaries, Ronald Stagg, to guide the legislature in developing the state's first pension plan for public employees.

Federal Taxation

The first national impact that Lincoln National had on the insurance industry through its relations with the federal government occurred in 1942, when Congress sought to tax life insurance companies in a different way than it had done since the beginning of the century. In the early 1900s life insurance companies were taxed in the same manner as any other corporation, the tax being imposed on the net income from all sources. A completely new tax basis was developed in 1921, in which the tax was levied only on income from such sources as rents, dividends and interest in excess of that required to maintain the reserves. The net effect of this formula resulted in life insurance companies paying little or no taxes. In 1942, in fact, only one major life insurance company paid any tax at all and Lincoln National had not been liable for federal taxes since 1932. Faced with heavy war expenses, Congress sought additional revenues from the insurance industry.

In 1942 McAndless was the chairman of the Joint Tax Committee of the American Life Convention when the U.S. Treasury Department invited the industry to cooperate in determining how a new tax structure would be formed. The concept which became law was worked out by Lincoln National's vice president, Walter Menge, and Ed Huston, the actuary of the American Life Convention who represented interests of the smaller life insurance companies, while on the overnight train from Fort Wayne to Washington, D.C.. Menge presented the plan to McAndless the next day at his committee meeting. He liked it very much and promoted the idea to the Treasury, with Menge helping to explain the details. A number of serious suggestions had been submitted, but this was the one that Congress

finally passed and the president signed. It was commonly known as "The McAndless Plan," although to some at the time, this should have been called "The Menge Plan." Menge, however, always protested that it really did not like the idea that much since it lacked the scientific foundations he preferred and, besides, it was only because McAndless liked it so much that he was able to sell the idea to the Treasury and the Congress. In 1943 Lincoln National paid the federal government $135,000 in taxes under the new formula.

Federal taxation continued to be managed through a series of amendments to wartime plan and earlier legislation, but in 1958 Congress determined to rewrite the income tax laws for life insurance companies. The process began with hearings by the House Ways and Means Committee chaired by Wilbur Mills. The issues that the committee faced quickly became immensely technical and bewilderingly complicated because the insurance industry itself had become so much more sophisticated in the previous three decades. The Treasury Department had developed the idea that life insurance companies should be taxed not only on their interest income, but also on their underwriting gains and, touchiest of all, on the dividends they paid out. This last point caused the great consternation: Mutual companies feared the impact on their policyholders, who received dividends, and stock companies were alarmed at the potential repercussions on their shareholders. In what came to be called "the tax war of 1959," two factions — one of mutual and one of stock companies — emerged in the industry's taxation committee, initiating a rivalry in the tax arena that continues to the present. The rivalry centered on whether federal taxation would be levied on investment income, which the stock companies favored, or on total income, as the mutuals preferred. The outcome was a mixture of both calculations, reflecting a compromise in which Lincoln National played a notable role.

At the time of the House committee hearings Menge, who then was president of Lincoln National, was a member of the trade association's taxation committee. Seeking to find a way through another thorny part of the issue that centered on taxation of interest income, Menge had a private meeting with Mills' committee and suggested a solution that provided for flexibility in the computations of reserves, an issue that was critical to the taxation of interest income. This concept came to be called "The Menge Formula" and generally was used to describe the process. But when the House committee made a number of changes in the bill that went contrary to what Menge believed was good for the industry, he arranged a meeting with Chairman Mills and asked that his name no longer be associated with the proposed legislation. Mills agreed and did not use Menge's name throughout the remainder of the hearings, but when the bill was passed into law, the "The Menge Formula" was used after all.

The U.S. Tax Act of 1959 was a landmark in legislation for the life insurance industry. The issues involved were so complicated and technical in nature, however, that the U.S. Treasury asked the two leading trade associations, the Life Insurance Association (LIA) and the American Life Convention (ALC) to provide experts to help interpret the new laws so that the appropriate regulations and literature could be developed. A group of five actuaries was formed under the chairmanship of Henry Rood, then a vice president of Lincoln National. The others included two employees of the trade organizations, a representative of the Metropolitan Life Insurance Company and one from the Hartford Life Insurance Company. This group rendered invaluable service to the Treasury Department over the next year and a half of intensive work refining the efforts of Congress and helping to establish many of the fundamental principles of taxation of life insurance companies still in effect today.

In addition to the work of Rood in the late-1950s, the efforts of Allen Steere, Gathings Stewart, Mike Marchese and Marcia DuMond over the next three-and-a-half decades kept Lincoln National in a place of industry leadership in federal taxation issues. Rapidly increasing inflation beginning in the late 1960s, however, disrupted the delicate balances struck in 1959,

and by the late 1970s the issue of inequity in federal taxation of stock and mutual life insurance companies again became a heated issue. Lincoln National President Ian Rolland assumed a central role in the negotiations between stock and mutual companies that followed — and resulted in a new tax law in 1984 — because of the high level of his positions at the ACLI and his reputation for even-handedness and fairness. As such, he was elected chairman of the special steering committee the ACLI created to address the taxation issues in order to prepare a united industry position for the Treasury Department and the Congress. In large part, Rolland also drew upon Lincoln National's own similar reputation extending back many years, a reputation as an honest broker that in no small way was tied to the firm's reinsurance operations. Indeed, one Washington lobbyist whimsically observed that Lincoln National was its own trade association, for it not only represented itself in national matters, it also represented hundreds of other insurance companies, both stock and mutual, who were its reinsurance clients. In this round of lobbying on federal taxation, compromises again were achieved which influenced the 1984 tax legislation, but the differences between stocks and mutuals persists and continues to color every new effort by the federal government to assess the insurance industry.

The Baldwin-United Affair

Lincoln National's leadership in the industry is also evident in the Baldwin-United insolvency affair that erupted in 1983. Rolland was chairman of the ACLI that year, so it fell to the Lincoln National CEO to lead the industry in its response to the scandal threatened by the failed company. When it became evident that the Baldwin-United Insurance Company had become insolvent, the National Association of Insurance Commissioners requested help from the ACLI and Rolland undertook the responsibility for addressing the issue.

Baldwin-United's six life insurance companies collapsed because of poor management. It was a time of volatile interest rates and in order to sell its

products, it had promised returns it could not meet. The portfolios of the Baldwin-United companies were loaded with over-valued stocks and securities of affiliate companies. It was, Rolland said in a speech to an American Bar Association seminar in 1993, "a house of cards."

Compounding the problem was that the state guaranty fund system was not in place across the nation. Three of the Baldwin-United companies were in Indiana where there was a guaranty fund; the other three were in Arkansas where there was no guaranty fund. Estmates were that if Indiana had to bear the cost of bailing out Baldwin-United, it would take sixty years for the failed insurers' policyholders to regain their investments. Rolland spent three and a half years fashioning an agreement that resulted in 165,000 policies being transferred to Metropolitan Life. In the course of finding a solution, the negotiations involved twenty-two brokerage firms, sixty-four life insurance companies, insurance regulators and attorneys general from fifty states and an army of lawyers.

The crucial issue was to find a company willing to be the leader and large enough to take on the Baldwin-United business. After several meetings with Rolland, John Creedon, CEO of the Metropolitan Life Insurance Company, agreed to take on the role of lead company, but only if Lincoln National and other major companies stood by to help, if needed. As Rolland recalled, "The Met did a really first-rate job. They provided the depth of expertise, resources and leadership necessary, while we at the Lincoln stood behind the scenes working shoulder to shoulder with the Met." The ACLI and the Met worked with the regulators, the hordes of representatives of the policyholders and the security brokers who had marketed much of the Baldwin-United business to develop a plan to resolve the issues. The industry was persuaded to pool $50 million to help finance the bail-out and the brokerage firms contributed heavily, too. As Rolland remembers, "It was a long, frustrating process, but in the end it worked well. The Met did a great job and profited from the new business it assumed (in excess of $4 billion in annuities), the policyholders came out OK and the industry came away with a guaranteed fund assessment that was a lot less than if Baldwin-United went into receivership."

In order to face similar issues in the future, Rolland established a special CEO-level Solvency Oversight Committee that would meet periodically to review conditions in the industry; Rolland was the committee's first chair. By the turn of the decade, indeed, the industry had to deal with two more major cases of insolvency — First Executive and Mutual Benefit — but because of the Baldwin-United experience the industry was able to meet these crises quickly and effectively. The experience also heartened the industry because of its ability to close ranks and work together to resolve a profound problem to the benefit of policyholders and businesses alike. In addition, the trade association demonstrated dramatically its effectiveness in working with regulators who established solid oversight models for states to enact guaranty fund legislation and an "early warning system" to alert states and the industry to potential insolvency situations.

Social Issues and Insurance Underwriting

Increasingly, since the mid-1970s

societal agendas have confronted the insurance industry demanding that it respond in ways which challenge the fundamentals of the underwriting process. Four issues in which Lincoln National played a leading role stand out: blindness, unisex pricing, the HIV/AIDS epidemic and genetic testing. Each of these issues imply much larger questions about individual and business rights, justice, fairness, just profits and reasonable expectations in the insurance industry.

Blindness: In the mid-1970s the American Federation of the Blind (AFB) challenged the traditional life and health insurance underwriting assumptions about the blind. As a rule, underwriters, including those in Lincoln National, presumed that blind people lived a life at greater risk than sighted people. It was assumed that accident rates were higher and that deaths were more prevalent. Some data, however, presented a different picture. The AFB challenged these assumptions and urged the National Association of Insurance Commissioners (NAIC) to require insurance companies to loosen their restrictions and insure blind persons without consideration of their sightedness. Michael Marchese, the chief governmental relations officer of Lincoln National, took a leadership role in the industry when he organized a lobbying effort to counter the AFB not on

the basis that underwriting for the blind had been unjust — clearly, it had been — but rather that the best remedy was to abandon pursuit of federal regulatory measures in favor of state legislation and regulation. In this process, Lincoln National was instrumental in bringing together for the first time a societal group, the AFB, with the insurance industry to create an acceptable compromise that served everyone well. In the case of the blindness issue, the compromises worked out between Lincoln National and the AFB led to the creation of an NAIC model that was adopted in every state.

Unisex: In the early 1980s the National Organization of Women (NOW) initiated a lawsuit against Mutual of Omaha in Washington, D.C., which had one of the nation's most liberal civil rights statutes, including a broadly based catch-all provision regarding "public accommodations." Using the "public accommodations" provision to apply to the pricing structures of health insurance, NOW contended that insurance companies discriminated against women solely on account of their gender because different pricing structures existed for men and women. Government Relations Director Marchese and Dr. Chambers assumed the lead in organizing an industry response to this challenge. Their contention was not that women ought to be treated differently than men, but rather that the issue needed to be focused on the real issues of health and mortality risk evaluation as a basis for underwriting and not on a general societal ideal of gender equality, which was how the issue was put to rest.

Privacy and Confidentiality: In the 1980s the onset of the HIV/AIDS epidemic and the emergence of the revolutionary importance of genetics in medicine raised critical issues of privacy and confidentiality that lie at the heart of the insurance industry's ability to underwrite. In the case of HIV/AIDS, as previously noted, the early association of the disease with homosexual lifestyles immediately thrust the issue into the political arena. Opponents to HIV testing and lifestyle profiles for the purpose of insurance underwriting feared that

Michael Marchese, director of government relations, confers with CEO Rolland in 1977.

such information would be used to discriminate generally against the homosexual community. In the face of a threatened onrush of legislative activity geared to restriction of the insurance companies' ability to evaluate the risks they were asked to cover, Dr. Chambers, played the key role in establishing the industry position on the disease through his leadership in the Medical Section of the ACLI. He and Marchese testified on behalf of the industry in critical areas like New York, Massachusetts and the District of Columbia in 1985. Also in that year Dr. Chambers represented the Health Insurance Association of America (HIAA) in Washington, D.C., at the congressional hearings held by Rep. Henry Waxman, chairman of the Health and Environment Subcommittee. Marchese, especially, worked on the sometimes difficult negotiations with leaders of the homosexual community to develop guidelines that would satisfy concerns about discrimination and confidentiality. In the end, by 1986, the public side of the issue was largely resolved with regulations in place which both protected individual rights and the ability of insurance companies to underwrite. Henceforth, attention could be focused on the medical problem.

Similarly, the ethics of genetic testing and its implications for an individual's right of privacy and the threat of discrimination has been a subject of discussion since the mid-1980s. Dr. Chambers again stepped to the forefront of the debate. Early in 1989, while chairman of the Medical Section of the ACLI, he formed the industry's first genetic-testing committee and appointed then-medical director of Lincoln National Reinsurance, Dr. Robert Pokorski, as chairman. The committee, which was charged to study the insurance implications of genetic testing, submitted its report in June. As a result, the ACLI and the HIAA established a joint CEO Task Force on Genetic Testing — Lincoln National's CEO Rolland was a charter member of the group. Separate joint working committees were also established and the groups began publishing their first reports in 1991. In the meantime, however, genetic testing had become an urgent issue when state legislatures began considering bills to limit or forbid underwriting on the basis of genetic-test results. In addition, in the past three years numerous important commissions and councils in the United States and Europe have openly recommended that insurance companies be forbidden to use genetic information in establishing eligibility for health and life insurance. In this charged atmosphere, even matters of family medical history were called into question by advocates of absolute privacy rights. In response, as with the HIV/AIDS crisis in the mid-1980s, the Task Force has insisted that the industry create strong measures to protect confidentiality and provide safeguards against descrimination but at the same time insist on access to genetic information when it has a legitimate bearing on health issues. To do otherwise, Chambers argued in 1994, would be to remove from the risk classification process the element of fairness to all policyholders and place in jeopardy the very foundations of the private health and life insurers. The profound issues surrounding genetic testing and the insurance industry have yet to be resolved.

In the past half-century Lincoln National has played a role of importance in the insurance industry out of all proportion to the size of the company. In part, this has been due to the exceptional reputation Lincoln National earned through the numerous personal relationships established through reinsurance services and treaties with insurance companies of all sizes and types. These reinsurance relationships above all else were based on trust and fairness — it was legendary, for example, that most Lincoln National reinsurance treaties were made on the basis of a handshake and little more. Thus, when the industry faced difficult, sometimes volatile issues, it was not uncommon to turn to Lincoln National leadership to be the broker in attempts to create industry consensus.

Lincoln National volunteer during the great Fort Wayne flood of 1982.

CHAPTER IV
THE COMPANY AND ITS COMMUNITIES

One of the sources of pride of Lincoln National since its earliest years has been its role as a citizen in its local, state and national community, and its concern for the community within the company. At age ninety Lincoln National is the leading citizen in the city of Fort Wayne, one of the leading citizens in the state of Indiana, and a national leader in issues of social conscience. Lincoln National annually donates two percent of its pre-tax earnings to charities, most of which are situated in Fort Wayne and other communities in which the company maintains a significant presence.

Moving beyond mere giving, however, the company also pursues a tradition of identifying critical community issues and stepping forward to become a part of the process of solving the community's problems. Acting as a responsible corporate citizen has meant more than providing funding for worthy causes; it also has meant providing the time and the talent of company personnel whose involvement as volunteers in nearly every facet of community life give added value to the traditional notion of corporate giving. There are good reasons for this. Just as the company was born in and nurtured by its home town, Lincoln National in turn has aided, nurtured, sustained, and, on occasion, quarreled with its parent community. The Lincoln National leadership is clear in its affirmation that when it undertakes charitable causes and addresses community issues it does so in keeping with its business goals and that these activities are indeed self-serving. Since the days of Arthur Hall, the company has acknowledged that it does not act in a vacuum, but is inextricably interwoven into the fabric of the community in which it operates. In short, being a good corporate citizen has been good for business. Perhaps more importantly, service to the community has also been perceived as the right thing to do; at the Lincoln National corporate citizenship has been another extension of the old company motto, "Its name indicates its character."

The tradition of community involvement by Lincoln National began with Hall's struggle to give the company presence in Fort Wayne. Just as he threw himself enthusiastically into the challenge of creating the new business, Hall also threw himself with enthusiasm into his adopted community. He first sought acceptance among the business elite of Fort Wayne through the contacts of the company's first president, Samuel Foster, and other officers of the board. The initial goals were to sell both stock in the company and life insurance policies, but Hall was soon caught up in the world of Fort Wayne, a world in which he could make his mark and his company's fortune at the same time. He fit in well and was well received. In later life he said he was proudest of the fact that he managed to sell $100,000 of Lincoln National stock in a matter of weeks without a penny of expense to the company. The initial years 1905 - 1910 were years of hardship for the company as it struggled to establish itself, but by 1912 Lincoln's National place was secure and Hall was president of the Fort Wayne Country Club, a position of acknowledged leadership in the community. Fortunately, Fort Wayne in the early twentieth century did not have a narrow business elite nor was it governed by a few aristocratic families. There was room for newcomer leaders and newcomer businesses. Hall was a natural leader and soon was asked to chair a host of clubs, fund drives and civic organizations. In 1916 he led the prestigious fund drive for the new YMCA building completed in record time of one year at Barr and Washington streets.

When World War I engulfed the United States in 1917, Hall was at the forefront of all the city Liberty Bond drives, several of which greatly exceeded government quotas. He was also treasurer of the Allen County Council of Defense. Employees of Lincoln National made contributions to the war effort that were in the top 25 percent of overall business participation in the city, although the company was yet small in comparison with the great manufacturing concerns of Fort Wayne. Among other financial institutions, Lincoln National employees were in the top 10 percent in their contributions to the war effort. A product of his ultra patriotic times, Hall was also the head of a jingoistic organization known as the American Protective League for the Fort Wayne District. This was a kind of vigilante group that carried out "dragnet searches" and sought out perceived "un-American" activities, including labor unions, outspoken pro-Communists and Communist organizations and pro-Germans, and denounced them as internal enemies. In Hall's mind, he was carrying out the same community service in these activities as he did in the community charity fund drives. After the war and during the great flu epidemic of 1918 - 1919, Hall was the head of the Fort Wayne effort to educate and regulate the community to prevent spread of the disease.

During the boom years of the "Roaring Twenties" Hall threw himself into community economic development efforts. He had been president of the Fort Wayne Commercial Club, the predecessor of the Chamber of Commerce, and he chaired various improvement efforts such as the Civic and Municipal Bureau and the Rural Development and Good Roads Bureau. In 1919 he became head of the Greater Fort Wayne Development Commission. In this capacity he undertook one of his greatest projects to benefit the home town, the attraction of International Harvester Corporation to Fort Wayne. Once this was accomplished, other related industries, such as the Zollner Piston Company, came to Fort Wayne.

Hall became the most visible business leader in Fort Wayne by the end of the 1920s and Lincoln National had emerged shortly after the First World War as the leading financial company in the region, as was proudly portrayed in the new home office building on Harrison Street. Hall was deeply involved in community self-help organizations such as the Community Chest, which was founded in 1926 and elected as its first president the head of Lincoln National Life. The company

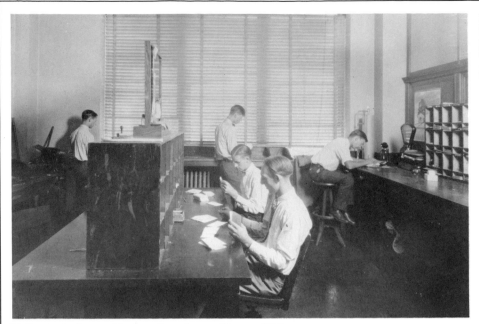

Mail room in the new Harrison Street home office, ca. 1925.

president also served in these years as the head of the Fort Wayne Art School and Museum, the Family Services Bureau, the Red Cross, the Christmas Seal Campaign, the YWCA, and the Fort Wayne (Community) Foundation. Hall's name was "emblazoned in the press," as one contemporary recalled, in connection with every significant fund-raiser and he was one of the most sought after figures in the state. *The South Bend Tribune* even speculated that he would be an ideal Republican candidate for governor, calling him one of the few "high-minded Hoosiers" in the state. Not surprisingly, with the onset of the financial crisis of the early years of the Great Depression, the community turned to Hall for leadership. Hall responded to the call with characteristic enthusiasm.

Initially, Fort Wayne business lead-

Arthur Hall and International Harvester

Through its president, Arthur Hall, Lincoln National played a significant role in creating a new industrial base for Fort Wayne in the decade following World War I. In November 1919 the International Harvester Company advertised in Fort Wayne and twenty-six other cities that it was looking for a community in which it could build its new central plant. The plan envisioned a $5 million facility that would employ as many as five thousand, producing thirty thousand trucks annually.

Prior to the arrival of Harvester, Fort Wayne was an industrial city founded largely on the Pennsylvania Railroad Shops, the Bowser and Wayne Pump companies, and the huge Bass Foundry. The prospect of attracting such a large company in the pioneering decades of the trucking industry, however, promised to secure Fort Wayne's future as a manufacturing center in the Midwest. Consequently, no effort was spared by the Fort Wayne business community to win Harvester's commitment to the city. The Chamber of Commerce quickly organized a special negotiating committee to offer an economic package to Harvester. An agreement was reached and Harvester agreed to come to Fort Wayne but only if several difficult conditions were met. Harvester required enlarged and paved roads to its plant site along the old Bueter Road (today's Coliseum Blvd. South), as well as gas, telephone, sewer, water and electrical service extended to the plant area, streetcar lines installed connecting to downtown, and special belt lines connecting to each of the four main railroads in town — all at no cost to Harvester. In addition, Harvester wanted to be sure enough housing would be available for its workers and so demanded that the city also purchase four hundred building sites and construct over one thousand homes. The Chamber was also required to form a corporation of "sufficient capitalization" to carry out the requirements. To make things even more difficult, Harvester insisted that all the efforts be conducted without publicity. The company was concerned that if the community failed to meet its side of the deal, Harvester could still turn to one of the other cities that competed for the plant and not have to cope with negative publicity.

In order to accomplish this immensely complicated task, as one participant remembered, the Chamber called upon Hall, "that superlative organizer, salesman and civic leader." Hall created the Greater Fort Wayne Development Corporation and set to work bringing together the heads of the utilities, the necessary city officials and business leaders. He personally raised funds and, when the project became public knowledge, raised community interest in the project. During the next year and a half, Hall oversaw the effort to extend the city limits to the new "East End" industrial park and all the other requirements demanded by Harvester. The most difficult of all the efforts was to convince all the railroads — the Pennsylvania, the Wabash, the New York Central, and the Nickel Plate — to build the belt lines from their main trunk lines to the Harvester plant. This required creative financing and delicate negotiations that lasted nearly a year. Another major impact of the project on Fort Wayne was the creation of several new housing developments in the East Pontiac, Anthony Blvd. and Bueter Road region, transforming the former waste lands on the East End into thriving communities.

The infrastructure projects were all completed on schedule and the housing projects were about to begin when the entire effort threatened to unravel. In 1921 a mild recession slowed business and Harvester asked for an extension for beginning construction of the plant. Panic gripped the news editors and speculation was openly aired that the project was doomed. Recognizing the dangers of a failure of trust, Hall convinced Cyrus McCormick Jr. to come to Fort Wayne to calm local fears. McCormick, the son of the famous inventor of the reaper and founder of the company, had just become chairman of the board of International Harvester. Shortly after he arrived in the city and inspected the East End developments with Hall, he gave a "memorable address" to area business and political leaders and assured them that Harvester would be in Fort Wayne. Fears were assuaged and the project went forward. International Harvester began construction of its enormous plant in 1922; by 1923 portions were in operation and full production was reached in 1924.

ers were not panicked by the crash of the stock market in October 1929. They approached the crisis in an aggressive spirit, refusing to expand relief efforts in favor of creating new jobs. The Greater Fort Wayne Development Commission, of which Hall was the past chairman and powerful board member, continued to attract new businesses to Fort Wayne. In 1930 Magnavox was persuaded to move to the Summit City, creating more than one thousand jobs and the Inca Corporation expanded its magnet wire operations. Two years later Theodore Zollner brought his piston company to Fort Wayne to be near International Harvester.

But there was to be no regional escape from the Depression. As early as 1931, some Fort Wayne factories were beginning to experience reduced demand for their goods and unemployment figures began to climb. In response to Gov. Frank Leslie's call for improved relief organization, the Allen County Emergency Unemployment Committee (ACEUC) was formed and Hall was elected chairman. This purpose of the group was to organize private voluntary relief and determined to resist any federal intervention in Fort Wayne's situation. Said Hall, who feared an interventionist state, "No one wants Governmental Taxation or Governmental Supervision for the care of the unfortunate." From the beginning, the ACEUC under Hall's direction was committed to providing work relief rather than the dole, such as cooperative ventures with the local Chamber of Commerce. The ACEUC was successful, too. Hall led two

major fund drives in 1931 and 1932 that raised $360,000, more than doubling the best of the 1920s' Community Chest fund drives. Local companies, including Lincoln National, made the major gifts that totalled forty percent of the goals, while their employees provided the remainder. Hall had a broad, national perspective on the economic crisis, but he focused on the local issues when he launched the 1931 drive by saying "We are protecting our city and our community against the perils of social destruction inherent in poverty, idleness, ill health, dependence and discontent." In this proclamation, the founder of Lincoln National also well expressed a belief about corporate responsibility evident in the company today.

As the Depression wore on and new measures had to be taken, Hall continued to play a leading role. He was the chairman of the Federated Relief Agencies (FRA), which was formed to coordinate public and private assistance, and he was founder of the Taxpayers Research Association in 1934 after volunteer efforts failed and federal assistance programs became unavoidable in the worsening economic disaster. This last group was one of his proudest achievements for the community, which by 1939 could boast that it was the lowest taxed city in its class anywhere in the nation. Hall's participation in community relief efforts continued even into the New Deal era after 1933 when he chaired the local chapter of the Federal Emergency Relief Administration (FERA). Matters had

become so difficult in the mid-1930s that even "hard-rock Republicans" like Hall welcomed federal programs with gratitude and enthusiasm; but such, too, was the measure of his devotion to the welfare of Lincoln National's community.

During World War II Lincoln National and its employees threw themselves into the war effort as did other corporations in the Fort Wayne area. The president of the company, A.J. McAndless, was chairman of the Victory Fund Committee in the 7th District of Indiana, and in 1943 every employee participated in the War Bond drive, making Lincoln National the first company in Fort Wayne to have its personnel set aside more than 10% of its payroll. Lincoln National was also the nation's first life insurance company to reach this goal and was granted the privilege to fly the special Treasury Department "Minute Man" flag with a "T," for ten percent, in the right-hand corner. Employees faithfully collected metal, rubber and paper for scrap drives, planted "Victory Gardens" and assisted with the local USO activities at the Army Air Corps fighter base at Baer Field. Senior officers of the company, like Allen Steere, took leadership positions in local funding efforts, and employees of all ranks joined the service, like Cliff Gamble, who became a fighter pilot in the European Theater, and Arthur Hall's son, William, who served as a Navy reconnaissance pilot in the Pacific. By the war's end, 128 men from the field force had entered the service and 61 from the home office were in uniform.

The Greater Fort Wayne Development Corporation

When Arthur Hall was asked by the Fort Wayne Chamber of Commerce to lead the effort to attract International Harvester to the community, he plunged into the task with his customary zeal. He staffed his volunteer committee with leading representatives from each sector of the business and civic community and launched a fund drive to raise $1 million. Among the top contributors to the drive was the Lincoln National president, Sam Foster, and several members of the board of directors. The company made a substantial donation also. Out of this effort was formed the Greater Fort Wayne Development Corporation, an organization that became the backbone of community growth during the next two decades, which was an era of the largest industrial expansion the city ever experienced. The Greater Fort Wayne Economic Development Corporation also exemplifies how in the first half of the twentieth century private business, not city hall, took the lead in developing the community.

As for the Greater Fort Wayne Economic Development Corporation, it did not stop its work with the successful Harvester project, and Arthur Hall continued to be a driving force within the organization. During the course of the 1920s the Corporation attracted other large manufacturers to the city, but most importantly it gave vital assistance to the emergence another of Fort Wayne's major twentieth century-businesses, the wire and die industry, which made Fort Wayne "The Magnet Wire Capital of the World." In the 1930s, during the Great Depression, the Corporation was a mainstay of economic stability in Fort Wayne, a community that weathered that disaster better than most in the nation. Through this organization and Arthur Hall's leadership, the Lincoln began a long tradition of playing a vital role in the economic welfare of its home town.

(continued)

$2.50-A-WEEK HOUSES ON $1 LOTS IN FORT WAYNE

Among experiments in meeting the grave problem of providing decent homes for the "ill-housed third of the nation" who cannot afford to pay economic rents, one of the most interesting is that now going forward in the average American city of Fort Wayne, Ind. (pop. 122,000). A major obstacle to building homes to rent at prices that poorest families can pay is the high cost of urban land. Like most other cities, Fort Wayne had scores of lots, vacant or occupied by dilapidated buildings, on the fringes of its industrial and business section— eating up taxes while their owners held them for a building boom. Last year the Fort Wayne Housing Authority approached these owners with a brand-new scheme. It offered to lift the tax burden by "buying" the lots at $1 each, with the provision that the owner could buy them back anytime he wished. Then the Authority set about devising a cheap prefabricated house, easy to set up, easy to move if owners reclaimed lots. Three local mortgage concerns put up the money, FHA insured their blanket mortgage, WPA furnished all labor. Result by Feb. 1: 45 neat three-room houses to rent at $2.50 a week.

Down by the railroad tracks lie the vacant lots and ramshackle hovels where poor folk dwell. On land like this by the Pennsylvania R. R., Fort Wayne is rehousing its poor at no higher rent, no cost to city except small tax loss.

Fort Wayne houses are prefabricated in a local warehouse by WPA laborers. Walls and partitions are 4-in. phenol-resin plywood panels filled with rock-wool batting for insulation.

Panels get a coat of sizing at the factory. Windows are among the few parts of the house bought as finished products. Total cost of materials which go into each house is $460.

"Minimum house" for family of four

Two bedrooms, bath, living-dining-kitchen room comprise Fort Wayne "minimum house." The main room is 12′ by 20′, bedrooms 7′ 8″ by 12′.

Oil heater, electric light and plumbing fixtures go with house. Most tenants come from shacks with none of these.

Furniture is supplied by tenants. Here family doubles up children.

A Fort Wayne house goes up in one hour and 40 minutes

FOUNDATION OF HOUSE IS 4-IN. CONCRETE FLOOR ON GRAVEL. AFTER CONCRETE IS LAID, THE ACTUAL ERECTION OF THE HOUSE TAKES ONLY ONE HOUR AND 40 MINUTES

HERE YOU SEE A FORT WAYNE HOUSE GOING UP. PANELS ARE PUT TOGETHER WITH STEEL TIE RODS WHICH RUN HORIZONTALLY THROUGH TOPS AND BOTTOMS OF UNITS

FORT WAYNE IS BUILDING 50 HOUSES AT RATE OF ONE PER DAY, MAY DECIDE TO BUILD 150 MORE. TENANTS, MOSTLY ON RELIEF, ARE CHECKED BY WELFARE AGENCIES

ROOF IS OF PANELS LIKE WALLS, BUT THICKER. HOUSE IS PAINTED AFTER ERECTION. FINISHED HOUSE (RIGHT: NOT THE SAME ONE SHOWN BUILDING) IS TRIM, NEAT AND SNUG

Life Magazine highlighted the novel idea for inexpensive city homes developed by William Hall in 1938.

In 1942 Lincoln National employees were told their contributions paid for a tank for the war effort.

While Lincoln National employees were personally generous in their support of various local charities and the company did its duty as a corporate citizen in all the major fund drives, the era of the two decades from the end of World War II to the early 1960s is distinctive in the absence of a high profile activist. In these years the company focused on business challenges, major growth efforts and internal change. With the new identity that accompanied the creation of Lincoln National Corporation in 1968, however, the company assumed a dramatically more public posture as a public-spirited citizen and began to seek ways to reach into and affect the community of Fort Wayne. Company publications, such as the *Lincoln National Life Review*, which began in 1968 and reflected the accession of Tom Watson to the presidency of the life company, now carried frequent images of minorities at work in the company or as a part of company-sponsored community programs. Editorial content

Some of the Lincoln National employees who served in uniform (from left to right: Owen Pritchard, Geraldine Gilmore and Cliff Gamble)

Volunteers at Casad Depot

Lincoln National employees participated in every home front activity during World War II, but one of the most unusual community services undertaken by the insurance company employees was volunteer duty at the local Casad Depot, which was one of the largest heavy ordnance storage centers in the country. Located near New Haven, Indiana, the depot was built in 1943 on a 650-acre site. Large quantities of anti-aircraft guns, auto parts, machine tools, and ammunition was stored there. At its height in 1944, more anti-aircraft weapons were at Casad than was used in all of England against Nazi planes during the blitz of 1939.

More than forty men from Lincoln National volunteered to spend after-hours work at the Casad Depot, amounting to an average of fifty days work every three months. Working evenings and weekends, these men did "double duty" moving loads of ordnance and equipment during emergency movements of material. This was the first depot in the country to solve the problems of "peak load" pressures and served as a model for other centers.

addressed social issues and such topics as the radical press and environmental concerns and articles frequently touted community focused initiatives by LNC and its employees in projects with names like Project Commitment, Operation Friendship, the Voluntary Service Unit and the Youth Project Commitment. Actuary Julia Oldenkamp headed the local assistance effort known as Call to Action and one group of Lincoln National employees who were concerned about area youth unemployment — Art Page, Ken Hallenbeck, Bill Lawson, Walter Bonham and Jim Lewis — simply took it upon themselves to visit local hotels, radio and TV stations, funeral homes and other businesses soliciting jobs; they secured 20 permanent and five summer jobs.

Corporate community involvement began a systematic activity under Watson's leadership and the development of Lincoln Life Improved Housing (LLIH). In 1972 Watson wanted to undertake a project that would demonstrate in a unique way his belief that the company had responsibility as a corporate citizen that extended beyond mere donations. A sales minded CEO, Watson also realized the public relations value of a highly visible project and knew instinctively that, apart from being an altruistic enterprise, being a good citizen was good for business. He wanted especially to develop a program that would benefit the home office community through a creative cooperative venture that would bring Lincoln National, government agencies and traditional lending organizations into partnership . Accordingly, he asked his top management officers to develop proposals. Ian Rolland, then-vice president of Lincoln National Reinsurance, drew upon his experiences in the East Wayne Street Center, which had earlier attempted to address the severe housing problems on Fort Wayne's East Side with the creation of the East Central Development Corporation. This organization involved a large number of concerned minority residents of the East Side in a largely volunteer effort, but only a few houses could be renovated. It was clear that volunteers were not enough. Sparked by the tax advantages then connected

The first Lincoln Life Improved Housing project before and after the project was undertaken.

with residence renovation projects identified by fellow vice president Jake Mascotte, Rolland's "white paper" described a unique housing renovation concept. Watson liked it and authorized Rolland to get the project going. The innovative idea focused on creating a community partnership that would help people help themselves in the belief that home ownership is one of the key foundations to family and neighborhood stability.

The program was initiated in 1973 by creating a subsidiary company, Lincoln Life Improved Housing, Inc. Harlan Holly, associate general counsel since 1972, was the first director

and the partnership included the City of Fort Wayne and Allen County, which sold the land and abandoned or dilapidated structures to LLIH for $1, and local banks, which provided the mortgages at below-normal rates. Federal assistance was provided through the Community Development Block Grants program administered by the city of Fort Wayne. In turn, LLIH managed the project and improved the housing inside and outside. The eligible family made no down payment, but leased the refurbished home for at least five years, paying through their mortgage half the refurbishing cost; Lincoln National paid the other half.

Rev. Benjamin Hooks speaks at the "Partners In A Dream" ceremony heralding the success of the Lincoln Life Improved Housing program in 1989.

At the end of the five years the family could buy the mortgage for $1 and assume the mortgage balance. In this way low- to moderate-income people in Fort Wayne could become home-owners. In 1989 the company herald-ed the first families to own their homes free and clear with a ceremony called "Partnership in a Dream." Dr. Benjamin Hooks, then executive direc-tor of the NAACP, was the featured speaker and he praised CEO Ian Rolland and Lincoln National noting that "this housing program is a big example of what can be done with commitment and money."

The impact on the families and neighborhoods has been profound. Not only is dilapidated housing elimi-nated, but also responsible residents are added to the neighborhood. Many low- income families, especially sin-gle-parent households, typically are ineligible for standard mortgages, but may be included in the LLIH program. One single parent best summarized the significance of having access to ownership of a decent home when she said, "I did a dance of joy when I

The Employee Gift Committee

The Committee of 22 was founded as the "Drive Investigation and Management Committee" on April 22, 1942 as part of Lincoln National's employees' war efforts. Originally, it was a committee of twenty employees who evaluated any fund drives to which employees might contribute. Near the end of the war, on April 12, 1945, the committee added one more elected member and included a Personnel Department representative to bring the total to twenty-two. The number of committee mem-bers has since changed, but the tradition of naming the group after the twenty-two has remained. The purpose of the committee after the war became one of evaluating donations to charities and worthy causes from the excess of money raised over the Lincoln National goal set for the annual United Fund campaign.

Among the proudest contributions the Committee of 22 made in its more than half-century of community

Lincoln National employees from the Committee of 22 make a donation to leaders of Boy Scout Troop 404 in 1978.

support was its donation of nearly $6,000 to the local chapter of the American Red Cross for tornado victims of the great Palm Sunday disaster of 1965. This was the largest of all the gifts received by the chapter. The tornadoes came late in the day on April 11 and ripped through the entire Midwest from Iowa to Ohio, killing more than 250 people. Indiana, which lost 131 peo-ple, was the hardest hit, however, and Allen County was smashed by several twisters that left forty-six dead. Fort Wayne was unscathed but lost all electrical power except for a small number of street lights, and the Lincoln National's Home Office was shut down for nearly forty-eight hours. Still, one hundred employees showed up for work on Monday and with the help of can-dles and gas lanterns operated the switchboard.

The Committee — known today as the Employee Gift Committee and working in conjunction with Corporate Public Involvement — continues its long tradition with gifts to the area's non-religious projects and organizations such as the Historical Society, the Fort Wayne Art Museum, the Boys and Girls Club, Big Brothers Big Sisters, the Fort Wayne Shelter, a rehabilitation center known as Washington House, and much more.

qualified. I had such pride to own my own home, a place my children could always come to and a place I could leave behind for them some day. Sure it is a struggle, but it is my dreamhouse and every day it gives me reason to keep going. I just feel so proud when my kids say 'If Mama can do it, I can too.'"

Since its beginnings, LLIH has achieved most of its goals. The program has proved, in fact, to be more successful than thought possible when it was initiated. It has renovated two hundred and seventy homes in two hundred and thirty blocks of inner city Fort Wayne at a cost exceeding $3 million. Most important, however, the program also raised the community's awareness of the severity of the housing situation in the central city and has stimulated additional public and private housing programs, such as Project Renew and the Housing Partnership. According to the director of Project Renew, "[Lincoln's] paving the way to the lenders, showing it can be done and be profitable, set the path for us. It wasn't a foreign language to them. It sure made it easier to implement new programs."

Lincoln National traces its traditional interest in education to its first president, Samuel Foster, who considered his most significant civic service to have been his election to the Fort Wayne school board. His goal as a trustee was to insure that the local education effort was properly funded; it was through his efforts while on the board (and the donation of his trustee salary), for example, that the property was purchased for the first public library, which at the turn- of-the-century served as the school library. Lincoln National's concern for excellence in education in its earliest decades, however, centered largely on university scholarship support for rising young actuaries, known after 1954 as the McAndless Memorial Scholarship. Support for public educational activities became Lincoln policy during Walter Menge's tenure and this marked the beginning of a long tradition of company interest in the local educational system that produced the majority of its home office employees. Walter Menge, in fact, recruited William Watson, the former dean of boys at Central High School, to attract and train young black graduates of Fort Wayne public schools to work at Lincoln National.

Lincoln National's role as an activist in local educational affairs began during the early tenure of Ian Rolland. The state of the local schools was not only a critical business concern for Rolland, but also a serious personal concern as well, and he was willing to put both his own and the company's resources to work to improve the local schools. The issues crystalized in the early 1980s when it became clear that Fort Wayne Community Schools had a serious segregation problem. The U.S. Department of Education's Office for Civil Rights reported in early 1984 that Fort Wayne public schools were "severely racially imbalanced during the 1982-1983 school year" and accused the school corporation of deliberately perpetuating the imbalances.

Throughout 1984 and 1985 public hearings on the issue were repeatedly postponed by school officials. Rolland recalls that he worked on several occasions with William Anthis, then superintendent of Fort Wayne Community Schools, on the issue of desegregation. School officials even sought Lincoln National's sponsorship in 1985 to support a $5 million referendum on the desegregation issue. At first attracted, Rolland became disturbed, seeing that not only was this a poorly conceived tax referendum seemingly designed to fail and thus divert the issue, but also that there was no representation in any of the

"A Day With President Lincoln"

Actor Richard Blake portraying Abraham Lincoln in 1980.

Since the time Robert Todd Lincoln allowed the company to use his father's name and likeness, Lincoln National has sought to promote the ideals and legacy of the sixteenth president. In addition to maintaining the Lincoln Museum and bringing theatrical productions back to Ford's Theatre, Lincoln National sponsored a nationwide "living history" program entitled "A Day With President Lincoln." Featuring Richard Blake, a professional actor acknowledged to have been the foremost portrayer of Abraham Lincoln, the one-man program was launched in February 1980 at Ford's Theatre before a congressional audience. During the course of the next year, Blake gave 443 performances across the country and made 418 appearances in schools as President Lincoln. Using a press conference format in the schools, "President Lincoln" met with students who posed as White House reporters of 1864 and asked unrehearsed questions.

In recognition of the importance of the program, the Freedoms Foundation bestowed on Lincoln National its highest honor, the George Washington Award, in May 1981 because of "the company's outstanding individual contribution supporting human dignity and the fundamentals of a free society."

planning of the people most affected. A frustrated Rolland remembered that "I supported him for superintendent, but it became clear that even if it were a favorable referendum on the issue, he would not act. The other significant people in the community, who were members of the school board, also did nothing." Discouraged by the lack of movement and impediments thrown up by the school officials, Rolland sponsored numerous public forums to discuss the issue. A critical moment came in 1985 during the dramatic forum held in the halls of the Chamber of Commerce when the Lincoln National spokeswoman for Corporate Public Involvement, Ladonna Huntley James, was verbally abused and her very character called into question when she attempted to present the anti-segregation position taken by Rolland. At the Chamber meeting only one person stood to defend Lincoln National's position, a black woman who was a senior official in the city of Fort Wayne's government. She summed the depth of feelings as she prefaced her brief, incisive rebuke of the Chamber with "My heart is broken today to hear these personal attacks on a fellow member."

In the face of these difficulties, Rolland asked Huntley James to find the best civil rights attorney available, and after a lengthy study contacted William L. Taylor of the Citizens' Commission on Civil Rights and former U.S. Civil Rights Commission director. In the meantime, several concerned parents had formed a biracial group known as the Parents for Quality Education with Integration (PQEI) in the fall of 1985. In concert with the parents group, Rolland addressed the issue in a series of public meetings, and PQEI focused its attention on defeating the poorly conceived tax referendum. Negotiations with the school corporation continued for many months, but when little was accomplished by further talks, PQEI filed a class-action lawsuit against Fort Wayne Community Schools and the State of Indiana in September 1986, claiming that the district had been unconstitutionally segregated and asked the federal courts to order a comprehensive plan for desegregation. Lincoln National funded the effort.

It was an emotionally charged time.

Hate mail was received by members of PQEI, supporters' homes were damaged and personal attacks on Rolland and Lincoln National became strident. Rolland remembers telling close associates, who voiced their concern about becoming involved in such an acrimonious dispute, simply that "It's the right thing to do. I don't really much care what people think about it. All this boils down to a sense of integrity. We have to ask the question, 'Are we really what we say we are?' We say we believe in equity and fairness, but if we don't stand up for that when we see clearly low income, primarily minority kids getting the short end of the stick in our own hometown, we must do something. We knew it would not be popular, but we were not going to let popularity or opinion polls dictate to us how to act."

Still, the decision represented a considerable risk for him and Lincoln National because of the unprecedented level of involvement and the intensity of opposition from some segments of the Fort Wayne community, which has had a long history of de facto segregation. The rhetoric became so vitriolic that Rolland at one point was characterized by the school corporation as "a cancer on the community." Although Rolland was often singled out, it was the biracial group of parents and children who were central to the desegregation effort. As Rolland said in a September 1989 interview with David Maraniss of the Washington Post, when asked about the PEQI group, "Yes, there was a core of people as offended as I was. They took the real risk, this biracial group of parents and kids."

The case continued for seven and a half years and was marked by dogged persistence of the PEQI group. While behind-the-scenes talks continued constantly, Lincoln National funded the expenses for research and legal fees. The Office of Civil Rights agreed to a Community Schools' plan for desegregation in May 1987, but PQEI continued its suit, believing the plan to be weak and insufficient. A trial was scheduled for April 1989, but thanks to the mediation of William A. Black, former CEO of the Indiana and Michigan Power Company, an agreement was finally reached with the school corporation by early 1989

which put into place a program to bring about racial balance and remedy the effects of segregation. To those who charged that the settlement would break up good schools, including those that were mostly black, Rolland replied, "I cannot believe that the so-called 'quality black education' or the 'quality white education' are, by definition, quality education."

Racially balanced classes began for the first time in the fall of 1992. The suit against the state of Indiana, which was funded by Lincoln National, continued for the next several years, finally ending in February 1994 when the state agreed to contribute nearly $13 million for meeting the costs of desegregation of Fort Wayne's public schools. This final agreement came ten years to the day from the date the Office of Civil Rights issued its first report on the segregated state of Fort Wayne community schools. "The major heroes in this are the parents and the plaintiffs in the class-action suit. We owe them a debt of gratitude for what they have done," Rolland said at the time. Heralded as a landmark effort by civil rights attorneys, within the insurance industry and in American business the role played by Lincoln National in the issue was also an expression of the high level of social responsibility the company was willing to undertake. As one attorney in the case noted, "No other corporation has ever done this, and if The Lincoln had not stood up, no one would have, and things would have simply stayed the same."

An outgrowth of the PQEI desegregation lawsuit was the formation of the Fort Wayne Local Education Fund (LEF). The settlement between Fort Wayne Community Schools and the Parents for Quality Education with Integration provided funds for educational improvements in the schools, but many thought more was needed. When one of the local newspapers, the Journal Gazette, editorialized on the idea of establishing a local education fund in Fort Wayne, materials were sent to Lincoln National for consideration. A committee of community leaders was appointed to investigate the possibility for establishing a Fort Wayne LEF. With a positive response from this group, Rolland won the support of the Fort Wayne Corporate

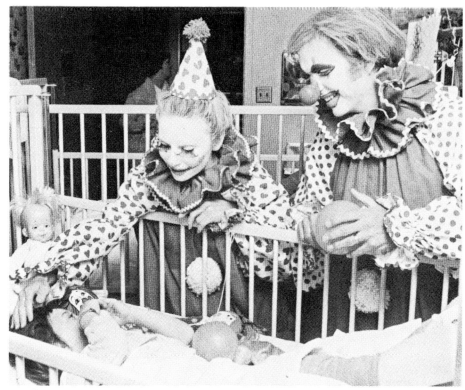

Lincoln National volunteers Terri and Ken Miller at a local hospital in 1975.

active role a part of the institution itself and its culture. Reflecting the CEO's desire to develop a more effective community role for Lincoln National, a formal Corporate Public Involvement department (CPI) was established in 1987 with Huntley James as its officer.

The creation of established guidelines for corporate giving in all Lincoln National communities are a direct outgrowth of the PQEI experience. The giving profile of the corporation is not unique on the face of it, although the annual 2% of pre-tax income is higher than most U.S. insurance companies give. Corporate Public Involvement annually gives to numerous agencies in its home office area and in affiliate office regions in three principal categories: human services, the arts and culture, and education. The agencies in themselves are not unusual. They are widely diverse, ranging from Arts United of Greater Fort Wayne, the Indianapolis Museum of Art, the Fort Wayne Ballet, the Hudson Institute, and the United Hispanic-Americans to the Insurance Industry AIDS Initiative, the Indiana Civil Liberties Union, the Indianapolis Neighborhood Housing Partnership, the Leukemia Society of

Council, which agreed to fund an LEF for Fort Wayne. Since that time, the LEF in Fort Wayne has funded over $250,000 in various educational programs within four public school districts and the community at large.

Although Lincoln National had been involved in its community since the first decade of its history, the formal, programmatic approach to public involvement evolved gradually during the years following the creation of the corporation in 1968. Traditionally, upon the advice of a "corporate gift committee," the board of directors decided each year which charities would receive donations from the corporation. The gift committee became a formal corporate entity in 1974 and a year later CEO Watson gave the group authority to make donations directly from an approved fund. A "corporate social responsibility committee" emerged in 1973 with the beginning of the Lincoln Life Improved Housing program under the direction of Harlan Holly, the director of corporate social responsibility. Gradually, during the late 1970s, the functions of the two committees merged and the corporate secretary relinquished some charitable-giving duties. In 1981 when Huntley James joined the corporation

in the area of corporate community involvement, Lincoln National began rapidly to formalize a program for public involvement and make this

(from left to right) Judy Davis, Dean Nelson, Marilynn Scherer and Joni Wood Lehman were among the many 1990 Lincoln National volunteers in the annual Junior Achievement "Super Bowl."

America, the United Negro College Fund, the Harvard Business School Fund, and the Fort Wayne Women's Bureau. What is notable is that Lincoln National was the first corporation in America to insist that it will not fund any organization or not-for-profit agency that does not have women or minority representation on its board of directors.

Rolland recognized as a result of the PQEI experience that the presence of even just one minority or female member on a board fundamentally changed the way it operated. Thinking back to the acrimonious meeting at the Fort Wayne Chamber of Commerce when his spokeswoman was battered by a room full of white men on the issue of desegregation, he wondered, "What would have happened if that one black woman had not spoken up in defense of The Lincoln's position?" For Rolland, the single voice in that charged atmosphere was a clear indication that Lincoln National's giving policies should be directed toward effecting change in recipient organizations. In 1986, then, Lincoln National reformulated its policies for corporate giving to include the stipulation that only institutions with full gender and minority representation would be awarded grants. It was a policy change that brought about change. The Fort Wayne Junior Achievement organization, for example, "one of the whitest, malest organizations in town," has incorporated in its strategic plan for 1995 30% female and 15% black representation on its executive committee, reflecting the local demographics for these segments of the community. When asked why this change came about, the J.A. president, Richard Menge (son of the former CEO of Lincoln National) said that it was

AIDS

AIDS was first recognized in the United States in 1983, and by mid-1985 Lincoln National had identified the emerging epidemic as the most serious health problem to face the insurance industry at the end of the 20th century. The disease was recognized as both one that would seriously affect the conduct of business as well as one that could affect personally the Lincoln National workforce and the community in which it lived. In order to address the immensely complicated issues raised by AIDS, Ian Rolland ordered that a corporate-wide task force be formed in October 1985 under the chairmanship of Joseph L. Romak, second vice president, Security-Connecticut Life Insurance Company. This apparently was the first corporate AIDS related task force to be formed in the industry.

The mission of the AIDS/HIV Task Force was "to direct overall issue management with emphasis on technical medical research, policy formation and information exchange." Every major component of the corporation was represented, including personnel from Claims, Government Relations, Reinsurance, Law, Human Resources, Corporate Planning and Analysis and Lincoln National Life's Medical Department. A central force in the task force was Dr. Donald Chambers, the company's medical director, an industry leader on the issue. All aspects of the company's business activities were to be surveyed, from marketing to underwriting. Romak recalls thinking after the first meeting "how this issue is enormously complex. Too much is unknown. What is known is terrifying: A universally fatal virus has arrived and there is no cure for the immune disorder it causes. ... and its impact would affect virtually every aspect of our business. At times, I felt overwhelmed. I think we all shared that feeling."

As a result of the task force's activities, unified management strategies for dealing with AIDS were developed for the corporation and each of its business units. In addition to considering AIDS in the context of such technical issues as pricing and reserving, laboratory testing technologies and claims tracking, the task force also focused on developing policies to protect confidentiality, prevent discrimination in underwriting and to provide for informed consent to testing. The task force also identified as vital issues that the company demonstrate its concern as a corporate citizen in the AIDS crisis and that it appropriately modify its employment policies and develop employee education programs.

While the AIDS/HIV Task Force addressed largely business issues in order to create an overall strategy for dealing with the epidemic, the human dimension of the disaster was brought home early in 1983 when a young man in the corporate headquarters of Lincoln National was stricken by the disease. Ladonna Huntley James, director of the Corporate Public Involvement Department and Merit Smith of the Employee Benefits Division were the first non-medical personnel at Lincoln National to tackle solutions to the AIDS crisis. Huntley James called together a group of local people interested in AIDS in 1985 and offered assistance, advice and funds. At that time, interest was largely centered in the homosexual community, but later broadened to include all segments of the population. This group became the core of the Fort Wayne AIDS Task Force, a community organization for which Lincoln National provided the seed money. This support by the company helped to garner additional grants from the American Council of Life Insurance (ACLI) and other local funding sources. Since that time, Lincoln National's support for the local task force has grown and a permanent residential hospice center has been established in Fort Wayne for people with AIDS. Smith served two terms as the president of the task force in Fort Wayne, in 1988 and 1989, and led the way for the organization to become an established part of the community's network of service agencies. Taking the lead of the corporate headquarters, affiliates of LNC have supported similar efforts in their own communities. One of the largest was the 1990 donation of $100,000 by American States Insurance and LNC to the Hudson Institute for the study of the economic, social and political consequences of AIDS.

In order to educate Lincoln National employees about the realities and dangers of AIDS, the company launched a program in 1988. Brochures on policy, prevention and services relating to AIDS were published, educational films were shown and numerous employee "awareness" meetings were conducted. At a White House ceremony In 1989 President George Bush awarded Lincoln National his Citation for Private Sector Initiatives in honor of the company's work on the disease as a personal as well as a business challenge.

"due to the example and pressures given by The Lincoln that caused the J.A. to make necessary and healthful changes. Lincoln National was the catalyst."

Minorities in the Lincoln Workforce

Minority representation in the company made its greatest progress since the mid-1980s, but Lincoln National in 1995 still was well behind many other insurance companies in number of African-American employees. Of the nearly nine thousand employees of Lincoln National Corporation in 1995, for example, 453 were African-Americans and of these only fifteen were officers. Senior officers acknowledge that the company has a long way to go to achieve full parity for minorities, but a process of change was initiated in 1992 that addresses such issues as recruitment, "glass ceilings," internal advancement and salary parity. Most recently, senior management gave its support to the newly formed African-American Group, an employee organization formed to identify and quantify issues of importance to blacks and propose solutions for the company to consider.

In the earliest years of the company there were no black employees at all. During these decades Lincoln National differed little from the rest of Fort Wayne, a city in which no blacks could be served in a restaurant along Calhoun Street, on whose streets the Ku Klux Klan marched openly, and which happily sponsored a

"Courthouse Play" with scenes of "pickaninnies fighting over watermelon and darkies singing songs of the old plantation and pleasing Abe, who freed them." Hiring discrimination for white collar positions was absolute at the Lincoln before World War II, as it was in nearly all Fort Wayne businesses. When Lincoln National began publishing *Life With The Lincoln* in 1923 a regular feature were Negro jokes and caricatures that were common in the era. In 1935, in celebration of Lincoln National's thirtieth anniversary, the company put on another popular entertainment of the era, the Minstrel Show, which presented the spectacle of its officers in blackface.

The only black person who worked in Lincoln National's halls before the mid-twentieth century was Walter Caldwell, a shoe-shine vendor who was the sole outside vendor allowed to ply his trade in the home office building. Caldwell was a successful businessman who owned a nearby barbershop and did well enough in the shoe-shining business to own a small hotel on the near east side of Fort Wayne. Very well liked, the mustachioed Caldwell also became a favorite visitor to the offices because he was a conduit for all manner of company news and gossip — he was the only person in the offices who moved regularly from one office to another.

Lincoln National did not hire African-Americans until the 1950s, but in doing so it was ahead of its times in Fort Wayne, where blacks still were denied access to white-collar jobs. Soon after the accession of

Walter Caldwell, 1960.

Menge as president of Lincoln National Life, young black graduates were hired from the local Central High School. As Menge recalled it, the director of personnel, Ronald Stagg, assembled a group of eight women he wanted to hire and Menge approved with one stipulation: "Don't put them all in the same section. Spread them around a little. I thought if they were in one particular area doing one piece of work, the prejudiced whites we had

Lincoln National employees stage a traditional Minstrel Show in 1935 in celebration of the company's thirtieth anniversary.

would always look upon that section as the Negro section (or worse) and these people would never get a chance to be assimilated by the Lincoln Life people as a whole. It would always be 'that black section.' I didn't think that would happen if we spread them around thoroughly so everybody had a chance to get acquainted." For Menge, it was "a matter of fair play" in the face of the normal discriminatory treatment blacks faced, and for the first time the company proclaimed in its published *Philosophy of Management* that qualified persons were to be hired "without discrimination as to race, color or creed." Still, there were no special programs put into place otherwise to assimilate the new workers into the formerly all-white atmosphere, and most of the new recruits did not stay. In order to identify and help black recruits the

company enlisted in 1965 the help of William Watson, a professional educator in the Fort Wayne Community Schools and a former Peace Corps volunteer. His job was not only to bring black workers to the Lincoln, but also to train them in office functions and deportment.

Although Lincoln National's affiliate Dominion Life in Canada employed African-Canadians without incident, there were few models in the home office. Lincoln National turned to its new Reliance acquisition to bring to the home office the first managerial level employee when Frank Mace was brought to Fort Wayne by Vice President Thagrus Burns in 1956. As director of Reliance files, he managed a team of as many as fifteen white men in the critical task of merging the Reliance records with those of Lincoln National Life. One former worker in

his team recalled that Mace was "the Jackie Robinson of the Lincoln," closely watched by everyone to see if he would measure up as a manager. Like Jackie Robinson breaking into major league baseball, Mace chose to do his job the best he could without making issues out of every slight, affront or insult — and there were many — choosing instead simply to do his job as effectively as he could and become a part of the Lincoln National family. Mace recalls that he had no special problems coming to the home office and that the people in Fort Wayne were supportive — all but two, but he managed them in his typically flexible manner.

The era of mandated change began during the tenure of Henry Rood (1964 - 1971) and became especially important during the presidency of Thomas Watson (1971 - 1977). What

William Watson and the first effort to recruit black employees

During the tenure of Walter Menge, Lincoln National decided to recruit black employees for the home office from the local high schools in Fort Wayne. Having had little experience with black employees and minimal exposure to the black community in Fort Wayne as a potential source for the work force, the personnel department sought the help of William Watson, the dean of boys at Fort Wayne's Central High School, who was employed at Lincoln National as a "personnel consultant" in October 1965.

Watson, a native of Parkersburg, W.Va., came to Fort Wayne in 1950 to be the director of industrial relations for the Fort Wayne Urban League. He had earned a bachelor of arts degree from Marietta College and held a master of arts degree from Ohio University, with additional postgraduate work at the University of Michigan, Ball State University and Indiana University. He joined the Fort Wayne school system as Central's dean of boys in 1960 and in 1963 he took a leave of absence to join the Peace Corps as a coordinator of the mission to St. Lucia. When he returned to Fort Wayne in 1963 he served the school corporation's student personnel department until he was recruited to work for Lincoln National.

Bill Watson (right) participates in a ceremony honoring a young graduate in the company's intern program for minorities in 1968.

At Lincoln National, Watson's job was to identify black graduates from the Fort Wayne schools who were likely to be successful as employees at Lincoln National and recruit them for the company. It was also part of his job to train the young people to work in the office environment. Following a paternalistic behavior typical up to the first years of the Civil Rights movement, it was thought necessary to acclimate black workers to a white environment. It was Watson's job to develop special training that was thought to be necessary — by Watson as well as by his white colleagues in the personnel department — on the assumption that even such basic habits as personal cleanliness, deportment and dress were generally lacking in the Fort Wayne black community. Watson was tough on the young people, who were mostly women destined for the lowest entry-level positions, because he very much wanted them to succeed. He was determined that if anything kept them from working at Lincoln National, it at least would not be their conduct and appearance.

By the time he left the company in 1967 to a take a position with A&P, he was not always fondly remembered by those he trained because he had been so demanding. He was, however, a pioneer in the introduction of black people as regular employees in a nearly all-white company and in raising the consciousness of the white employee population to the normalcy of blacks also contributing to the successes of Lincoln National.

One Hundred Years of Service to Lincoln National: The Mace Family

When all the years are added together the family of Frank Mace has given Lincoln National 100 years as employees. Frank served forty-four years, his wife Evelyn twenty-five years, their daughter Donna has almost thirty years (so far) and their son Frank Robert two years. They have given well beyond the years of work, too, as each has also served the community.

Frank Mace was one of the first African-Americans to work at Lincoln National. Born and raised in Pittsburgh, Pennsylvania, Mace joined the Reliance Life Insurance Company in 1943 only to be called into the Army later that same year. As an anti-air-craft gunner, he fought in the South Pacific in the campaigns in New Guinea and the Philippines. When the war was over, he returned to his entry-level job at Reliance in Pittsburgh. Working his way through the ranks as a filing clerk, he was called up for service again when the Korean Conflict broke out in 1950. When he returned from a year overseas, he returned to a Reliance that was in the midst of being sold to Lincoln National. When in 1956 it was decided to merge the old Reliance completely into Lincoln National and move the Pittsburgh operation to Fort Wayne, Thagrus ("Thag") Burns offered Mace the job of supervisor of the Reliance records with responsibility for merging the old system with the Lincoln system.

At first, Mace had a staff of one; within a year, he had thirteen working under his direction solving the seemingly endless difficulties of blending file systems by hand in the oppressively cramped quarters in a leased building known as "the Tailoring Building" at Clinton and Brackenridge streets (site of today's parking garage). What was unique was that all the staff working under Mace were white. Two or three young black women were working in clerical positions at Lincoln National by the mid-1950s, but a black supervisor of white employees was unprecedented. Throughout his early years in Fort Wayne, as Thagg Burns later revealed, Mace was in fact a test case being closely watched by senior management who were interested to see how well a black supervisor would perform. Senior management was very pleased by what they witnessed and Lincoln National slowly began employing an increasing number of minority workers by 1960.

As for Mace, he recalls that with only two exceptions, he was treated fairly and well by everyone in the company. The only thing he recalls that he did not like about Fort Wayne when he moved here was the lack of Major League baseball team. He filled this gap, after a fashion, by playing many years as a centerfielder for the Lincoln Life Blues softball team. His wife, Evelyn, joined the company also in a filing related job in 1960. She and Frank appreciated that she had the night shift as a "jacket chaser" while he worked the daylight office hours. "That way," the Maces recall, "when we were raising our children we would have at least one parent home all the time. Also, we didn't have many fights this way since we weren't home much together."

Perhaps the Maces are best known for their generosity, both to fellow Lincoln employees and to the people of Fort Wayne. An accomplished magician, Frank became widely known for his ability to cheer people in hospitals, nursing homes and schools. An orphan himself, he paid especial attention to entertaining in the area orphanages. Every Christmas for many years the Maces held an open house at their home on Buchanan Street so that folks could enjoy Evelyn's hospitality and Frank's extensive model trains all decked out for the season. At first, the Maces only invited Lincoln colleagues. "I believe I've had all the Lincoln brass in my home at one Christmas or another," Frank fondly remembers. The tradition grew, however, and the Mace home became a regular holiday stop for many in the city. Local radio host for WOWO, Bob Sievers, always spoke glowingly of the wonderful Lionel and other large-gauge model trains that filled both sides of the Mace duplex basement. The TV stations soon joined in the celebration and Frank was especially proud to take some of his trains to the annual Fort Wayne Children's Zoo Christmas programs. For Mace, "What was really enjoyable about the trains was watching other people enjoy them."

All the Maces became involved in an neighborhood-driven housing rehabilitation program called Project Renew, which raises funds to build or refurbish housing in the South side area of Fort Wayne. Frank's daughter Donna, currently a Lincoln National employee, is the president of the board of Project Renew, among several other neighborhood betterment organizations. Frank was also among the most active Boy Scout leaders in the community, believing that solid parent-child activities were the best way to keep communities healthy. His son, Frank Robert, who is currently a fireman, eventually won Scouting's highest rank as an Eagle Scout, and Frank himself was awarded the prestigious Silver Beaver for twenty-five years of service.

Frank Mace and the Reliance files.

Menge had characterized in 1955 as the "fair thing to do" had become the "legal thing that must be done" after 1964. Statements in the LNC employee manuals from 1969 affirm that it is against company policy to discriminate because of race, but the notion that Lincoln National had an obligation to go beyond legal requirements to become a part of the corporation's vision began with the accession of Ian Rolland. The belief that social change was "the right thing to do" began to become ingrained in the corporate culture. As early as 1972, the company's state government relations officer, Dan Seitz, forecast affirmative action legislation and urged CEO Watson to get ahead of the process and begin recruiting the best minority candidates available. An Equal Employment Opportunities Committee was formed, and in 1976 George Dunn, a black veteran of the U.S. Army, was hired to address Affirmative Action issues. Other officers, such as General Counsel Jack Hunter, already viewed minorities and women in law schools as good sources for top lawyers for the legal department of the future. One of the first attorneys recruited by Hunter was Arthur Page, a Fort Wayne native who had recently graduated from the Indiana University Law School in 1971. Page found few black contemporaries on the Lincoln National payroll when he joined the company in 1971, but the law division provided the necessary mentoring and network connections as well as challenging assignments that gave opportunities to demonstrate evidence of high levels of capability. Through the work of staff like Page and Mace sound examples of the quality of executive level work performed by blacks was firmly established.

Under Rolland formal and intensive efforts to address racial minority issues were inaugurated. An Affirmative Action Office was established, but recruitment of black professionals was stymied, in part, by the very location of the home office. Although in many ways the Midwestern, small-city image of the company worked to Lincoln National's advantage, the perception that Fort Wayne was too small, too narrow-minded and just too Midwestern caused many prospective black

employees to turn to companies in Chicago or in cities on the coasts. High turnover of black employees was also often blamed on the Fort Wayne environment, but the "Fort Wayne issue" may also have been a smoke-screen for other difficulties. It was clear, for example, that affiliates located in large cities, like American States in Indianapolis, for example, also faced the same difficulties as the home office. In response to such suspicions, staff studies in 1979 revealed deep concerns among black employees about middle management attitudes, lack of the informal "mentoring" that for others was critical in advancement and exclusion from the normal flow of informal communications that employees believed was so necessary to know the affairs of the company. To address these issues, racial awareness seminars were organized in 1979 and 1980 to develop heightened sensitivity among all employees of the unique issues pertaining to race. This was the first organized integration effort in the company and one of the earliest such efforts in the industry. The law division through its Affirmative Action work directed by vice president Carl Baker also actively promoted minority awareness throughout the corporation. Gradually, racial equity moved beyond policy statements to begin to become part of the corporation's culture as more black employees were advanced. In January 1995, for the first time an African-American was advanced to the position of company president when Roland C. Baker was named to direct First Penn-Pacific Life Insurance Company. Although it is a process that is by no means complete as of 1995, it is clear to many African-American employees that notable changes have indeed taken place in the past two decades. While the "Shared Values" initiative launched in 1994 stresses, among others, the values of "diversity," "fairness" and "respect," and is intended to reaffirm the company's character, racial equity is also assumed to be good for Lincoln National's growth and critical to the ability of the corporation to compete in the next century. By thus tying racial parity to the business goals of the company, Rolland has intended to weaken the barriers that largely have been erected by middle management.

Lincoln National's reputation for exercising its social conscience in racial matters has been acclaimed in the industry and on Capitol Hill. Rolland and other Lincoln National senior staff, for example, enjoy a comfortable rapport with the Congressional Black Caucus. Other insurance leaders, like Walter Gerken, the former CEO of Pacific Mutual Life, and Richard Schweiker, immediate past executive director of the ACLI, have praised Rolland and Lincoln National for undertaking unpopular stances for what they believed to be the right thing to do.

Women in the Lincoln Workforce

Women have been the majority of employees at Lincoln National since its beginning, but only in the last two decades have they been counted among the leadership of the company. Throughout its history, the insurance industry has maintained a large clerical workforce and traditionally there has been a preponderance of women in the clerical ranks. Reflecting this tradition, the Lincoln National workforce in 1993 was approximately 71 percent female, most of whom served in a clerical or administrative assistant level. Also reflecting present-day conditions in the industry, women as leaders in the company remained a minority; at Lincoln National among the officers only twenty percent were women in 1993. While the numbers of female officers remains a significant minority in 1995, the historical trend is one of growth: Compared to twenty years ago, there are more female officers today and they have achieved steadily increasingly higher positions, more women serve on strategic committees; and there is less sexual harassment. In sum, there is greater responsiveness to women's issues in general than there was twenty years ago. For example, programs have evolved or been put into place that address such issues as "glass ceilings," recruitment, compensation, mentoring and networking, training and recognition of the unique role of women as mothers.

The oldest surviving veteran of Lincoln National is a woman, Alice

Testimony to the times, late 1940s.

Lincoln National women of the 1920s.

thing was done by hand. She quickly rose to a supervisory position, which she held until her retirement in 1959. "We didn't pay any attention to hours," she said as she fondly remembered. "We were happy because we had jobs. We knew everybody we were working with and everybody was nice. When I worked, I wanted to see every girl at her desk and working. Believe you me, I watched them and they worked. I loved the girls I had. I liked my job, I liked the people I worked for and they valued my work. I don't know what more you can want." Her experiences are echoed by Marcelline Kleinrichert, who joined the company in 1920 and worked for forty-five years at Lincoln National as a secretary. She still takes great pride in having served the company well for nearly five decades and in the life long friendships that in 1994 still bring her to the offices for bridge games with other members of the Loyal Service Club. Not everyone of that generation agreed that women were always treated right. Margaret Walker, for instance, was one of several women who believed that salaries, benefits and work load might be better and often sought to draw other women together to bring grievances to the male management. Generally, these efforts had little impact; most women in the early decades viewed work at the Lincoln National (as elsewhere) as a temporary situation to be replaced by homemaking and raising a family after getting married. Few viewed their work as a career.

O'Reilly, who is one hundred years old. She was hired in 1916, when the company was starting its second decade and still remembers the heady days of the company's initial growth and struggle for survival. Although there were no special benefits to assist women on the job, other than her salary, O'Reilly recalls proudly the long hours as a secretary in new business processing located in cramped quarters on Berry Street where every-

Lincoln National women's golf team of 1930.

As was expected in most white-collar businesses before the middle of the twentieth century, women employees at Lincoln National who intended to marry were required to give two weeks notice of their resignation prior to their wedding. If any of these women were reinstated, it would be only as a temporary employee ineligible for any benefits. As the 1925 office manual states, "It is the general policy of the company in reducing the clerical force to terminate the services of married women first." This continued to be the policy of Lincoln National until well after World War II. By 1950 women who intended to marry were still expected to resign, but the reinstatement of valued female workers was so frequent that the company sought to protect its employee health and life benefits program from the risk of too many claims due to pregnancy by requiring all married women to agree to a two-year probation at the end of which they had to pass a medical examination before being allowed to enjoy full sickness and death benefits; otherwise, they were considered temporary employees and ineligible for benefits. In the mid-1960s married women were a regular part of the workforce, but pregnancy was still cause for termination of employment. Not until the mid-1970s did it become a normal part of the company's policies, which are still in effect, to allow women who became pregnant a leave of absence and the right to return to work.

Advancement within the company for women before the mid-1970s was possible but limited to a range of positions below that of officer. Before World War II women usually did not expect, nor were they expected to be, officers, regardless of their professional training. In the early 1920s, for example, Helen Williams, one of the first women in the United States to pass the actuarial exams, came to Lincoln National but moved to an eastern company when she could not advance beyond supervisor of the Mathematics Department. In the early 1930s Agnes Kinder, who specialized in mortgages, became the first female attorney to join the company but did not advance to officer rank, and she was joined in 1934 by Hilda McDarby, an attorney since 1920 and a member of a local law firm, who became assistant to Arthur Hall and later Walter Menge. In 1939 Margaret Walker completed her actuarial exams for the highest degree and was awarded a fellowship in the American Institute of Actuaries (AIA), ahead of younger actuaries Gathings Stewart and Samuel Adams. Walker never entered the ranks of company officer, however, while Stewart eventually became president of Lincoln Life and Adams the chief actuary of the company. The highly skilled Walker eventually left Lincoln National to become president of Royal Neighbors of America Insurance Company. Dorothy Ball, who executed a great number of deals in the investment department in the 1950s and 1960s, was disappointed that she and other women delegated officer level work were not advanced to officer rank. More typical were the number of women, such as L.C. Williams, Esther Kruse, Gertrude

Kocks and Helen McCrory, who reached managerial rank from the late 1920s, usually serving as assistant managers of various departments with ther own secretaries.

Not all women wanted to become officers, though. Typical of women's early achievements were those of Vera Pruger, Elizabeth O'Rourke, Ruth VanOrsdol, Florence Warner and Ann O'Rourke, who all became department heads and supervisors in the early 1920s and were intensely proud of their success and their contributions to the company. They had been recruited by Franklin B. Mead, who ran the day-to-day office operation and who believed strongly in the abililty of women to organize and direct department activities. Ann O'Rourke, for instance, was given the task of organizing the first Issue Department (for processing approved policies), an area she and her successors directed in a time of rapidly increasing sales. Ann's sister, Elizabeth, came to the company in 1926 and rose through various ranks of supervisor until 1933 when she was named the assistant company secretary and was head of the department of Office Administration. Many women, of course, achieved excellence in their clerical positions and did not aspire to higher rank. For example, women like Winnie Beeth, who came to the company in 1929, became the first person in Fort Wayne and one of only eight hundred nationally to win designation as a Certified Professional Secretary, and Eileen Chaney, who won numerous awards and national recognition for her skills as an executive secretary, found career fulfillment when she was elected in 1957 to president of the Indiana Division of the National Secretaries Association.

One notable channel for achievement by women in the company before the 1970s was in the sales force. Among the earliest women to sell life insurance for Lincoln National was Zura Ziegler Brown, who joined the company in 1924 and became Lincoln's and Indiana's first chartered life underwriter (CLU). For years she led as one of the top ten salesmen and women and was for many years the president of the Ladies Guild of the Clubman, a promotional organization within the sales force in the 1920s (it

The women's rest room, ca. 1925.

is notable in the Clubman promotional year that top agents were singled out as "men who have helped other men" and that regularly several of these "men" are in fact, women who have helped other sales personnel recruit agents and find prospects).

As with changes in minority representation in the company, changes in opportunities for women required changes in attitudes and the fundamental culture of the company. In its earliest decades Lincoln, like most companies of the era, took a paternalistic view of the place of women in the company. The 1925 office manual saw fit to caution women that the restroom was a privilege not to be abused and is only to be used during the lunch hour or after work, unless

permission is given by the company nurse. Nothing is said about the men's restroom. In 1930 the company magazine, *Life With The Lincoln*, highlighted twenty-five Lincoln women, noting that "The fact that we have very attractive girls at LNL cannot be hidden. They are charming from a personality angle; each is distinctly individual; and from a strictly business point-of-view competency is a highly developed characteristic. The little group photographed here were all helping entertain the Central division men who were attending the Sectional meeting held at the home office recently. They were pressed into special service in our new main and junior officers' dining rooms during the luncheon hour." While these

archaic practices diminished greatly during World War II and in the years soon after, the company still felt moved regularly to teach women how to behave. A column appeared in the company magazine of mid-century, *The Lincoln Log*, entitled "For Girls Only." In its initial article the author admonished the nearly 1,500 women at Lincoln National's home office to dress sensibly according to their shape. Using comic names, like "Karen Kneeser," "Bertha Bigg" or "Lelah Loudmouth," the advice columnist held forth on "bony knees" and the need to hide them, overweight figures squeezed into tight garments, and on the offensiveness of she who "giggles and shrieks with raucous laughter." The column concludes

Alice O'Reilly: 100 years and still growing

Alice O'Reilly serving on the St. Joseph's Hospital Auxiliary after her retirement.

Alice O'Reilly celebrated the beginning of her second century in 1994 and can still remember clearly that first week she started working for Lincoln National in October 1916. O'Reilly arrived in Fort Wayne in 1905, the year Lincoln National was founded, when her father brought the family from Ashkum, Illinois. She attended St. Patrick's grade school and completed high school studies at St. Catherine's Academy on the city's south side. After graduation she went to work as a bookkeeper and clerk for a local shoe store. Her younger brother, Edward, found work at Lincoln National in the Agency Department, and he encouraged his sister to come to the company also. Alice was soon hired by Ann O'Rourke, who then headed the Issue Department and later became Arthur Hall's second wife. O'Reilly's job was to file index cards. Later, her younger sister, Katherine, also joined Lincoln National and worked there for many years.

When Alice began her career at Lincoln National the company was small but growing rapidly. There were only fifty people on the payroll and all desks were on the fourth floor in the Elektron Building on East Berry Street. Above all else, O'Reilly recalls the intimacy and friendliness of the operation. She was particularly taken by the personable nature of the men who were the managers. She recalled Hall as "a different type of person, even though he was president — you could stop him in the hallway and chat with him. Mr. Hall always greeted you no matter whether it was morning or afternoon, he always greeted you with 'Good Morning' or 'Good Day,' and called you by name. Well, that was one of Mr. Hall's fine qualities. I think he made it his point to know and call by name everybody that worked at the Lincoln Life. He had such personal contact with people. At that time the company gave flowers on Mr. Hall's birthday, in May, when we started the May drive — Hall Month, we called it. Now, one particular Hall Month I was ill, but Mr. Hall divided his bouquet that day and brought half of it to me at my house and took the other half to someone else who was ill also. Well, it has always meant so much to me because he just walked up — Mother happened to be in the front yard and I was upstairs in bed — and all he said to Mother was 'I brought half of my birthday bouquet out to Alice.' And they were gorgeous."

O'Reilly was a hard worker and spoke her mind. Once, when President A.J. McAndless was walking around the large open office areas, as was his habit, stopping in at various desks to see what was going on, he stopped at O'Reilly's desk and chatted about her work. She tried to keep up the conversation and do her work at the same time, but finally losing her patience she blurted out "Mr. McAndless, I am very busy and just don't have time to talk to you. So if you stay any longer, I'm just going to have to put you to work." McAndless left in a hurry.

On another occasion President Walter Menge stopped at her desk and asked casually what she thought of the new color paint with, "The well groomed, poised Lincoln Lifer attires herself appropriately for business while hopefullly making the most of her plusses and the least of her minuses."

The Lincoln National culture put a high premium on women's job performances, to be sure, but in 1963 there was only one female officer, Marilyn Vachon. As late as the end of the 1960s and 1970s, when the local *News-Sentinel* still had a "Society Page," the focus on women in the company literature continued to present stereotypes of people unlikely to be officers of a large corporation. This was particularly true of the annual Lincoln Life Queen Contest, a tradition that stretched back to the mid-1920s (by 1965 it was part of the United Fund drive, which sponsored a city-wide beauty contest). Each September a panel of judges from outside the company evaluated contestants for poise, personality and appearance in the lobby of the Harrison Building extension. In the same spirit, a special "women's section" was a regular feature in the company magazine of the 1970s known as *The Review*. There, in the column called "Strictly Feminine," the topics for women continued to define and limit their interests with stories on such topics as creative party table decorations, Easter egg designs, and macrame.

The same era of the 1960s and 1970s, however, also witnessed the emergence of new interests and expectations by women in the workplace. Increasingly, the women who joined

Florence Warner, ca. 1925.

Alice O'Reilly: 100 years and still growing (cont'd.)

just put on the walls of the New Business Department the night before. "Mr. Menge," she replied, "I wasn't going to say, but since you asked, I'm going to say it. I hate these walls. I think the colors are horrible. These gray walls remind me of a prison." Menge did not answer, but the next day when O'Reilly reported to work (she was always the first to arrive) she found a crew of painters just leaving and the walls a bright new shade of green. One of the them didn't hide his displeasure when he said to her: "We know, Miss O'Reilly, you're the cause of all this." "Yes," she shot back, "I guess Mr. Menge agreed with me."

When the Northern States Life Insurance Company of Hammond, Ind., went into receivership in 1933 and Lincoln National was named receiver, the company sent O'Reillly and a young actuary to the Hammond office to take over. The two worked closely and became good friends; the actuary jokingly described himself as the "president" of Northern States and O'Reilly as the "vice president." Years later, when O'Reilly retired she received a warm note addressed to "Miss O'Reilly, Vice President of Northern States Life Insurance Company." It was signed President Henry F. Rood.

Relations between O'Reilly and the presidents were not always smooth and, again, her career is a measure of the singular character of the supervisory grade women who made Lincoln National their career. In 1950 McAndless sent around a memo announcing that retirement could be taken by women at age sixty. "They led everybody to believe that they were going to retire at age sixty-five and then out of the clear sky they came along and gave some figures and said that they were going to retire women at age sixty — and, of course, Mr. McAndless left town the day the memo came around. I got mad, real mad — I was just snortin'.

"I called Mr. McAndless' office and said to Mr. Bryce, his assistant, 'Now, when Mr. McAndless gets back I want to see him and I want to see him because of this memo and I'm not going to sit around and talk about it to anyone else because the memo came from him and I always try to make my people live by the rule that if you have any problems go to the people who can solve them for you. You tell Mr. McAndless that I want to see him.' The next day when Mr. McAndless returned, he must have talked to Mr. Bryce, because he was down at my desk before noon. He said, 'I understand you want to speak to me. Perhaps we could use Mr. Unger's office up front (it was empty that morning).' Sure, I said through my teeth, I've been waiting to see you all morning."

O'Reilly explained to McAndless that the five years meant a lot to many women who had anticipated working the extra years. She then fired at McAndless, "I know there are some people here now who should have been retired ten years ago," and added that "I want to work if my health were all right; if not, I'd have sense enough to get out. I don't want the Lincoln Life being burdened with me if I can't do my job. Forcing women to retire that early is just wrong, Mr. McAndless." As it happened, the memo was never officially rescinded. It was, however, ignored.

For O'Reilly, "it disturbed me in that I felt like somebody was trying to pull something over on us. It was just wrong, and I told him so." Eventually women were given the option of retiring as early as age sixty, if they wished.

O'Reilly retired in 1959 after forty-three years of service. In retirement she began her second career doing something she believed stood at the center of what makes living worthwhile: helping others. She became a volunteer at the St. Joseph Hospital in Fort Wayne as a member of its auxiliary and as a leader of the Catholic Business Women's Club she did volunteer work at the Indiana State School for the mentally handicapped, in addition to a variety of other charitable activities. She also became active in the administration and board of directors of the St. Anne Nursing Home, where she resides today. "Our great purpose in living is to serve others," she said recently, "When we are not helping others, our existence is meaningless."

Her enthusiasm for charitable work has only been surpassed by her love of the University of Notre Dame and Irish football. Until recently, she held season tickets to Notre Dame football for games that reached back to the era of Knute Rockne.

Margaret Walker receives from A.J. McAndless her certificate for completing her actuarial exams. Looking on (left to right) are Gathings Stewart, Samuel Adams and John Phelps.

Miss Lincoln Life of 1960, Marjorie Schaefer, and her attendants, Mary Couture (left) and Kay Augspurger (right).

Marilyn Vachon, Lincoln National's first female officer.

JoAnn Becker, was promoted to president of The Richard Leahy Corporation in 1991, the first woman to be placed in charge of a Lincoln National affiliate.

the workforce were better educated, more independent and more activist. Again, as with minorities, the law division was a leader in recruiting professional women and advancing them to positions of leadership. For General Counsel Jack Hunter, who believed that the law division would become a leader in the industry only if it developed a group of attorneys of diverse backgrounds, the law schools were ideal places to recruit female attorneys since it was then difficult for women to break into traditional law firms and corporate law divisions. By the early 1980s the presence of professional women and minorities in the division was no longer unusual, and Lincoln National extended its philosophy of diversity to law firms hired by the company by chosing only those firms that also shared the value of diversity.

Other officers welcomed the opportunity to tap this source of talent though not without opposition. Executive Vice President Richard Robertson, who joined the company in in the reinsurance division in 1963, recalls a common attitude in the mid-1960s when he asked his supervisor at the time why not use more women in the business. The patient answer to the young actuary was that "reinsurance customers wanted to speak to knowledgeable people and if they wound up talking to a woman they wouldn't think they were getting the expertise they wanted." When Robertson advanced in his career, he became one of the first officers in the company actively to recruit talented women for entry level jobs. As Robertson noted in his *Financial Newsletter*, "One thing I discovered was that for what we were willing to pay for these positions, we were able to attract women with substantially more talent than the men we were able to hire."

An important milestone for women in Lincoln National occurred in 1975 during the tenure of Tom Watson when the first women joined Lincoln National boards — Jill S. Ruckelshaus, who headed President Gerald Ford's Commission on International Women's Year, went on the board of Lincoln National Corporation and Joyce Schlatter, a civic activist with the Fort Wayne Community

Foundation, joined the Lincoln National Life board. With women on these boards issues about female roles in the company were raised at the board level for the first time. One result of this was the formation of the Women Executives Group (the WE Group) to serve as a networking vehicle among the top women at Lincoln National, including board members.

The project that greatly assisted Lincoln National to open opportunities for women was Quality Commitment, launched in 1978 by the new CEO, Ian Rolland, and directed by Vice President Cliff Gamble. The central purpose of this project was to increase productivity in the workforce, but the process for achieving this goal was based on a "grassroots" concept for bringing about change that included employees at every level in group and self-study activities. For the first time, women on a far-reaching scale were not merely directed as to how they were to do their work, but were involved in analyzing and defining their work and, in effect, taking ownership of their role in the company. As Gamble recalls, "Quality Commitment unearthed many talented women and opened new avenues for their advancement."

In the company's seventy-fifth anniversary publication of *The Company News* (June 1980), the "women's movement" and the need to seek talented women for the health of the company's future were stressed as among the most significant forces of change. While women experienced progress in Lincoln National throughout the 1980s as the numbers of female officers increased, compensation packages improved and benefits expanded, but it was clear that more needed to be done for women to achieve parity and for the corporation to realize the full value of its female workforce. The impetus for Rolland to launch a new initiative was the essay "Women As A Business Imperative" that appeared in the *Harvard Business Review* in March 1992 by Felice Schwartz of Catalyst, a not-for-profit organization that offers consultation to corporations regarding women's upward mobility and work/family issues. Rolland asked Ladonna Huntley James to lead a corporation-wide task force to analyze both the

National Women's Political Caucus
is proud to present

The 1994 Good Guys

November 15, 1994
The Mayflower Hotel
Colonial Room
Washington, DC

The 1994 "Good Guys Award" was given to Rolland by the National Women's Political Caucus.

Barbara Kowalczyk, senior vice president and director of Corporate Planning and Development, with Bruce Barton, vice president. Kowalczyk became director of the strategic planning operation in 1994 and is the first woman on the senior management committee.

opportunities and the barriers for women within the Lincoln. The "Women At Work Task Force" was formed and undertook an intensive

self study of the corporation between September 1992 and April 1993. Data were accumulated, focus groups were held, surveys and executive interviews

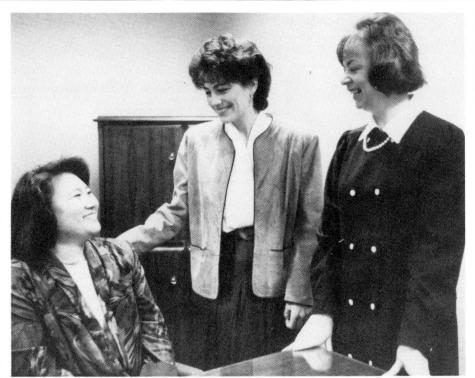

Three Lincoln National women were recognized as "Women of Achievement" in 1991 by the Fort Wayne YWCA. From left to right they are Madeleine Baker, Judy Davis and Carolyn Nightingale.

Corporation for the eighth straight time on its annual list of the nation's one hundred companies "that most appreciate, understand and adjust to the needs of working mothers" in recognition of the child care center and other programs such as flexible work schedules, elder care support programs and lactation centers. On Nov. 15, 1994, the National Women's Political Caucus hailed Rolland as one of its six annual "Good Guys" — along with Vice President Al Gore and Ben Cohen and Jerry Greenfield of Ben and Jerry's Ice Cream — as men who have provided a role model for other men in support of equality for women.

The Harrison Street Building: "The Company's Most Expensive Mistake"

Between 1912 and 1921 Lincoln National continued to grow dramatically. During this time the company's insurance in force increased twenty-seven-fold and the workforce had increased from nine (and a part-time mail room boy) to 219. Projections called for increases to 974 by 1932 and by 1937 there would be 1,656 employees. There was clearly a need to expand its facilities beyond the "Elektron Building," but this time Lincoln National was determined to design and build its own offices. The decision to build gave Lincoln

were completed, policy-setting committees and recruiting practices were analyzed and work/family issues were explored. In the end twenty-eight recommendations were unanimously accepted by the Task Force and presented to the CEO. The Task Force continues its work and monitors progress on its recommendations. Among the most dramatic responses to the recommendations and earlier

studies was the construction of a $1.5 million child-care center, which opened in September 1994 near the home office.

Although Rolland is the first to acknowledge that the company needs to do more, Lincoln National has received national recognition for its efforts in behalf of women in the workplace. *Working Mother* magazine recognized Lincoln National

Lincoln National's new home office on Harrison Street as it appeared shortly after its completion.

National an opportunity to make a statement about itself not only to those who visited the home office, but also to the community which gave it birth.

There was never a question in these years of leaving Fort Wayne. The issue for the new building centered on whether to build downtown or on the outskirts of town. It was a question that sharply divided the board and for the first time put Arthur Hall in direct opposition to the majority of his directors. Hall and his chief officers wanted to build the new home office on the then partly rural south side area of Fort Wayne, at a location near Piqua and Calhoun streets (near the location of Fort Wayne's first shopping center, Rudisill Plaza). Hall reasoned that the company needed to prepare for future expansion and that the least expensive expansion of facilities would be horizontal rather than vertical. A simple majority of the board, however, favored building closer to the downtown business district. Many of them, led by Board Chairman Samuel Foster, owned businesses in the commercial center of Fort Wayne and wanted to tie Lincoln and its employees to the core of the community. In the ensuing contest Hall managed to win to his view the necessary seven votes to agree to a south side location; Hall immediately closed the deal on the property and left for a life insurance conference in New York. While there, he received a telegram from Foster informing him that one of the board members had changed his mind and now favored the downtown site. Hall rushed back to Fort Wayne, but the issue was carried in favor of a new location facing Harrison Street near the downtown business district and across the street from the main railroad station. Hall later lamented that this decision by the board resulted in "the company's most expensive mistake" because, as it turned out, the home office was not expanded vertically, thereby incurring the wasted expense of high-priced downtown property, the necessity of purchasing additional high-priced downtown property for horizonal expansion and the costs of elaborate foundations that were never required. Once the decision was made to stay downtown, however, the commitment to the cen-

Hall is joined (from left to right) by the architects, Harry A. Hopf and Benjamin W. Morris, Lincoln National officers, Franklin Mead and Daniel Ninde, and John Bacon, an associate of Morris.

tral business district and to the Fort Wayne community became a key characteristic of the company.

A committee to study building needs was formed in July 1921 and by November Harry A. Hopt of New York, who had planned the home offices of Phoenix Mutual, the Southern Life and Trust and the LaSalle Extension of the University of Chicago, had been selected as the planning engineer. Upon his recommendation, the New York firm of Benjamin Wistar Morris was selected to be the architects. Benjamin Morris had emerged in the early 1920s as one of the premier American institutional architects of his time. Among his early works were the J. Pierpont Morgan Memorial Art Library, the home office of the Aetna Life Insurance Company, and the Cunard Steamship Building in New York.

The design of the $1 million-building was inspired by the Lincoln Memorial in Washington, D.C.. Its "Grecian" appearance was neo classical in its stately, well balanced Doric columns, severe geometric patterns in the great bronze doorways and sweeping staircase leading to the main entry plaza. The monumental first story was

constructed of Indiana limestone and faced with Vermont granite. The entire complex formed in a U-shape with a cupola as a temporary feature over the central hall. In the initial conception, a larger-than-life statue of Abraham Lincoln as president was planned for the center of the entry plaza. Initially, the building was only four stories high, but the foundations were built to accommodate additional floors so that one day the building might rise to fifteen stories. The building was an expression of the enormous success of the company. It was a proud announcement to Fort Wayne, Lincoln National's customers and investors, its employees and the insurance industry that the company had come of age and had embarked on a new era of growth and prosperity.

On May 3, 1922, at a special "employees' get-together party" at the auditorium of the local department store of Wolf & Dessauer, Hall proudly presented to the employees the plans of the new home office. With characteristic zeal, Hall called the new edifice "the most beautiful life insurance building in the world," and he was especially proud of the bowling alleys and other recreational facilities

Ocotober 13, 1923: Moving into the new home offices.

in the building that helped cement the staff of the "Lincoln family." The evening's festivities began with a "splendid dinner" planned by two secretaries, Misses Shreve and Warner, topped by an individual box of chocolates for each of the employees. The dinner was followed by the awarding of the annual bowling trophies by Hall and a special treat of listening to the exciting new technology of the radio. All 275 employees crowded to the front of the auditorium to hear the orchestral broadcasts of an Eastern radio station, but an electrical storm in Pennsylvania blasted the show off the air. The radio operators, two men from the reinsurance department, turned their antenna to the Southwest to pick up an orchestra from that direction when Hall interrupted to announce that Agency Manager Walter T. Shepard was about to make a broadcast to the home office from San Antonio, Texas. Startled that one of their own would appear on the new marvel of the radio, employees gathered in awed silence around the enlarged amplifying horn that was the speaker. After listening to the announcement in Shepard's familiar drawl including the startlingly recent news that Nora Shreve of the Accounting Department intended to

"bob" her hair, the employees buzzed exceedingly about the new technology and that "it came all the way from Texas!" A great laugh (and not a little disappointment) was had by all when it was revealed that in actuality the "broadcast from Texas" had come from an adjoining room to the Wolf & Dessauer auditorium and that "Mr. Shepard" was in fact Bob Fowler of the Underwriting Department. Hall quickly appeared on stage to present to the employees for the first time the plans for the new home office building, beaming at the gasps and exclamations by the staff as he recounted the amount of space and new equipment that would be a part of the future home office. The evening concluded with a dance to the strains of the locally popular Dickerson Orchestra and, for some, a slumber party at the home of Susan Dunlap of the Investment Department.

Construction began in spring 1922 and was completed by mid-October 1923. In keeping with the efficiency talents of Franklin Mead, who directed the entire project, the moving weekend the following fall, on October 13 and 14, was carried out so that business ended on Friday in the old Berry Street building was picked up on Monday morning in the new

home office without a faltering step. Employees of all ranks volunteered to carry out the move beginning early Saturday morning when twelve moving vans, some of them horse-drawn, were loaded for the shuttle between old and new buildings. Those who experienced the move recall with pride how nothing was lost and everything from the old office, properly tagged, was quickly and efficiently placed in its new location. The only mishap occurred when a large tray of hundreds of "Addressograph" plates, all carefully organized by policy number, was dropped and the plates scattered. This was a critical part of the 1920s version of a "data base" and one crew of women under the direction of Alice O'Reilly spent an anxious day putting these back into place.

Inside, the foyer and elevator corridor were meant to impress all who did business with The Lincoln. Tall granite walls, on which were inscribed the top salesmen for each year, extended two stories above the grand marble staircase leading to the first floor. Along the frieze in the elevator corridor in the center of the first floor were the bas-relief sculptures of Paul Jennewein, of the American Academy in Rome. The figures of young children (modeled after his own) bore the legends of "Love," "Truth," "Pride" and "Gracious Fortune" were praised in the *Architectural Record* of 1923 as "one of the most striking artistic friezes of the year."

On the day of the dedication of the new home offices, on November 7, 1923, a special ceremony was held in the nearby Palace Theater, Fort Wayne's largest stage. U.S. Postmaster General Harry S. New gave the inaugural address, followed by presentations by Hall and Foster, after which the building was thrown open to the public with a house-warming reception. A three-day agency convention was then held in the new facilities. One of the most noticeable features of the new building for the agents who for decades arrived and departed Fort Wayne by train, was the grand new electrical sign that proclaimed The Lincoln National Life Insurance Company mounted on the top of the home office facing the Pennsylvania Railroad tracks and station located just south of the building. Reflecting

Hall's interest in air mail, another sign, one which could only be seen from the air, was erected on the roof. It pointed the way to the new Fort Wayne airport on the north side of town.

Additions were made to the new home office almost immediately. In 1929 the south wing was extended and in 1931 a similar addition was made to the north wing. The 1923 office was in many ways a delight to the employees. Especially appreciated was a company cafeteria which offered cut-rate meals on the premises during the short lunch break. In the 1930s an employee could get a superior meal (compared to other downtown restau-

rants) for twenty-five cents. Even in the late 1960s, a luncheon could be purchased for only thirty-five to forty cents, far under the usual price in area eateries. In some respects, however, the new complex offered new difficulties. Before the age of air conditioning, the windows were kept open during the summer months, but the proximity of numerous rail lines with their coal-burning steam engines left a daily problem: coal soot all over everything. Before the middle of the twentieth century as many as two hundred trains arrived and departed Fort Wayne each day and Marcelline Kleinrichert, who worked in the Actuarial Department in the 1920s

and 1930s, recalls that in the middle of the summer a daily chore was to sweep off the coal dust that blew in the open windows overnight from the trains and settled on desks and paperwork everywhere. During the day, it was terribly noisy and hot, but in the winter it was comfortable. The women's lounge was an added benefit, though closely restricted, with its ping-pong tables, bridge tables and couches. The garage facilities underground included automotive upkeep and repair services, such as oil changes, radiator flushes and tune-ups for those entitled to use the garage.

Expansion of the home office facilities was a continuous activity. In addition to the first additions to the central home office building, the acquisition of the Reliance Life Insurance Company required the acquisition of additional major office space. The old Wayne Pump Company facilities located at Coombs and Cochran streets on Fort Wayne's east side were acquired in 1952 and remodeled in 1960 at a cost of $1 million to accommodate the inclusion of the Reliance records and the expansion of the group life business.

The most significant expansion, however, occurred in the late 1950s under the direction of Walter Menge. Since the end of World War II the company's business had doubled and redoubled; there were more than 1,200 employees crammed into the 1923 building. Chief Investment Officer Edward Auer chaired a special building committee and among the first discussions was one to decide whether to stay in downtown Fort Wayne. Several suburban sites were considered, but the proximity of rail transportation and efficient mail delivery from the main post office across Harrison Street, in addition to a strong sense of commitment to be a part of the central Fort Wayne business district, led the committee to recommend expansion of the old building rather than construction of a new one. In 1956 the Chicago firm of Holabird & Root & Burgee was chosen to design the new structure, which would include additional stories to the original building and expansion of the complex to the east to occupy the entire block. The new construction was designed to blend with the origi-

The kitchen staff, 1923.

Dining area, 1923.

147

Ross Moyer celebrating his birthday in the new building, ca. 1925.

The bowling alleys in the basement, ca. 1925.

Ruth Blue (left) and Joan Korn Handled all the calls in 1960.

nal in style and materials. Ground was broken in 1958 and a cornerstone ceremony was held in February 1959. Apart from the deaths of two men who fell during the construction, the chief casualty was the old cupola, which was removed to make room for the additional four stories. One of the most exciting new elements in the renovated building was the installation of the novelty of escalators. The new home office complex was dedicated on October 9, 1960 in a grand ceremony that filled Harrison Street with nearly two thousand employees and guests who heard Walter Menge dedicate the building to the people who made Lincoln National and Frederick L. Hovde, president of Purdue University, praise the virtues of capitalism and American business. The climax of the ceremony was reached when the enormous 12- by 18-foot American flag was unfurled on the new flag pole behind the Lincoln Youth statue as the Fort Wayne Philharmonic orchestra played the National Anthem.

In March 1975, ground was broken for another major addition to the home office that would extend the Lincoln's buildings almost another entire block to the east. Increasing the office space by one-third, the new seven-story building facing Clinton Street was dedicated in 1976. One of its most distinguishing features was the installation of the Lincoln Museum on the ground floor, but this was the last expansion of the company's old home office complex.

Continued growth of Lincoln National required further expansion of office spaces in the 1980s and 1990s, but rather than merely adding room, these expansions reflected the changing nature of the corporation. In 1979 the company purchased and remodeled a large office complex on the city's southwest side that had been occupied by the Magnavox Corporation.

Known as "Lincoln West," the offices officially became the home of Lincoln National Reinsurance Companies in 1993, reflecting the unique place as a distinct entity that reinsurance has come to occupy in the structure of the corporation.

Perhaps the most important and symbolic changes in building structure since the Harrison Street home office was built in 1923 occurred when a former department store was extensively remodeled in 1991 to become a new central downtown office building for Lincoln National. Called "Renaissance Square," this building, which stands across the street from the old Berry Street home offices of Lincoln Life, was remodeled further to serve as the new headquarters of Lincoln National Corporation in 1994. Under one roof were thus placed the operations that most clearly were related to the functions only of the holding company, including corporate board, executive and human resources offices, investor relations, auditing, treasurer, corporate public involvement, corporate law, Lincoln National Investment Management Corporation (LNIMC) and the Lincoln Museum. The move from the old Harrison Street complex to Renaissance Square physically separated the Lincoln Life Insurance Company from the holding company for the first time since 1968. The purpose of the separation was integral to the new corporate reorganization that began with Project Compass in 1989-1990, which envisioned a sharper image for both the life company and the holding company in order to eliminate unclear lines between the two entities. In this way, LNC sought to provide stronger policy direction and oversight to all the lines of business and consolidate its investor and public

Indoor golf facilities, ca. 1925.

The stage for the Lincoln National Social and Athletic Association, ca. 1925.

A Sign of the Times: Lincoln National's home office was Fort Wayne's best fallout shelter in 1964

In the late 1950s and early 1960s fear of nuclear attack was widespread. Community preparedness organizations and the Civil Defense made elaborate plans to protect populations from the after effect of the great blasts, should they ever come. People were taught how to turn their homes into fallout shelters to survive the aftermath of an attack; some homeowners even invested in individual fallout shelters that were installed underground in backyards. For the general public, however, the Civil Defense designated certain large buildings in the community to serve as fallout shelters also. The Allen County War Memorial Coliseum was the first to be designated and was rated to hold nearly 4,500 hundred people.

As part of the Civil Defense effort to assign enough shelter space for the entire community population of more than 165,000, Lincoln National's home office building on Harrison Street was designated in 1964 as the community's largest fallout shelter. It was rated to hold just over 5,000. More than merely naming the building as a shelter site, the Civil Defense sent two semi-trailer loads of supplies to be stored in the basement. Included were scores of water cans, hundreds of cases of concentrated foods, sanitation kits, first-aid kits, radiation detection equipment and dosimeters (to measure radiation build-up). The supplies were designed to last two weeks for the five thousand people in the shelter. The water supply would be augmented by the one-hundred- gallon per hour well located in the basement of the Harrison Street building, though little thought was given to the consequences of the loss of electrical power.

Typical of the dour pictures drawn at the time of the terrible decisions that nuclear holocaust would require, employees were warned that in case of an attack not to try to go home to check on family members — they would have to fare for themselves. Schools with all their windows, everyone was reminded, were the worst places to be in the event of a nuclear attack. On the bright side, however, Civil Defense experts did not consider Fort Wayne to be a "prime" target.

The spacious lounge of the 1960 addition.

relations roles. Similarly, Lincoln Life, which occupied the entire group of buildings between Harrison and Clinton streets, was henceforth as clearly defined physically as the other major business. Thus, the mid-1990s headquarters of Lincoln National, a multibillion-dollar international financial corporation, now stands across the street from the first building the company purchased for its headquarters in 1912, the Elektron Building on East Berry Street, when Lincoln was known as "the little company over the grocery store."

Working at Lincoln National, 1905 - 1995

Approaches to management and to work have both changed greatly since the turn-of-the- century, but by and large Lincoln National has been regarded as the premier white-collar place to work in Fort Wayne.

Compensation scales, benefits and working conditions have been superior to comparable businesses in the region in the past half-century and recent surveys of employees reveal the perception that the company is comparable to industry peers.

When the company began ninety years ago as a small office made up of Arthur Hall and a stenographer, conditions were hectic, cramped and uncertain — not unlike any other business trying to get off the ground in 1905. The office furniture — a kitchen table and a few straight-backed chairs — was borrowed or second-hand and the equipment for creating and keeping records was primitive. Each year the number of employees grew, but those who recall those first years also remember a strong "family atmosphere" about the business. It was a place where everyone knew each other and put a great emphasis on helping fellow employees.

The work day was simple and strictly regulated. Offices opened at 8:00 a.m. and closed at 4:30 p.m., with a half an hour for lunch and no break periods. Using the rest room was a privilege restricted to the lunch period and before or after work. The

Clerical staff sorting applications during a sales contest in the 1920s.

office was open for half a day on Saturdays. Dress was formal business attire — the men were not allowed to remove their coats and the women were expected to be buttoned from shoe top to neck. Decorum in the office was closely monitored. Alice O'Reilly remembers her first week on the job in 1916 when the woman across the aisle from her desk struck up a conversation and Alice cordially replied only to be confronted by her supervisor, Ann O'Rourke, who scold-

ed her, "When there is anything to say, we get up from our desk and go to the other desk. We do not talk across aisles." When she herself was a supervisor in later years, during the 1930s through the 1950s, O'Reilly liked to have all the women in her area clearly in view so that she could be sure everyone was working at their appointed tasks all the time.

In the first half-century it was the usual practice for the president of the company to stop by the desk of any

employee and ask about progress of work. In the case of President McAndless he might well suggest an entirely new method for finishing a project or even a new project altogether. There were no partitions between desks and only the very top officers had separate offices. Formal training programs for new employees did not exist. One woman in the World War I era remembers her supervisor coming to her and saying, "I have to have a policy checker and I want you to take

The Lincoln Lifers baseball team of 1928.

The Lincoln Lifers and Babe Ruth

On May 6, 1927, the semi-pro team of the Lincoln Lifers met the legendary New York Yankees for an exhibition baseball game in Fort Wayne's League Park. This 1927 Yankee team boasted a host of stars including the great first-baseman Lou Gehrig and Babe Ruth, who was to hit sixty home runs that season. League Park was filled to capacity and the game turned out to be full of drama and excitement. The Lifers were a veteran team and had played, in earlier years, exhibition games with the likes of John McGraw's New York Giants and Connie Mack's Philadelphia Athletics.

The Yankees led from the first inning with Gehrig providing the key hits. In the eighth inning, though, the Lincoln Lifers took a 3 - 2 lead with a flurry of hits. New York tied the game, sending it into extra innings. In the Yankee half of the 10th, one man was walked, but two men were put out quickly. Ruth came to the plate to much clamor. Quickly the Bambino took one pitch for a strike and then swung and missed another. Then on the next pitch he walloped the ball over the centerfield fence and onto the roofs of the buildings across Clinton Street. Ruth, as he often did, carried the bat around the bases with him. When he reached home the stands emptied and as the crowd swarmed around him (including happy Lincoln Lifers); he was heard to say, in typical Ruthian fashion, "I told you when I came up to bat you might as well start for home."

Ruth often remarked later that was the hardest hit ball of his entire career, and stories grew in time that Ruth often joked that it was also the longest ball he hit as it landed on a passing freight train en route to Chicago. In actuality, the ballpark did not face the tracks.

Clerical area in the Lincoln National offices on E. Berry Street, ca. 1920.

the job." She protested, "Oh, how could I do that, I just don't know anything about it." The supervisor replied, "Well, we have to have a policy checker. Here's the stuff and so proceed." The distraught clerk said, "Don't I have anyone to train me?" and the supervisor simply answered, "No, we don't have anyone to train you — you'll just have to pick it up as best you can."

Early management governed the company in a paternalistic fashion. Creating a "Lincoln family" was an important part of Hall's concept of leading a loyal, efficient and productive workforce. His "fatherly" role was that of disciplinarian and nurturer. Consequently, a great deal of attention was given to techniques of management that centered on firm regulation of "family" life as well as a deep respect for the individual employees, a concept that Hall summed up in the mid-1920s remarks on "The Chivalry of Power" (adapted from the works of the English historian Sir Arthur Helps [1813-1875]). In this statement on the conduct of management, Hall stressed that the power of the manager, while necessary for good order, efficiency and the well being of the business, was also something to be used in a kindly manner, fairly and with understanding and compassion. Good managers did not gloat over others' failures or seek to take credit where others did the work. In this way Hall and his followers created the foundation for Lincoln National culture — a sense that managers not only ruled, but also nurtured employees, and the parallel to the figure of the father in the family setting of this era was the and widely accepted guidepost.

In 1935 Hall addressed the annual meeting of the American Life Convention in Chicago and elaborated further on his ideals for personnel development in a life insurance company. Although principally applied to the officer ranks of the company, Hall's views were eventually extended to all ranks when he stressed the fundamental requirements of good management in creating and sustaining "a thinking, reasoning staff," one that was strengthened by incentives, given opportunities for variety and innovation in work and clear guidelines for accountability.

Hall worked especially hard to motivate, lead and inspire — this is what he did best. He knew as few others have that the heart of their business lay in teamwork, camaraderie, integrity and enthusiasm, and that these characteristics were impossible if the working conditions were poor, morale was depressed and loyalty was compromised.

When the company built the new office building on Harrison Street, Hall considered this also as an important tool for further cementing the "Lincoln family." Great care was given in the construction plans to the efficient and wholesome atmosphere for employees: The building itself became a symbol of all the company's achievements, ideals and aspirations. Not only was this facility to be the architectural expression of the company's astonishing success, it would also house within its walls all that was needed for the employees' well being. It was an impressive place to work, especially for Fort Wayne, Indiana. The composed, harmonious Doric features of the neo-classical building expressed modest grandeur and well balanced energy. Inside, its spacious rooms, large windows, impressive hallways, abundant lighting and a grand entryway with the names of the top sales people permanently engraved in the granite walls reminded the employees daily of the new scale of operation and the growing importance of the business. After 1932 all who entered Lincoln National passed by the impressive and inspiring statue of young Abraham Lincoln executed by the renowned sculptor Paul Manship. When a person, either clerk or customer, entered the new Lincoln National home office he or she knew unmistakably that this was a business that was a cut above the rest in town.

Gaining employment at Lincoln National had become a privilege and a mark of achievement by the early 1930s. In a speech made in Toronto in 1931 Elisabeth O'Rourke, company secretary, she proudly noted that Lincoln National only hired "honors" graduates of high schools and universities. She also noted that the company preferred to hire only people with no previous business experience so that "we absorb them into our organization before any ideas or policies for-

eign to our methods of doing business have been acquired." Personal appearance was a consideration of the highest priority. In one manual of the 1930s, it was noted that "we do not care to employ applicants whose appearance reflects an impaired or debilitated physical condition." In regard to appearances, however, O'Rourke cautioned that "inasmuch as the department managers are mostly of the males species, it is quite evident how important a factor personal appearance can become, ... but it has been my observation that women are better judges of women than are men, who are too apt to be swayed by matters of personal charm, which of course are of some importance, but not always to the exclusion of all other qualifications." After all, O'Rourke warned, "some people have the ability to so camouflage their individual shortcomings that they can create for display purposes a character or personality entirely foreign to the true one."

In keeping with the new expectations of the company and the growing size of the workforce, an employee handbook was issued in 1925, which codified the structure of the "Lincoln family" at work in a way that bore striking similarities to the descriptions of work patterns in factories that were such a prominent part of Fort Wayne in the first half of the twentieth century. The ringing of gongs ten times signalled the start and end of the working day. Five minutes before closing a single ring of the gong notified workers to clear their desks, cover typewriters and adding machines and return files to the cabinets and vaults. Personnel were cautioned that "loyal and efficient employees" do not watch the clock and do not congregate in the corridors. They prepare to do better work by demonstrating that they do their present work well. Great attention was given to efficiency, the evidence of which was keeping desks and work stations clear of all clutter, personal effects and anything else not related to work. No papers should be left on the desks after work, the manual continues, and no photographs or cartoons were allowed under the glass tops of the desks. Each employee was assigned a locker and was given a clean towel twice a week, "to be

Efficiency expert F. L. Rowland, 1923. He later became the first executive director of LOMA.

deposited in the hat compartment of the locker." Personal mail and visitors could not be received and those visitors doing business with the company were to be received promptly in the specially designed reception room. Workers leaving the building during working hours were required to use an "Out Pass" obtained from a supervisor.

While many of the early regulations seem overly restrictive a half-a-century later, these were the normal models for managing a large number of employees, and the procedures that sound oppressive to the modern employee were generally welcome as good, reliable business practices — the orderly work site was the sign of a stable business. In addition, for the insurance industry especially, the need for great accuracy and rapid, satisfactory service to customers lay at the heart of the success of the business, and Lincoln National had done well because it paid attention to these issues. Franklin Mead, second-in-command in the early years, was devoted to efficient practices in the office. He recruited Frank L. Rowland, an efficiency expert, and the two men organized the Life Office Management Association (LOMA) in 1924 as a part of the company's redoubled attention to office operations in its new building. They also developed such other

efficiency techniques, new in their day, as the "Standard Practices Instruction Manual." This loose-leaf binder contained policy instructions on every facet of company work, from ordering supplies, using paper clips, posting mail, inking stamp pads, pulling the window shades, handling receipts and turning off the lights to completing expense vouchers, filing and disposing of records, contributing to the group life plan, and the proper form for addressing different types of letters.

To enhance the workplace and balance the strict regulation of work activities, much attention was given to the life of the employees beyond their desks. While the new employee handbook codified the structure of work for the "Lincoln family," the spirit of the "family" had to be nurtured in other ways. Within the workplace spaces were created for new functions that were not directly related to work, ranging from sports facilities and a cafeteria to a nurse's office and banking and postage facility. In the 1920s this was revolutionary for a business in northeast Indiana, and it was highly unusual anywhere before World War II.

Key facets of Lincoln National culture that are still important today — health, physical fitness, social interaction, the Abraham Lincoln collection, training and development — had their origins in the 1920s when the Lincoln National vision of itself was so dynamically stated in the construction of its new Harrison Street home office. The health of the employees received special attention. Company policy in 1923 stated that one of its goals was to "aid and maintain a high standard of health among its working force." To this end, a nurse was hired to operate a "first-aid hospital" and even made "house calls" to ill employees. With the great influenza epidemic of 1919 that carried away millions world-wide still a vivid memory, the company also retained a consulting physician not only for administering examinations, but also for monitoring potentially dangerous contagion situations. Smoking, though primarily perceived as a fire hazard and not a health risk from the 1920s through the 1960s, was severely restricted on Lincoln National property. In the mid-1980s

the issue of smoking became a central one for Lincoln National precisely as a health threat and its practice in company buidings was banned entirely largely as a result of employee demand. Health benefits generally for employees and their dependents expanded dramatically from the 1960s to become the most important and extensive programs for employees in the modern company, including programs for dental and vision care as well as major medical, long-term disability and extensive psychological services, to name but a few.

Also simultaneous with the construction of the Harrison Street home office building in 1923 was the establishment of a formal company recreational program. Known before World War II as the Lincoln Life Social and Athletic Association, the organization was sanctioned by the company as a means of giving employees control over the recreational facilities built into the new facility. The organization was open to all full-time employees who paid the dues; officers were elected yearly to serve as volunteer leaders of the group. For the recreational use of the employees the company provided specially equipped rooms for meetings, theatricals, dances and gymnastics. Six full-sized bowling alleys were built into the basement level and two clay tennis courts were located in the rear of the building in the three decades before the expansion of the facility in the late-1950s. Perhaps most extraordinary was the indoor golf course on the fourth floor of the main building. Here the popularity of the nine-hole putting course competed with a driving cage for the employees' free time as one of the favorite spots for workers to gather.

Sports for Lincoln National employees extended beyond the building facilities. The company, beginning in 1917, sponsored for many years a respectable semi-professional baseball team and a professional bowling team that won a national championship. For employees there were teams that formed as early as the mid-1920s — ranging from the men's and women's basketball teams that played in the YMCA leagues (the LNL "Wizzers" women's team won the city title in 1921), to the men's softball teams, men's and women's golf and tennis teams, all of which played in city leagues. For more than two decades after its beginning in 1958 the athletic awards banquet at the local Berghoff Gardens was a featured event of the year. These activities represent an unbroken tradition of Lincoln National athletics that today is found in company leagues for men and women in softball, golf, bowling and, since the early 1960s, volleyball. These, in addition to the "Corporate Challenge," which pits Lincoln National competitors against employees of other corporations in the area, the family oriented "Olympiad" and the popular "Club Ped," which is part of the Lincoln National Employees Wellness Program.

The corporation's Wellness Program reflects the "health revolution" of the mid-1980s and 1990s, but it fits well with the long tradition of the company's emphasis on employees managing their own and their families' health. In the 1920s it was a part of the daily routine for a physical exercise instructor, usually the local YMCA director, to take his place on a desk at the head of the room and lead the employees in calisthenics as a part of their required daily exercise. In the late 1960s and throughout the 1970s, the publications of Lincoln National Life and American States increasingly addressed dietary concerns, smoking and other lifestyle issues, but not until the mid- 1980s did *The Company News* and *Multilines* begin to reflect society's intensified concern with personal health. In 1995 Lincoln National Corporation supports a wellness department for all its employees which sponsors a wide range of semi-

nars, activity programs and discussion or demonstration groups on health and wellness issues.

Social interaction became a formal part of Lincoln National culture in the early 1920s. Building upon the notion of the "Lincoln family" that came from the earliest days of the company's history, Hall sought to unite his workers as a team in a variety of ways. Before the company had many resources, Hall would simply do it on his own. The annual picnic gathering at his home on Beechwood Drive in Fort Wayne became a favorite event. It started in 1920 when the Lincoln National women's tennis tournament was held on Hall's private tennis court. Following the match the employees were treated to a picnic and the tradition continued until well into the 1930s. Remembered for being

Lincoln National's championship bowling team, 1922.

The World Champion Lincoln Bowlers, 1922

Arthur Hall loved bowling. In 1917 he organized the Lincoln Lifers semi-professional bowling team to compete in the tourneys across the nation. Recruiting bowlers from Indianapolis, Cincinnati, and Grand Rapids, Hall was the team manager and the team quickly became a Midwest powerhouse. The Lifers won the Central States Championship in 1919 and the Indiana title in 1920. The team was frustrated three years in a row, however, in its bid to win the largest bowling event, the American Bowling Congress tournament. In 1919 and 1920 they finished third and in 1921 they ended the season in fourth place. In 1922, the Lifers were at last able to take the ten-pin championship tournament held in Toledo, Ohio, giving them the title of International Bowling Champions.

In the years afterward, Lincoln National continued to support a team on the national circuit, but the championship team's members drifted to other organizations. Bowling, however, continued to be a popular part of employee life at the company, which sponsored its own league in addition to the Lincoln National teams that bowled in city tourneys. Reflecting his own interest and the great popularity of the sport, Hall had bowling alleys installed in the basement of the new (1923) home office building.

a pleasant, casual afternoon's affair, officers, managers, and the rank and file easily mixed, chatted and enjoyed Hall's hospitality. Hall also sponsored a company dinner each spring at the popular auditorium of Wolf and Dessauer, a local department store, and for the officers, beginning in 1931, he held a special "long-weekend retreat" at his Leland, Michigan, home he called "The Duck," located in the northern part of the lower penisula near the shore of Lake Michigan. To these were added the "hilarious parties" at the Sergeant Hotel at Lake Wawasee. These parties were possible when the company was small, but with the success of the company the workforce grew and even before the Great Depression many of the special activities ended.

After World War II social interaction at Lincoln National became increasingly a club affair. The company simply had become too large to do otherwise. Only on the rarest occasion, such as the Lincoln National's fiftieth anniversary in 1955, was there an attempt to have a company-wide event that included family members. The great half-century celebration was held at the recently completed Allen County Memorial Coliseum and featured the popular big band sound of Fred Waring and his Pennsylvanians. For many years this was one of the most fondly remembered events sponsored by the company, particularly because it also involved the families of the employees. The Men's Stag golf outing was started in the 1950s and was extremely popular well into the 1960s and this was matched by the women's golf open, but these events were organized by interested individuals and differed from the old "Lincoln family" outings when the company was smaller.

In an effort to recall the older camaraderie, two organizations were founded not long after World War II, the Loyal Service Club and LINCS. The Loyal Service Club was formed in 1949 with Jerry Klingenberger as the first president. Its purpose was (and continues to be) to maintain a club that brings together those veterans of Lincoln National who served twenty-five years or more who demonstrated through all their years with the company strong sentiments of friendship,

loyalty, helpfulness and respect for the company and its employees. The earliest meetings were highlighted by the humorous skits done usually at the expense of the inductees to the Club; today, the event has evolved into a solemn, formal occasion which stresses the special nature and length of service to the company. LINCS began in 1950 as a women's group that would occasionally sponsor gatherings, shopping tours, trips and fund-raising activities for worthwhile charities. Trips to Europe and Hawaii, to Chicago or Detroit for Christmas shopping, the Kentucky Derby and the museums of Cincinnati characterize the club's activities in the 1960s and 1970s. The organization, which now includes men, still meets monthly and continues to sponsor weekend trips, a crafts bazaar, bingo and card parties, Family Carnival Night and a book fair, but membership roles are smaller in the 1990s as the focus of many women at Lincoln National has changed greatly, as has that of the company.

As Lincoln National rapidly grew larger in the 1960s and 1970s, the workforce became increasingly more specialized and work more fragmented; personal ties to the company were weakened. The old concept of the "Lincoln family" continued to be strong, but gradually new ties to the company evolved and new ways of developing the teamwork so impor-

tant to a successful sales operation were formed. The workforce itself was changing and women were a large part of this change. In the first half-century of the company's history women generally did not stay in the workforce long. They worked at Lincoln National until they married and, because of the endless manual tasks needed for the huge records keeping functions of the business, were relegated largely to mechanical jobs. The nature of this work changed with the advent of computers during the 1960s and women began to approach work at Lincoln National, as elsewhere, as a career. No longer satisfied with rote jobs — jobs that increasingly machines could do — women increasingly sought greater roles in decision making, job definitions and the work environment.

Seeking to anticipate necessary change rather than react to crisis and to establish new dynamics for working at Lincoln National, Ian Rolland, as the new CEO, initiated in 1978 Quality Commitment, an innovative program designed to change the foundations of work in the company and create new, broader-based ties through team efforts. Developed largely in accordance with the "job enrichment" philosophies of Roy W. Walters & Associates, Inc., this long-range program for institutional change was founded on the principle of the greatest possible involvement of employees

The "Wall-Bash Cannonball," robotic mail delivery vehicle, one of the many 1970s office technologies introduced to enhance efficiency.

in all ranks addressing problems and generating new ideas "in the belief that all work can be done better by the continuous application of creative thinking, problem solving and energetic job performance." Its goal was to create a new basis for the Lincoln National way of life. Employees found themselves after 1978 often organized into teams under team leaders coming together in committee meetings to address issues that in an earlier time simply were left up to management. One of the "old-timers" who worked in the "steno pools" of the 1940s and

1950s commented critically upon visiting the company in the mid-1980s that "there is just too much committee work going one. Everywhere I went there were groups of workers meeting and not working at their desks."

The creation of Strategic Business Units (SBUs) in the early 1980s greatly magnified centrifugal forces pulling the old "Lincoln family" into smaller segments. Intense loyalties to individual, vertically organized business units, such as reinsurance, pensions and investments, in addition to those companies not located in Fort Wayne,

grew quickly as Quality Commitment teams in the home offices and affiliates focused on the narrow needs of their SBU rather than the corporation as a whole. The result was the formation of immensely stronger business units with their own cultures, some of which were competitive with other SBUs. In addition to two officers' meetings and two management forums each year, one of Rolland's techniques for cementing the parts of the corporation was the creation of regular Total Employee Meetings (TEMs). The annual Total Employee

Jean Roth, director of the Choraliers, rehearses members for the annual Christmas program in 1969.

Harold Turner holds forth during a Choralier performance in 1991.

The Lincoln Choraliers

In 1995 the Lincoln Choraliers charm and delight not only Lincoln National employees, but scores of others in the home office community of Fort Wayne.

The choral group began in 1948 when about thirty women sought the backing of LINCS, the Lincoln National's women's organization, to present Christmas carols during the holiday season. Originally directed by Chelsea Brown, the group was immediately popular and soon were singing at other Lincoln National functions, such as the Loyal Service Club banquets and as a welcoming chorus to the old Reliance Life agents when Lincoln National acquired the company. The organization flourished for three years until, in 1951, many of the original members were transferred to the Wayne facility as the Group Department grew.

The Choraliers was revived in 1955 as a group for men and women at first under the directorship of Paul Gilbert and then, in 1958, Jean Roth, who was a professional musician. The new Lincoln Choraliers quickly regained their earlier popularity. Rehearsing long hours after work, they became a mainstay of the Lincoln National celebrations of the holidays. By the mid-1960s the Choraliers were performing all over Fort Wayne and began a regular spot that continues as a part of Christmas programming on local television. Since 1990, the Choraliers have assumed a more professional look, thanks to the company's underwriting of their first choral robes. In 1994 they continued their nearly half-century tradition by giving nineteen concerts not only in the home offices, but also in area retirement homes and other community centers.

The annual party at Hall's home in Fort Wayne included tennis matches with the CEO as chief umpire, ca. 1925.

A women's basketball team of 1929.

Meetings in numerous sites across the country not only gave Rolland the opportunity for explaining personally to employees the latest corporate developments and the role of individual business units, they also gave the employees the opportunity for directing their questions and concerns directly to Rolland. In addition, as a vestige of the old "paternal" role of the CEO, Rolland maintained an open-door policy to all employees, as well as full access to him through the electronic mail system. He is universally known in the company for his willingness to answer and act upon comments that come unfiltered to his computer terminal. Despite the openness, it was clear in the early 1990s that more had to be done. There were enough corporate-wide barriers that Rolland believed the overall business goals of Lincoln National were being hampered. He decided that a new initiative to break down walls and bind employees together was necessary in order to maximize the total effectiveness of the corporation.

A task force led by Executive Vice President Jack Hunter sought input from throughout the company to identify the values that were shared by employees at every level in the corporation. The committee looked for universal inward values that centered on individual behavior, rather than codes

A Lincoln National women's softball team of 1991.

that looked outward, such as those that might deal with product quality . Many of the behavioral values, such as those touching on ethical conduct, were already in existence and simply needed to be listed, while others were condensed from a wide array of experiences. As a result of the committee's work, seven shared values emerged: fairness, respect, commitment to excellence, diversity, employee ownership, responsibility and integrity.

Shared Values draws upon both the earliest traditions of the company and its latest strengths and pulls them together as a strategy for the next century. Just as Lincoln National Life had to overcome mistrust of the insurance industry in the wake of national scandals in 1905, the modern Lincoln National Corporation has identified integrity as the premier shared value in the wake of new scandals in other companies. Trustworthiness and incorruptibility lie at the heart of every facet of the company's business and in 1994 and 1995 there has been a renewed dedication to the earliest motto of the company, *our name indicates our character*, and to the namesake of the company, Abraham Lincoln, through the creation of the new, world class Lincoln Museum. Also harkening to the earliest "Principles of Management" expressed by the company's founders and echoed

In 1973 the concept of equal opportunity had become a highly visible company standard, as illustrated in this cover of *The Review*.

LINCS members ham it up displaying their "wide-eyed view" of spring fashions at the 1960 Mother-Daughter Party.

by each successive president, Shared Values identifies commitment to excellence, responsibility and employee ownership as key concepts that tie all Lincoln National employees together. Ownership, especially, has become critical because it ties employees' personal fortunes to the overall success of the company, thereby enhancing the value of their own work. While fairness was always a part of the Lincoln vision for how it conducted its business, in the 1994 Shared Values program the idea has been expanded to include how employees are expected to deal with one another as well as with customers and clients. The newest item among the shared values is diversity. In terms

of talent and experience, this was implicit in the philosophies of management expressed by Hall and McAndless. From the time of Menge, however, the idea that business strength derived also from diversity of races became a part of Lincoln's philosophy of management and this was given greater emphasis in the affirmative action atmosphere of the administration of Watson and especially in the social consciousness exhibited by Ian Rolland. Under the Shared Values program, however, the concept of diversity in every respect — intelligence, experience, cultural background, gender, race, creed, — as a fundamental strength of the company has been extended to include all varieties of

individuals who might add value to the corporation and its business goals.

The constant that Rolland shares with all his predecessors is the awareness that employee satisfaction is the company's greatest asset and that The Lincoln team, defined differently in different times, lies at the heart of the company's ability to succeed in business. In place of the old close-knit crew in a single building driven primarily by the excitement of sales, renewals, exciting reinsurance contracts and club activities, the shared values that draw upon and expand 90 years of company heritage form the foundation upon which the modern Lincoln National Corporation has sought to create a new "Lincoln family."

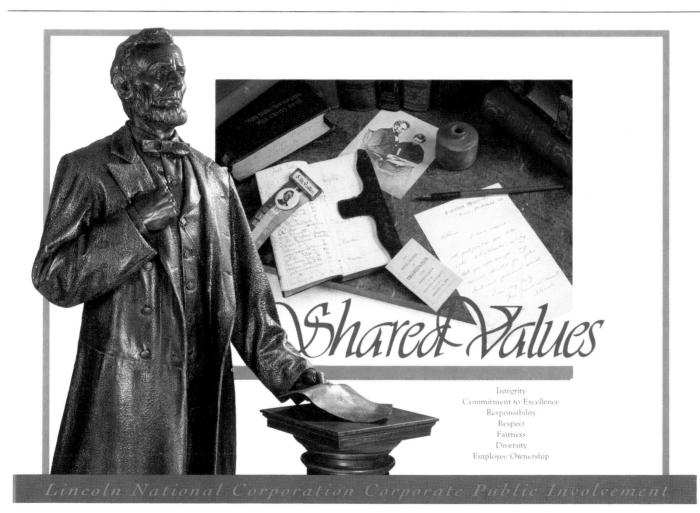

Integrity
Commitment to Excellence
Responsibility
Respect
Fairness
Diversity
Employee Ownership

Lincoln National Corporation Corporate Public Involvement

PHOTOGRAPHY CREDITS

Ian M. Rolland portrait, p. 46:   Ron May

Prime Time photograph, p. 58:   Ann Kolesar

Housing program photograph, pp. 124-125:   Bernard Hoffman, *Life Magazine* ©Time, Inc. Reprinted with permission. Contributors. Hoffman, Bernard.

Image of 1940s workplace, p. 137:   Sheldon Hine

Color section:
    Executive area, rotunda: George Heinrich
    Ken Dunsire, executive area: Dean Musser, Jr.
    One Reinsurance Place meeting room: Tom Galliher
    Lincoln National buildings: Ken Harper

Other photographs have been used with permission of the Lincoln Museum, Lincoln National Corporation.

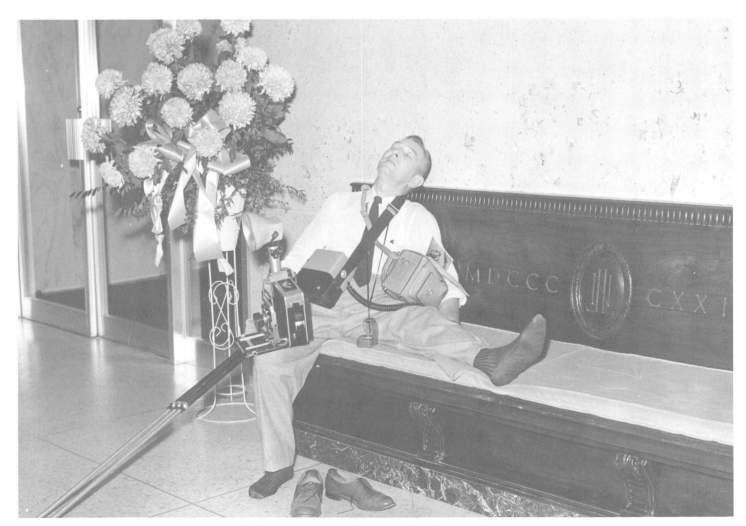

Sheldon Hine, Lincoln National's photographer

INDEX